BLACKTOWN, U.S.A.

BLACKTOWN, U.S.A.

by Frank L. Keegan

Little, Brown and Company — Boston — Toronto

All of the photographs appearing in *Blacktown, U.S.A.*, unless otherwise
credited, were taken by Clarence Sanders.

The poem "Mother to Son" is taken from *Selected Poems* by Langston
Hughes. Copyright 1926 by Alfred A. Knopf, Inc. and renewed 1954 by
Langston Hughes. Reprinted by permission of the publisher.

The author is deeply grateful to Norman Jordan and Mary Mason for
allowing him to reprint several of their poems in this book.

Published simultaneously in Canada
by Little, Brown & Company (Canada) Limited
PRINTED IN THE UNITED STATES OF AMERICA

For Helen and Leland Schubert

The black people, graduates of ghetto schools, in some cases of no schools, through wit and grace, singing their song in a strange land, have made a triumphal entry upon the scene.

— WILLIAM F. BUCKLEY, JR.

America is just like a turkey. It's got white meat and it's got dark meat. They is different, but they is both important to the turkey. I figure the turkey has more white meat than dark meat, but that don't make any difference. Both have nerves running through 'em.

— HENRY ALLEN

White folks don't want peace; they want quiet. The price you pay for peace is justice. Until there is justice there will be no peace or quiet.

— JESSE JACKSON

One ever feels his twoness — an American, a Negro; two souls, two thoughts, two unreconciled strivings; two warring ideals in one dark body, whose dogged strength alone keeps it from being torn asunder.

— W. E. BURGHARDT DU BOIS

Negroes will not break out of the barriers of the ghetto unless whites transcend the barriers of their own minds, for the ghetto is to the Negro a reflection of the ghetto in which the white lives are imprisoned. The poetic irony of American race relations is that the rejected Negro must somehow also find the strength to free the privileged white.

— KENNETH B. CLARK

Acknowledgments

To Diana Wilson, Roberta Phillips, Tamsen Bredvold and Carol Miller, who turned the sounds of the tapes into pages of print, magically and skillfully.

To Harold Enarson and Dolph Norton, who supported me in Cleveland both as colleagues and as friends.

To Larry Dennis, who told me ten years ago that it was the white man who had the color problem, not the black man.

To W. H. Ferry, who taught me that integration is a white man's lie.

To Alex Haley, who revealed to me, and who embodies, the black oral tradition.

To Studs Terkel, the master interviewer, who showed me in print and told me in sound how much dignity, and impotence, urban folks have — whether black or white.

To Franklin Delano Roosevelt Anderson, my black brother, who permitted me and my family to cry the night Martin Luther King, Jr. was murdered, the night this book began.

Contents

INTRODUCTION

"Thank God I'm a White Man!"

Blacktown, U.S.A. is another country. Two years ago I entered it to meet the natives and record their conversation. Most were willing to talk to the white foreigner. They allowed him into their homes and places of business. They permitted him also to exploit them by taking away the tape recording of the talks. These were transcribed and edited, they constitute the bulk of the present volume.

Recently I left Blacktown, saying as I went, "Thank God I'm a white man!" Some will say I am a racist. They are right. And so are we all — all the good white folks.

The whole thing happened accidentally. My university duties required that I enter the Blacktown adjoining our urban campus in Cleveland, Ohio. After talking with students and high school officials, I discovered a number of voluntary organizations set up to compensate blacks for their lack of formal education and to develop black pride. They ranged from paramilitary organizations to poetry and arts centers where there were meditation rooms and where the white man was welcome.

After one visit to Blacktown, three blacks followed me to the high tower of my university office on the ninth floor. They walked in unannounced, stood round my desk and asked for money and a program. When I asked why, they said solemnly: "For survival training." The idea appeared ludicrous. "How," I asked, "can the white man tell the black man about survival in the ghetto? You know that better than we do." "The black man can survive in the cities, but we don't mean in the cities," they replied. "We mean survival in the hills of Pennsylvania when we were driven out of the Middle West."

The answer was unexpected. The request was sincere. The need was urgent. What could I say? It was the first time I could provide neither answers or money for the questions or requests put to me by black men and women. There would be many, many more.

No doubt it is symptomatic of the state of the racial crisis of our time that my first encounters were with the most nationalist and alienated groups of black people. And I was dealing with the young whose passions run strongest and ideals are high. I learned later that I was being tested by the "nigger nationalists," those professional militants who make regular demands upon the liberal establishment and who escalate the price for maintaining civil peace during those long, hot summers. They are expert negotiators for the annual presummer payoffs which allegedly keep things cool. They resemble nothing so much as the barbarians north of the River Po in Roman times. History reminds us that their demands were increased to the point where the Republic, near exhaustion from the demands of its widespread colonial empire — with its wars and

4

pacification program (the *Pax Romana*) — was unable to pay the annual tributes. The barbarians then overran Rome.

In the beginning there was the enthusiasm of discovering a new culture, a new language, a new style of life. I had just returned to the United States from a two-year stay in Mexico where I was a member of a white minority. North Americans were amused to call that minority "gringos," especially when Mexicans could join in the laugh. It was a practice I would see repeated by black people in the United States, when referring to themselves, or others, as "niggers."

It was in Mexico that I came to know a distinguished Negro mathematician from a middle western college who was on a six-month consultantship to teach the new high school science programs to Mexican educators. He learned Spanish, entertained Mexicans exclusively and avoided contacts with North Americans. He was he said, attempting "to become a Mexican." At the time it seemed idiotic. Later it appeared pathetic, another result of the loss of identity which Alex Haley calls the "psychological abuse" visited upon the black man by the white.

In a foreign land, the American becomes accustomed to being a member of a well-heeled minority group living along Embassy Row. What the American is not prepared for when he returns is the colonial situation within the United States. As I moved from my white suburban village to Blacktown, the transition was as abrupt as traveling from San Diego to Tijuana, from El Paso to Juárez. By all the standard sociological and economic indexes — housing, recreation, education, family structure, welfare, crime, taxes — the change from white suburbia to Blacktown was dramatic and abrupt: a movement from affluence, space and freedom to poverty and all the forms of constriction, including slavery itself.

In Blacktown today, the Civil War never happened but the civil war goes on daily. I became aware of black oppression when a group — identified only as the Black Information Service — sought me out. There were rumors, circulated widely in the white dailies, that they were intimidating store owners and extorting funds in the accepted manner of Chicago gangland. There was truth in the rumors and the black defense of the practice was

5

simple and pragmatic: we want to control everything in our town, including its vice.

Representatives of the Black Information Service (BIS) picked me up at the designated spot, a drugstore; I was then taken to an apartment in the "projects," that universal urban term for public housing, the place where the white conscience is put to rest because it improves the homes of the people in Blacktown — on condition that they remain there. I was beginning to learn that black urban dwellers, in or out of the projects, are separated *from* white people, *by* white people, *for* white people.

I was not aware when the meeting began nor entirely sure when it ended. I was an appendage, a spectator, a suspect. Guards were posted at the exits and a lookout at the single window. It was going to be a special performance for this white man. They seemed to be waiting for a leader to arrive, but there was no leader. It was a peer group of men and women — all chairmen were cochairmen — who worked for "the Man" during the day and organized for their people at night. They were intelligent, dedicated and planned their programs well. They had read widely and deeply in the social and economic literature of revolution. My discussion with them was better than anything I found in the faculty lounge of my university.

Courtesy and friendliness were everywhere (I had not yet learned how intensely blacks fight blacks) and the Afro or Eastern names often gave way to "brother" and "sister." Gestures were frequent and flamboyant, dresses rich and colorful, usually in Afro style. Reports were given and discussion was brief. Unanimity ruled the procedures and all heads nodding was a signal to begin or to end the discussion of a topic, or to introduce a new item.

My turn came. (How the new blacks enjoy keeping the white man waiting!) What did I want? The university would offer short-term courses in necessary skills — bookkeeping, consumer education, reading and college prep subjects. They asked sharply: Who will control the courses? Who will receive the money? Who will do the teaching? Where would the classes be held?

I had learned in Mexico that the foundation official does not tell the local agency what is needed. The Mexicans knew what they wanted, it was up to the North Americans to provide the money and the experts. One enters only with an invitation, does what one can, what one is asked to do, then leaves. But I was unprepared for this concept of self-determination. Everything was to be in their hands, the money and building, the teachers and program of study. I realized that the Black Information Service wanted only one thing: university funds to start their own neighborhood centers. It was black self-determination with a subsidy from Whitey.

As we talked, speech patterns changed. Conversations erupted and there was much movement. Points were made standing, or during long stridings around the room. Denunciations were hurled with the sweep of an ebony arm lightly held by a flowered Afro sleeve. Clenched fists became gestures of affirmation. When brothers or sisters pounded fists together, affirmation became total approval, even exaltation.

The white man was never forgotten, always under observation. When he spoke there was silence. When he spoke favorably of the black cause, there was intense silence. When he spoke defensively of America, there was muted hostility. Sometimes the white man said something they approved of and murmurs arose. Unlike a white audience, careful to suppress enthusiasm, the black man and woman were silent only when they were negative or suspicious.

But these reassurances were few. Suddenly a black figure leaped to his feet and exploded at me, "White man, do you believe in civil rights or human rights?" "Human rights," I replied quickly. The black man thundered, "Watch him. He is a counterrevolutionary." I learned later that I was the first white man he had spoken with in two years.

As I drove home through Blacktown that evening at dusk, I recalled that in Mexico the North American officials always left the *vecindades* at sundown to return to their own part of town. When I passed through the invisible wall separating Blacktown from Whitetown, I looked for a border crossing, an armed guard, almost reaching for my passport.

Arriving home, my wife recounted the day's happenings. Because we had both spoken up for school integration in our all-white suburb, there had been some local reaction. More than one person had hinted, she said, that my previous work in Mexico had made

7

me suspect. One neighbor was convinced that I was a paid political agitator.

It had been a long day, partly in Blacktown and partly in Whitetown. How could one choose between the black interpretation — a "counterrevolutionary" — and the white — a "paid political agitator?" I had been out of the country a long while. Americans, both black and white, were uptight. I decided to learn more about Blacktown. What I didn't know is how much I would learn about Whitetown.

The Cultural Deprivation
of White Folks

Americans are a provincial people. Americans can be independent, pragmatic and at times visionary, but they remain remarkably culture-bound. As the anthropologist Clifford Geertz said, "We do not know very well what kind of society we live in, what kind of history we have had, what kind of people we are. We are just now beginning to find out, the hard way . . ."[1]

The general education of our people, by which I mean something more than literacy, has never been remarkably high. We do pro-

9

vide short, rigid courses in "Americanization" for the newly arrived immigrants who want United States citizenship. But these courses, even supplemented by the public school system, are not sufficient to establish the knowledge and awareness necessary for life in the American Republic. Americans have always put too much faith in their school system. They persistently confuse schooling with education. It was inevitable that they would regard the mandatory requirements of civics and American history as sufficient for achieving equality in the American melting pot.

The best argument for learning another language is that it helps you understand your own better. The same argument applies to culture. And Americans need desperately to study comparative civilizations. Failure to understand another culture results in ignorance of one's own. The white American presumption is that he is somehow magically capable of understanding another culture, especially the black man's.

There are a few exceptions. A women's club in Cleveland having heard of my minor forays into the black community wanted to know what it was like down there in the ghetto, and asked me to speak to them. I suggested that they ask a dweller of Blacktown rather than a white man and they agreed. Later I learned they had asked a Negro minister of a suburban church who had come from the East and had never been inside Cleveland's Blacktown. When I was asked to speak again, I accepted, and brought along tape recordings of some of Blacktown's citizens.

It was a pity the white women could not understand ghettoese. They could not hear the important things black women were telling them, like:

I met a white woman once who said, "I thought I had myself a Negro friend." And I said, "Kid, if you thought you did, put it out of your mind!"

If our black students are too young to make decisions about the institutions that are murdering them, they are too young to be murdered.

Don' talk 'bout my mama no more!

Discerning their discomfort, I produced the printed texts of the voices heard on the tape. When reduced to literacy, the sounds made sense to them.

What would happen, I asked, if your husbands returned home tonight and announced that the family was moving to Iraq, Tanzania, or Argentina? The response was immediate: we would, they assured me, begin to study the language, customs, foods, dress and culture of the foreign people. They were right. That is precisely what to do. If you want to understand Blacktown, I suggested, begin with your own ignorance about black people and try to correct it.

As I returned to Whitetown after visits to Blacktown, I was constantly reminded that intelligent white people knew all about conditions in the urban ghetto. I was told that educated white people were quite aware of the poverty and crime, the generally low estate of the black citizen in our cities. The real question, I was advised, was how to improve their condition before they became disorderly and riotous. The dictum that education is a race between civilization and catastrophe never seemed so appropriate, nor so misleading.

At the time, universities were avid to get more black students on the campus. My work was seen as somehow related to that ambition. So the questions became: How do we attract more black students? What can the university do for them? What can we teach them? But all I could hear was the other side: Why do we repel black students? What can they do for the university? What can they teach us?

The reversal of questions became a kind of game. For every point made by the white man, there was the dark side. The "black problem" became the "white problem"; *de facto* segregation is really *de jure* segregation. Unemployment among whites is called recession; among blacks it is called laziness. And how, I wondered, can we good white people deny full integration while supporting desegregation? That contradiction gave me a long pause.

I discovered that what my liberal friends and colleagues didn't know was the present state of American race relations, but *they thought they did*. They thought they knew the real feelings among

11

poor black folks. One distinguished academician told me he knew exactly how a southern-born black high school dropout felt about American society. A university administrator, noting the rash of campus thefts, often accompanied by acts of violence by black janitors against the white security police, told me that he understood these acts of aggression. They happen, he said solemnly, because the janitors are tense and nervous from trying to hold down two full-time jobs simultaneously. What the administrator didn't know was the strength of the local black power caucus among his employees. These incredible misunderstandings were matched later when a professor wryly noted that "the only great idea produced by Africa is cannibalism." But every day my experience revealed that it was the blacks who were being devoured.

Many Americans think there has been a dialogue between black and white people in America. Some even think that integration is the common goal of both. Probably a greater percentage of black people in the past have wanted genuine integration than white people, but we will never know. Today that shining ideal is well on the way out. We good white people should have admitted long ago that "We are all — let us face it — Mississippians." [2] With or without guilt feelings (which don't help the black man much), we might have admitted that we really do sympathize with the fellow who said, "Thank God I'm a white man! I'm the luckiest person in the world."

Long ago we should have suspected one another when we proclaimed righteously that we had no special feelings about Negroes — because, as we said, "I didn't even know one until I was grown." We should have concluded with Norman Podhoretz: "Special feelings about color are a contagion to which white Americans seem susceptible even when there is nothing in their background to account for the susceptibility." [3] White Americans are sick in their feelings about Negroes and the actuality of having known black people or not has nothing to do with it. It is part of this nation's cultural heritage, the hidden one, the one we didn't learn in those civics courses.

With these admissions, we might then have been able to deal with ourselves and our own conception of integration. We might have considered whether integration ever meant more than "equal opportunity," i.e., the chance for the black child to sit next to the white child in school, for the black laborer to work beside the white laborer, for better housing in the ghetto and the right to vote.

Did it ever mean not only that our daughters would marry black men but our sons black women? Did it ever mean we would be grandparents to dusky children? Did it ever mean we would work for a black boss or, if the occasion warranted, submit to arrest by a black policeman? Did it mean we would permit our children to be bussed into a black neighborhood or that we would travel together in the South? Did it ever mean not only that they would integrate with us but that we would integrate with them? No, it never meant these things.

There has never been a dialogue between the black and white people of America. The reason is simple. They have never met. Today introductions are no longer necessary because the black man has stopped knocking at the back door, or at the front door. He is now leaving Blacktown and walking into the houses of Whitetown uninvited. Those who ask him to wipe his feet before entering, to await an invitation, to speak softly and sit properly, have missed the point. The black man is here, in the living room, and he is looking around. The best illustration of the present state of America's race relations is contained in this exchange:

White man: "What do the niggers want now?"
Black man: "What have you got?"

Under these circumstances it is difficult for most white Americans to carry on a conversation, but much more than talk is being required today. And how can they even converse? Most white Americans cannot hear or understand a black high school dropout speaking angrily about white oppressors, or the equally angry black welfare mother.

James Baldwin has noted that every white man knows one thing: he would not like to be a black man. And, he adds, "If he knows that, he knows everything he needs to know. He has no need to ask a black man what he wants."

13

All white Americans are, culturally speaking, racists. We may not consciously hold to racism as the doctrine that white people are superior to black people, but our attitudes indicate, and our language confirms, the fact. Long before the Kerner Report of 1968 spoke of America as a "sick society," we should have made the same diagnosis.

Americans need to study another culture, another language. That study would reveal that nationality and culture are not the same. Where our forebears came from may give us an Irish, Polish, or Jewish name but if we have lived a generation in the United States we are culturally white racists. Our institutions, schools, neighborhoods, churches, laws and morals are set by white people for white people. We may occasionally respond to our environment as white nationalists, but most of us, most of the time, respond as products of a white racist society.

And we are all — black or white — far indeed from the hope of Frantz Fanon, "In the absolute the black is no more to be loved than the Czech, and truly what is to be done is to set man free." [4]

The ways in which language reveals our cultural racism are legion. Our sportswriters will not, for example, allow a black heavyweight champion to change his name from Cassius Clay to Muhammad Ali, but the same gentlemen, after Sunday Mass, will speak to the virgin they grew up with in parochial school, little Theresa Murphy, as Mother Mary Humiliata.

But not all examples are so frivolous. The most notoriously racist ones are used in the school system and in social work when we speak of the "disadvantaged" or the "culturally deprived." It has not occurred to most white Americans that they have been deprived of the black culture, or that they suffer a severe disadvantage in not knowing any but their own regional society. Of course, no one can be familiar with every culture, but it is a white racist presumption to label blacks and other nonwhites as "culturally deprived" because they do not share the middle-class mores of the white suburbs. In some instances it disguises but thinly a doctrine of white supremacy, northern style.

The special irony of these phrases when applied to black folks is that the blacks are not, in this sense, culturally deprived. They know the white culture. They had to know it in order to survive these hundreds of years. The kind of work black people have been forced to do in Whitetown has given them the cultural advantage. They know the bedrooms and kitchens of America. According to the remark of Imamu Amiri Baraka (LeRoi Jones) "there have only been two occupations a black woman could go into in America without too much trouble: the other was domestic help." [5] The black woman has returned to Blacktown to talk about the white man and his community. It is for this reason, among others, that the black woman can cope more effectively with the white community than the white woman can cope with the black.

Plantations, Northern Style

It was a black woman who first told me that the plantations of the South were transplanted to the North when the black migration from the South began. I looked around then and saw both the house niggers and the field niggers. You can tell the difference because the house niggers are lighter in complexion and more sophisticated in the white man's way, in education, dress or conversation. Field niggers are always uneducated, unskilled and very dark. Black people sometimes add a third type, the yard nigger, but I don't recommend the distinction to white urban dwellers. It is too subtle. All kinds of niggers appear in the most unexpected places.

At a meeting of a national conference of high school and college English teachers last year, I arranged a meeting between six black high school students and about fifty white social studies and English teachers. The students, fresh from a course in African civilization and a black United States history course, were articulate, and strident proponents of black identity. The middle-aged white teachers were startled and confused at first, but they quickly recovered the standard white middle-class response. They came forth as Christian, as integrationist and, ultimately, as patronizing and colonial. The black students responded to this as Henry David Thoreau would have done had he encountered that man who was trying to do him the greatest good. Thoreau, you will recall, would have run for his life.

The teachers told the young blacks that they were not like other white Americans, indifferent to social injustice. They said that integration was still possible, that there was need for goodwill on both sides. The young blacks were in a state of almost total recoil. It was as if some white slavemasters had entered the room with their whips and chains. They drew back physically, pointing out that they had experienced white man's justice and they didn't like it. The name of Martin Luther King, Jr. was often on their lips; the man who tried to follow the white man's impossible dream and was murdered.

As the discussion continued without interruption, and well over the allotted time, I left the room for a moment. I was immediately confronted by the program chairwoman, a white woman, who informed me that there were some members of the audience who did not like this "problack program." She strongly suggested that I end it. When I refused, the house nigger appeared. She was a black English teacher, from the same high school as the students. She intervened suddenly, and gracefully, summoning them back to their regular classes. Loud protests from the audience, as well as the students, were to no avail. Slowly, almost wearily, the students rose and followed her out of the meeting hall. Only one student remained behind to continue the discussion because, he said, "I just don't care anymore."

House niggers are difficult for white people to identify because it is part of the black code to play the game with the Man. And black people play the game quite well. They are sometimes called "Oreos," white on the inside and black on the outside. But it is a foolish white man who would call a black man to his face, either a house nigger, a "Tom" or an "Oreo." Yet there are plenty of all three in Blacktown.

Perhaps the most obvious manifestation of the plantation mentality in the North occurs when the hint of insurrection arises. Recent examples include the arming of the black students at Cornell University in late 1969, and the many televised incidents of Black Nationalists marching in formation with flags and bandoleers through Blacktown. The spectacle of armed blacks is sure to send the temperature of white people rising to spectacular heights. It is a reflection of those old fears of other plantation uprisings, like Nat Turner's.

Grace Halsell in her book, *Soul Sister,* recounts the episode in Mississippi when she was almost raped by a white man in his house. It was dramatic but, like most of her narration, trivial and misleading about the depth and extent of the American race problem.

You don't need to go to Mississippi to find white men overpowering, buying and exploiting black women. It happens on the urban plantations of the northern Blacktown every weekend when the "Johns" leave white suburbia in their cars, or their downtown motels on foot, to pick up black women. The women are plentiful and very young, especially when the unemployment rate is up and the welfare checks down.

But no system of peonage can be long maintained when the economic system no longer requires the unskilled worker or the industrial slave. As a result of new technological developments which have upgraded the skills of the working class, the question now becomes: what do you do with people you don't need anymore? The American economic system, based on stimulation of artificial tastes, consumer services and defense research, has taken a new technological direction through the use of computers and advanced scientific knowledge. The black parent knows that his level of education will keep himself and his children in economic servitude for generations to come. He knows there will be, as Daniel Moynihan has said, "Another generation of the howling slums, the worn-out hollows, the endless days of half-broken men and their families harvesting other men's crops." [6]

In the first half of this century, unskilled labor was necessary and either a white immigrant back, or an ebony one, was welcome to provide industrial muscle power. Today muscle power is being replaced by brainpower. And the remnants of unskilled labor will be held by poor whites and blacks clawing at one another over the seniority system, and entry into the trade union, while the skilled workers become increasingly white and affluent, even if they are immigrants.

Recently, I experienced a vivid illustration of this point. Because of an airline strike, I was forced to take the slow-moving train from the East to the Middle West. As I boarded in Grand Central Station, I noted a number of small, dark people in clean, unconventional clothing, perhaps forty couples and their children. I was told they were Italians, from Naples, migrating to Cleveland, Indianapolis, Chicago and Canada. The ancient crowded railroad car resembled the Iron Horse's equivalent of steerage as they stacked their luggage expertly under and behind the stiff seats — with much direction and urging from the shrill voices of the women. The men would enter the building trades in America.

After one of the stops in upper New York State, a black girl sat beside me. She appeared to be about eighteen. A black man and woman gave her two sandwiches and a carton of milk. Her parents, I surmised. It was only when she took the food that I noticed the handcuffs. The left hand was free but the right was anchored to the arm of her seat. Then I noticed others. It was a large family indeed, including two policewomen and one policeman with four more handcuffed girls. Oppressors and oppressed were black.

What do the Italians think of this? They look straight ahead, saying nothing. In the New World, unable to speak the language or sense the customs, will they be accepted or will they too be manacled?

New passengers board the train. One of the newcomers is about thirty, dark and stocky. He moves to a forward seat by one of the young immigrant husbands and begins speaking in Italian. For the first time, I see an immigrant's face relax and he smiles as I hear the Italo-American say, "Now the American woman is very special, my friend." They laugh together and I realize that the newly arrived Italians may have left one home, but they have just found another in America, even in Indianapolis.

The Italian may not know the language or customs of the Americans now, but some of his countrymen do and they are here. When together they visit the hiring hall of the building trade unions which exclude black apprentices, they will all be Italo-Americans — and long before that first paycheck arrives. By the time the second paycheck arrives the new immigrant will be the most racist of Americans.

But the person whose thoughts were most important was probably the black policeman guarding his black sisters. What did he think of the Italian immigrants? Did he realize that the one who was truly shackled was his black brother, the semiskilled and unemployed ghetto dweller, perhaps the brother of the black female convict? Did he realize that he is the slave boss for the northern white slavemaster?

As the train moved slowly westward, past the black colonies of our northern cities, I reflected on the fact that the black girl was chained to the seat next to mine. Whether handcuffed or not, she has never been free. From the Harlem where she came from to the upper New York State prison she was entering, she has been shackled to one place or another. Only the accident of an airline strike had brought us together.

The proximity of black people to white is more important than it may appear. It is much more important than this writer's temperament or his taste. The nearness, the physical nearness, of black people to white gets us to the heart of the integration question: are they integrating with us or are we integrating with them? It gets us also to larger questions, about the climate of freedom in the United States.

As a good white liberal I used to be concerned about the "climate of freedom," about the fact that justice unequally applied is injustice and that freedom divided is slavery. With other good white liberals, I supported causes in Russia, Latin America, the Middle East and Asia on the grounds that freedom is important in every part of the globe. The principle was sound but the application faulty. While our white hearts were bleeding over faraway places, injustice and unfreedom have been rampant in the black colonies, the urban plantations of the United States.

But surely not all Americans have been concerned about injustice in faraway places. Famine and thirst, murder and rape, death and disease are all tolerated, so long as they occur at a distance. If Viet Nam were an offshore island in California, the war would have ended long ago. It was Timothy Leary who defined violence as "murder at a distance," though another, and perhaps more authentically American, statement would be: to hell with everybody else. The young, affluent, largely white people who congregated at Woodstock — four hundred thousand strong — were not establishing an independent nation, but rather exhibiting a typically American practice: fouling another's nest, calling upon outside resources for food, health and sanitation, all the way claiming individual liberty, "doing your thing."

Just as we have permitted injustice and unfreedom in faraway places, so also did we exploit the land, sea and air of our countryside. It is an interesting speculation for the future whether the ecological concerns of the present will be translated into political and social terms, an event which will require a new analysis of the phrase, "the *climate* of freedom." As we now discover that nature is taking its revenge for our profligate conduct by destroying the leafy suburbs and fouling the country air, is it possible that we will see that society, like nature, is organic? Will we learn something about the indivisibility of freedom from the indivisibility of life and nature? Will we perceive that the climate of freedom in Blacktown is a measure of the climate of freedom in Whitetown?

But to know this, we must enter Blacktown, the urban plantations of the North. It is a difficult admonition in these racially tense times, and I do not recommend it lightly. It is nonetheless essential that the white man enter Blacktown because it is certain the black man is entering Whitetown. The first entry of the white person may

21

be made through books like *Blacktown, U.S.A.*, but the second, third and other entries must be made in person. The white man will be jostled a little, ridiculed a bit, and often ignored, but all he will ultimately lose are his false ideas about black folks. His gains will be many and significant, including, just possibly, his soul.

The white man and woman must enter Blacktown because there is fear and guilt on both sides. As Martin Luther King, Jr. said, "The Negro needs the white man to free him from his fears; the white man needs the Negro to free him from his guilt." If the white man — for whom this work is chiefly intended — is able to free himself from guilt, he must come to know black people intimately. He must know them as well as he knows his best white friends. And when he knows them this well, he will never again say, "Some of my best friends are Negroes." He won't need to say it, he will manifest it. The white man must enter Blacktown to meet the citizens there. How he does so, when and where, are his to decide. He may select his own time and place, but he must enter those northern urban plantations and stay awhile even if, at the beginning, he visits only in the daylight hours.

Unless he enters Blacktown, the white man will never understand why Dick Gregory suggests that a reading of the Declaration of Independence should accompany the sounds and sights of the TV showing of the latest ghetto riots. Unless he spends some time in Blacktown, he will not understand the charge that there is a police state in America's inner city, that, increasingly, black folks regard themselves as an oppressed and colonized people under the heel of a white army of occupation.

Unless the white person enters Blacktown, he will not understand what James Cheek meant when he said: "Black Americans see themselves today in relation to their government in much the same way as Hamilton, Jay, Madison saw themselves in relation to the 'Mother Country.' There is beginning to emerge among the black leadership a delineation of the grievances against the 'establishment' which echoes the Declaration of Independence." [7]

What will he find when he enters? A slave society in transition. There will be all the consequences of white racism, all the aspects of a colonized people. He will find also a growing movement

22

toward black identity and concepts of self-determination. These concepts are now being hammered out in psychological and sociological terms in Blacktown. He will find no serious political self-determination or economic independence. At the moment, the urban plantations are simply that: totally dependent sectors of a dominant white political and economic majority.

The white man and white woman will also see the emergence of a black urban culture. It is not their task to interpret it, or note its direction in any definitive fashion, at least until they have done some substantial homework. For the blacks themselves, it remains largely undefined and uncharted, partly because of white historians who insisted that "Negroes are, after all, only white men with black skins; nothing more and nothing less." [8]

I have been arguing that the white man and woman should enter Blacktown — regardless of the personal inconvenience, danger or cost to themselves, their pride and their fondly held conceptions and misconceptions about Blacktown. I would be remiss if I did not warn them about some of the other dangers. One is condescension, another is Negrophilism. The first arises from viewing the black man as inferior and the second from viewing him as superior.

The temptation to deal patronizingly with the subject peoples of America's Blacktowns will be almost overwhelming. It is inevitable that, as the true conditions of the urban plantations become known, white people will respond as neocolonial people always have: first by expressions of shock and then by costly, condescending and patronizing attempts to correct the conditions without eliminating the causes. The Kerner Report is a case in point. It failed in its suggestions for a solution to the polarization of the races because the response was in the terms of a white racist culture and society. The means for social change in America today are flawed; they are affected with the very disease they hope to eliminate. What the correction of the social and psychological ills of America's Blacktowns requires is nothing less than a new and better society, a racist-free society. The Kerner Report didn't tell us white people how to rid ourselves of our sickness, racism.

The second danger is Negrophilism. With American institutions

23

under attack, it will appear an easy way out. As white America scrutinizes its own society, its strengths and weaknesses, it will turn to black America for the humanity it appears to have lost. As a friend of Frantz Fanon put it, "The presence of the Negroes beside the whites is in a way an insurance policy on humanness. When the whites feel that they have become too mechanized, they turn to the men of color and ask them for a little human sustenance." [9]

Surely it is true that the black cause in America, especially as it reflects our indifference to the best in American political and social institutions, is the most moral cause in America today. We have all but forgotten that America's own revolution was based upon a new conception of humanity, a worldwide conception. The black cause is a permanent moral revolution which will endure long after public policy, ecological and technological changes, have reduced or eliminated hunger, poverty and war. It is permanent because the conflict between white and black people is not a battle for men's minds. The conflict is almost mindless. It is based rather on long-held, centuries-old social and moral attitudes about superiority and inferiority. They will not erode quickly, unless we seriously consider the use of truth serums, lobotomies, concentration camps for blacks, or government subsidies for miscegenation. Perhaps we will. Some blacks think we are using some of these methods now.

In 1963, Eric Severeid said, "If the Negro passion of today is not a true people's revolution, it is as close to one as we have ever known in our land." [10] Mr. Severeid was only wrong about the timetable. The Negro passion has been around a long while, for as long as there have been black people. What white folks don't understand is that the black cause in America is moral because every black child is born with a moral cause. Being born in blackness, he is born a victim. As a consequence he suffers not only socially, politically, and economically. He suffers as a whole human being.

Negrophilism will be a temptation for the white man as he enters Blacktown because he will discover some of the virtues that come from a slave experience and from constant oppression. To paraphrase Fanon, there will be a lot of white skins in black masks.

24

They will discover the greatness of W. E. B. Du Bois in his famous Credo of 1910: "I believe in pride of self so deep as to scorn injustice to other selves." And today in Blacktown, despite the drumfire of angry militants who sometimes sound like black racists, and despite the increasing radicalization of the black middle class, he will still hear the sounds of a higher law and a deeper freedom. He will encounter black men and women everywhere saying what a black woman journalist in Chicago, Lilian Calhoun, said recently: "Must we always emulate bigots, stupid, ignorant know-nothings? The real beauty of being black in this insanely racist country is not in how one wears the hair or the length of the borrowed African dashiki but in being whole human beings." [11]

As white people enter the urban plantations of the North and find ordinary black men and women talking like Lilian Calhoun, they will demand an incredible thing. After centuries of dehumanization, they will turn to black people and ask them for the strength, forgiveness and largeness of heart to heal white society. When white people do this, they will be able to understand the anger and frustration of the young black writer who said recently, "Here we go again . . . Black people have to become superhuman . . . Why must black folks be super Christians? When has the white man been redemptive?" [12]

And it will not only be in moral matters that white America will look to black people but, equally incredibly, in politics. In my own city where there is a black mayor, Cleveland white voters expect urban miracles after decades of corruption by white ethnic politicians. And when we look for a black President of the United States by 1980 as William F. Buckley, Jr. has suggested, will we not really be looking for a national, and an international, miracle?

The call for a black President of the United States marks the height of the white man's Negrophilism.

The Young Malcolms

The urban plantations of the North have two kinds of street patrols, one protects the black people from the whites, the other protects the white people and their property from the blacks. The first patrol is on foot; it is quite young, black, tough talking and tough acting. The standard weapon is the switchblade. Its members are all, potentially, younger versions of Malcolm X. The second patrol stays in the streets in squad cars, cruising slowly. Its standard weapons are the pistol and shotgun. Its members are older, middle-class whites who live in the suburbs. They also are tough talking and tough acting, and they belong to the Fraternal Order of Police.

Perhaps the best description of a white man's encounter with the first patrol is contained in the following:

If you are white and go walking alone through the Cleveland ghetto, the older residents will often pass you on the sidewalks and murmur a brief greeting in that old way of the country South. Yet a cluster of scowling teen-agers may very well mutter as you pass by, "What you doin' around here, white man?" and stamp their feet smartly on the pavement behind you to see if you will flinch.

Do not throw out your chest. But do not slump your shoulders. You must walk in the precise manner to indicate you don't mean any harm, you are only looking around, but nevertheless you can take care of yourself. When you see two goofy-looking guys, one wearing a black burnous, the other a goatee and an embroidered skullcap, remember that you are not permitted to stare. When two blacks pass by, roaring with laughter at the same pair of goofs, do not assume you have the right to laugh with them.

Wear a pair of Murray space shoes and enter Hough on a warm, jumping Friday night. The blacks have a big thing about shoes, one of the traditional status symbols of a slave society. A voice might call out from the idlers standing against the wall of the buildings. "Hey, man! Them shoes from Holland, right?" But try to be calm. Forget the incidents that have occurred, the many kinds of blood that have flowed over the very spot on which you are standing.

A half block further and you could get another old, familiar, Hey; a nod of the head, the summons from the tough-guy that indicates the command to come over and heel. Do not feel that standard reaction, Who the hell do you think you are? You are on his turf. Go over to the scruffy-looking alley cat about seven-eighths stoned. He might even meet you halfway. "Them's molded shoes. Right? How much they cost?" Say, "Eighty-five dollars . . ."

If the dude suddenly kneels down and grabs your foot, don't jerk away, Stall for a thought, a plan, a policy, Say, "They fit just like a glove." Forget that the cruddy son of a bitch is feeling up your toes. Remember those grins and the eyeballs, the glinting switchblades whirling out of the neon and the headlights, the purple suits without lapels, the hats with the unbelievable brims and Kelly-green sashes, the bell bottom pants of any color whatsoever.

27

But then the black cat with the starved-looking fur and back-alley eyes might stand up and grin the most beautiful of grins. "Well, okay baby, We'll see you around. Now, you be real good now. You hear?" Stand there and smile for just a second before walking on with a wave. You will feel warm. Or you will feel something. You might almost want to kiss the bastard.[13]

These are the young Malcolms. They are not nationalists now, only hustlers. They are the target of recruiting efforts by Black Nationalists only slightly older than they. When they are recruited, they become good disciples — though the dropout rate of the Black Nationalists' schools is not known by white people.

Malcolm X once said, "This generation of our people has a burden, more so than at any time in history. The most important thing we can learn today is to think for ourselves." Within each urban area in America there is an inner city of young blacks who are thinking for themselves. They are the offspring of parents who migrated from the South in the thirties and especially in the war years of the forties seeking a better life. The children of these immigrants reached manhood during the sixties. Unlike most of their white peers, they emerge from a street culture, not a school culture, and they all live in Blacktown.

The contrast between the white and black teen-ager is illuminating. The young black may never have visited the suburbs, and when he walks through Whitetown he hurries because he was once caught there and beaten up pretty badly. His parents know the language and customs of the southern farm and woodland while he knows the language of the streets, Aretha Franklin, and the sound of police sirens. He knows also the juvenile court and the city prisons. If he follows the path of a young Malcolm, he dropped out of junior high school four years ago and has been drifting ever since from job to job. On the street corner though he is a regular full-time worker, a very resourceful hustler.

His mother told him he had a father but his mother never told him who. His little sister and brother look different. When he was in school, there was a U.S. President named John F. Kennedy who was assassinated. But he dug the black deaths more, Martin Luther King and Malcolm X. He was supposed to like Dr. King, but on the

28

street corner Malcolm was the read dude. Tonight he plans to watch the late late show.

The youth in Whitetown, on the other hand, have improved their standard of living as social and economic changes have rewarded the industry of their parents.The young white has known a Republican and two Democratic Presidents, and he has a vague idea of the difference. He wouldn't know much about Malcolm X, except that he was a wild nigger, and he has never visited Blacktown. He knows Captain Kangaroo because he grew up with him on television. He knows the film as an art form and the automobile as an escape hatch. He knows the comfortable feeling of having an allowance, a bankbook and sometimes a credit card. He plans to go to college.

Whitetown's inhabitants and structure are as variegated as Blacktown's. Now, in the suburban areas closest to the central city, young whites see their black counterparts, in Afros, slowly sauntering their way through; they like to look at white girls. Young blacks appear to the inhabitants of Whitetown as creatures from another planet but by nightfall they are gone, gone to the ghetto.

The ghetto is a monolithic world. It is one where time is measured two ways: either workdays and weekends or the summer (hot) and the winter (cold). Like Malcolm, the young bloods are known by initiative and a quick wit. They are willing to learn almost anything, but teaching them is not easy. They are largely self-educated, an education not infrequently gathered from the time and leisure provided by a period in the workhouse or prison. No matter. To move from Blacktown to the penitentiary is to go from one prison to another.

They share the culture of the poor, and the poor in America today have television, radio and the film. They are influenced by the mass media, but they also join enthusiastically in the new black identity movement. They reveal their black pride in dress, song, manner and speech.

They also share some distinctively American virtues. They hold that violence can sometimes be justified, that self-determination is a democratic value, that ethnic separation is not wrong, that those who live in a community should control it, that a free press should extend to all. And like most other Americans, they have racial attitudes.

This new American black voice arising in our inner cities speaks sometimes with a foreign accent. Nothing is more characteristic of the young Black Nationalist than his hybrid quality. While being American and sharing a vision of promise and hope, he is also consciously Afro, with soul. Like those who argue that Western man, before engaging in the study of Asian thought, must first understand Western civilization, young black America is now pursuing the study of its own culture and history in Blacktown. The results of that study may well determine the possibility and the limitations of dialogue with white America and its culture.

The first phrase which came from the lips of the new young black was "black power." It frightened the white man, but only because he hadn't been listening. Black power is not new in American history. Programs of black rebellion and strategies for power have bloomed briefly throughout the life of the Republic, but they never reached maturity. And the recent calls for "black power" did not cause the white backlash, it was rather the other way around. As Kenneth Clark has noted, " 'Black Power' is the cry of defiance of what its advocates have come to see as the hoax of racial progress — of the cynicism of the appeals to the Negro to be patient and to be lawful as his needs are continually subordinated to more important national and international issues and to needs, desires and conveniences of more privileged groups." [14]

In recent years the phrase has been given new meaning and a broader definition. Today black power embraces a number of cultural, social, economic, and political programs which take self-determination and the black community as their true center. There is now appearing, especially in northern Blacktowns, a national platform of black rebellion, and a growing Black Nationalist ideology, which has both plausibility and substance. The Black Panthers are only the ones upon whom the media has recently seized. Five years ago the bête noir of white folks was the Nation of Islam, the so-called "Black Muslims." But there are today many, many Black Nationalist organizations, some better and some worse than those created and sustained by the white media. The reader of this volume will discover some of them.

Black power has not yet received an adequate response from white America largely because it is widely regarded as a physical challenge to the system of white dominance, rather than what it is: a cry of anguish and defiance. And white America's response to the physical challenge is predictable: retreat and repression based upon fear. Some part of that fear, as it applies to any impoverished people, is justified. There are reasonable fears about the deteriorating quality of neighborhood life, the effects of poverty and drugs, the gang wars, extortion, and brutality. But these grim facts are not facts about black people, they are facts about ghetto life, whether black or white.

The new black voices have come upon America at a difficult time in her history. Never before have our institutions seemed so dysfunctional, precarious, threatened, and archaic. They seem structured for another time and place. While these internal changes occur, worldwide events place additional pressure upon civil order against a background of ever increasing racial polarization. The guerrilla exploits of the Cuban revolutionaries, and the stalemated war in Viet Nam, encourage the young black to see the decline of American military power. The black man in America sees himself as part of a world revolution in which the white man is the real minority.

All these events, internal and external to life in the urban ghettos of American cities, are paraded before the eyes of the young black man and woman through the mass media. Is it any wonder that he is at a crossroads? Is it any wonder he seeks a new expression and a new program to rid himself finally of the ancient wrongs?

And the media itself poses a special problem for the new young black. When he is depicted or described in the white media, whether in sound or print, he is seen negatively: a man who lacks something — education, housing, health or justice. His positive qualities are rarely mentioned except when a crime, or alleged crime, has been committed. From reading the white daily newspapers one would think that black people are not born, do not marry, don't achieve, don't die. Since black pride is not served by the white media, where will white Americans learn something positive about black people?

It is true that other U.S. minorities are also ignored, the Indians, Puerto Ricans, Appalachian whites and newly arrived East Europeans. Nonetheless, black men in America today by reason of their numbers, the justice of their historic role in America's economic and cultural life, their world revolutionary impact, thrust themselves with a special claim upon us.

The absence of a free press for the black man has hurt both him and the white man. It has kept the white man uninformed and frightened. It has prevented the black man from a better formulation of his newly won opinions and his growing nationalistic aims. A great contribution today toward a genuine dialogue between Blacktown and Whitetown would be to listen to the new black voices of America's inner cities, *both* in the white and in the black press. And we should listen to what they are saying, not only to what they have allegedly done.

The sound of these voices is harsh and unrepentant, hostile yet somehow heroic. They are sometimes wrong and frequently inflammatory. White ears are not accustomed to the voices of Blacktown which are clearly in the French tradition of *j'accuse!*

As the young Malcolms begin to think for themselves, they are analyzing their plight. They are searching out the real enemy. "They know they are catching Hell, but they don't know where they're catching Hell from," wrote Malcolm X. They are beginning to find out. Take Viet Nam. It is a special war for them. When the young Malcolm is facing induction into the U. S. Army he wonders why. Sometimes he is a member of his own army in Blacktown. He has his uniform and flag, drills and guns. Why should he join that other army and fight yellow people in Asia?

One young black man put it this way:

Ain't no use. Man gonna get me, kill me off, no matter what I do. Here in the street one night, maybe. Maybe on the freeway, he stop me: BAM. Or maybe over there, ya know, Viet Nam. That's the cool way. Me and the Viet Cong out there. Bang. Bang. Me dead. Or the Viet Cong dead. Either way the white man won.

A Cleveland black poet, Norman Jordan, puts it another way:

> Hell
> We are on
> To you whitey
> trying to off
> yellow power
> with black power
> (killing two birds
> with one stone) . . .
> Bullshit,
> fight your
> *own* fucking war.

It is paradoxical to note that the number of young Malcolms in our northern cities is not rising as rapidly as the number of young black militants, but it is true. Had Malcolm lived we would today see legions of young Malcolms, as we see a rising number of Black Nationalists. To be a young Malcolm is a high calling: the attributes of a Malcolm X are rare in any race. And we don't realize how young the black militants are. Many are twelve to sixteen years of age and Malcolm X, who died six years ago, is but a shadowy figure for them.

Malcolm's death greatly retarded the improvement of America's race relations. He was an extraordinary man, a leader of remarkable intellect and courage, a genuine spokesman for his people. When history places his name alongside those of Frederick Douglass and W. E. B. Du Bois, it will do so because he represented the emergence of a new phase of the black movement, its appearance in the northern city. Unlike Martin Luther King who was a product of southern Christian traditions, Malcolm was a product of the northern ghetto, a citizen of Blacktown. The record of his conversion from a hustler's life to one of total dedication to the black and the human race is only paralleled by another black man's spiritual odyssey, the *Confessions* of Augustine, Bishop of Hippo in North Africa. What is remarkably similar in the two autobiographies is that the very character of the regeneration of spirit develops from the dissolute conditions of their previous lives. Despite their many other achievements — one in the social and the other in the theological order — Malcolm remained a remarkable hustler to the end of his life, as Augustine remained a sex-seared monk.

But if the actual number of young Malcolms increases slowly, the number of potential Malcolms is large and growing. The reason is simple. The young Malcolm is a product of the northern ghetto and we are producing many young alienated blacks in New York, Philadelphia, Newark, Detroit, Cleveland, Chicago, Watts, and Oakland.

In a remarkable set of passages, Dr. Robert Coles of Harvard has described life in the northern blacktowns:

I have asked [the ghetto child] to draw pictures of himself, of his school, of his home, of anything he wishes, and I get from him devastating portrayals — schools that look like jails, teachers whose faces show drowsiness or scorn, streets and homes that are as awful on paper as they are in real life, outsiders whose power and mercenary hostility are all too obvious, and everywhere the police — looking for trouble, creating trouble, checking up, calling people to court, calling them names, getting ready to hurt them, assault them, jail them and beat them up, even if they are children.

No wonder I encounter anger, frustration, violence in ghetto children. Everywhere things go wrong; the lights don't work; the stairs are treacherous; rats appear — they're not timid; uniformed men patrol the streets, certain that trouble will appear; teachers work in schools they're ashamed to call their own, jobs are few, and welfare is the essence of the economy.

And yet, I'm writing this article chiefly to say that the ghetto does not kill its young children, that comes later at age twelve or fourteen when idleness becomes a way of life, when jobs are nowhere to be had. From the first decade of their existence, ghetto children huddle together and learn about the world they've inherited, go on to explore it, master its facts, accept its fate, and burn from day to day their energy and life, able for a while to ignore the alien outside world. And I find in those children a vitality and exuberance that reminds me of the fatally ill I once treated on hospital wards. For a long time they appear flushed with life, even beautiful, only to die. I remembered hearing from a distinguished physician, who supervised a few of us who were interns, that they're fighting the battle of tuberculosis and they're going to lose,

34

but not without a brilliant flash of energy. It's a shame we can't intervene right at the critical moment and help them win. He, of course, had the faith that some day medicine would intervene with one or another saving treatment. Ghetto people have no such confidence and I'm afraid that I, at least today, share their outlook.[15]

Dr. Coles speaks of that interim moment when the child of the ghetto appears "flushed with life, even beautiful, only to die." He reminds us of the various kinds of death, of the various kinds of violence. One of the black people I interviewed, who does not appear in this book, explained it this way:

People are dying all the time. But whites get real upset if somebody takes a gun and shoots someone and they lay out there with a bullet in them and die. But nobody gets upset when you tighten up the money supply and they starve to death, or if the mortality rate moves up. If you were on a reservation out in Arizona or Oklahoma, an Indian is not going to live to be over thirty-three years old because white people have put him in that type of situation. They don't get upset over that, but they keep telling me they're concerned about certain types of death.

It is true. White people are concerned about white deaths, just as black people are concerned about black deaths. Who is concerned about death itself, anywhere? It was Dick Gregory who noted that the Texas children who applauded the assassination of John F. Kennedy, and the white children who were gleeful over Dr. King's death, were matched by the New York children who were delighted by the assassination of Norman Lincoln Rockwell. What we need, says Gregory, is not to select one assassination over another but to oppose assassination itelf.

Death has a way of polarizing people and of escalating hostile feelings. What frightens white people today is that the young Black Nationalist, the potential Malcolm, is out of control. He is not afraid to die. It is not a complete definition of a revolutionary to say that he is not afraid to die, but it is an essential characteristic. For a genuine revolutionary, death is a given, on condition that he makes it as costly as possible for the enemy.

35

Death is also an escape and it can be suicidal. The young Malcolms are frequently the children of southern blacks who migrated North as to the promised land. Claude Brown poses the ultimate question: "The children of these disillusioned colored pioneers inherited the total lot of their parents — the disappointments, the anger. To add to their misery, they had little hope of deliverance. For where does one run to when he's already in the promised land?" [16]

Where does he run indeed? He doesn't run, not anymore. He stays and fights.

The Two Blacktowns

There are some young and some old Malcolms in this volume. But there are a number of other black people too. Most of them live within the city limits of Cleveland, Detroit, Chicago, Boston, and Philadelphia. But no matter where they live in the northern cities, they are all residents of Blacktown, U.S.A.

Even those black people who live in the so-called integrated sections of the northern cities are regarded by their white neighbors as immigrants. They have not immigrated from the South, from another country, or even from a continent. They have immigrated from Blacktown, that mysterious place where black folks live and work, play and sing, and die. It can be found anywhere in America where there are groups of black folks.

There are really two Blacktowns in America and every black person lives in one or the other. The first is the physical one, often found at the core of our large cities, what is sometimes called the ghetto. Other times it is called the inner city, and it used to be called the other side of the tracks. Michael Harrington described it as part of *The Other America.*

In 1928, Louis Wirth wrote, "The ghetto is not only a physical fact; it is a state of mind." [17] What Wirth meant was that the physical ghetto produces a state of mind in its dwellers. The deeper truth is that the ghetto also produces a state of mind in those who do not live there, in those who establish and maintain a segregated society. The second Blacktown exists in the mind of the white man. It is not nearly as crowded as the first, but its creatures are nonetheless fantastic folks, bigger than life.

White people know the first Blacktown, at least near its boundaries. Passports are not required, and there are no border patrols. Yet the lines of demarcation between Blacktown and Whitetown are as firm and distinct as the borders of Mexico and Canada, maybe more so. Sociologically it is another country. Lately there has been talk about the doctrine of separation in Blacktown; blacks have been accused of wanting to go it alone. The natives find that amusing — just before they get real angry — because the separation of Blacktown from Whitetown was the white man's plan. Many of the inhabitants of Blacktown didn't read the Kerner Report but they didn't have to. They already knew what it was talking about: "White institutions created it [the ghetto], white institutions maintain it, and white society condones it." [18]

Like a foreign country, there is a different accent and language, another set of values and family structure. In Blacktown there is both more and less. There is less income and property taxes, less schooling, narrower streets, fewer trees and parks. But there are more bars and small businesses, more prostitution and crime, more older houses and broken windows, more transients. By white middle-class norms, there is more of what is bad and less of what is good.

You know the place. White people drive through, or around, it daily — at fairly fast speeds. If they were ever set adrift there, they could not "cope," they would not survive. The contrary is not true. Black folks do leave Blacktown and return at night after working for the Man. During the daylight hours, there is considerable traffic between the two towns. But there is a difference. White people enter Blacktown for service and deliveries, only a few work there and these rarely dwell in Blacktown. Black people enter Whitetown because they have to work there and they too return at nightfall. Then separation becomes complete and they are sealed off from each other, except for the integration represented by prostitution.

Because white Americans do not enter Blacktown, and because they have been deprived of black culture, they have been forced to construct an image of black people for themselves. This is the second Blacktown, the Blacktown of the white man's mind.

The inhabitants of the second Blacktown are creatures of imagination. Because they are fantastic creatures, they sustain contradictions. Sometimes they appear half-human and half-animal, at other times they are half-human and half-divine. Like the mythical gods and goddesses of ancient times, they have magical qualities. They are beings endowed with both vices and virtues far surpassing their real selves. They are "super-blacks."

Who are these creatures? They are what we used to call Negroes: shiftless but strong, violent yet cheerful, fun-loving and cowardly, clever and stupid, sexy and dirty. They are all the same, all niggers.

The Blacktown of the white man's imagination has its own structure and government, a simple one. It is led by nobody, conned by everybody and inhabited by suckers. Its chief citizens are ministers, hustlers and charlatans. Lately, some crazy Black Nationalists have been throwing fire bombs.

The white man's Blacktown contains a lot of inferior people who are, somehow, victims. And they don't care. They don't care if they are inferior, of if they are victimized. They haven't even, until recently, cared about what white people called them. But no matter. They are all the same. White people know that Saturday night and Sunday morning belong to black people and that on Monday morning the blacks will get up and sit under a tree with a watermelon, or on the curb with a welfare check in their hands.

The Voices of Blacktown

Some white people and some black may not recognize this description of black people. They will regard it as extravagant and deeply racist. They are right. It is both. It is an exaggerated view of black people and an accurate description of what most white people think.

Regardless of the particular characteristics however, white people are convinced that all black people are the same. They are all niggers. As Vice-President Agnew is alleged to have said, "Once

you have seen one ghetto you have seen them all." What he probably meant was, "Once you have seen one nigger, you have seen
them all." The stereotyping of peoples is not a new phenomenon,
and it may be visited upon the Irish as drunkards, the French as
erotic, the Germans as stubborn, as easily as upon the blacks as
carnal, dirty or whatever. No group of people escapes pejorative
comment by others, or even by themselves. Yet the number and
degree of defects, vices and aberrations ascribed to black people by
whites easily places them in a separate category among the minority groups in America — ever since that seventeenth century appellation, "the Apes of Africa" noted by Winthrop P. Jordan.[19] More
importantly, there is no particular talent, nor quality of a positive
sort, attributed to black people as black. Whatever intelligence or
virtue the black man has, he received from his association with
white people. The notion that Africa may have provided a culture
in which black men everywhere, even in America, may share and
perpetuate among themselves is for almost all white Americans and
for most blacks, too, beyond comprehension and belief.

Above all else, white people think of black people as the same:
undifferentiated, homogeneous, lacking individuality. The cultural
deprivation of white people is never so marked as when they consider the black American. This stereotype has been developed consciously and unconsciously in both whites and blacks. As Bayard
Rustin perceived: "The notion of the undifferentiated black community is the intellectual creation of both whites — liberals as well
as racists to whom all Negroes are the same — and of certain small
groups of blacks who illegitimately claim to speak for the majority." [20]

The stereotyping of blacks by whites is particularly infuriating to
black people because whites do not themselves expect that any one
white leader or group speaks for them. Why should blacks alone be
considered as a monolithic and undifferentiated community?

Blacktown, U.S.A. attempts to destroy this stereotype. It presents twenty-one voices from Blacktown, all different, except for
the single fact that they live in northern cities. The "young Malcolm" will appear here but so will the businessman, the lawyer
and politician, the administrator and social worker, the artist and

preacher, mothers and fathers, sons and daughters, husbands and wives. There are no national figures in this book and only a few who are widely known in their respective cities. They are ordinary — by which I mean typical — black people. Any black community of any size in the United States contains black people with the same determination, charm and intelligence, and foibles, as the people of *Blacktown, U.S.A.* What is remarkable about them is not that they are there, but that they have never been heard by white people.

There are Blacktowns in the South but all the persons I interviewed are from northern ghettos. Some people in the book argue that there are no differences between black life in the South and the North since regional conditions are equally destructive of black people. But there are differences, probably differences of kind as well as degree. Nonetheless one is impressed with the manner and frequency of the appearance of southern folkways in the northern city. Migrations have been recent enough to permit memory and custom to work their way deeply into the life-style of northern urban dwellers. The reader will discover that the South is very much in this book as it is in the mind and culture of American blacks everywhere. Even when the northern black is removed two or more generations from the rural South, he will still regard it as the "old country," his ancestral home.

The black middle class is also contained in this volume and it is an increasingly beleaguered class, one that is being challenged to respond more consistently to the demands and the needs of the entire black community.

Recently an interesting debate developed in the pages of *Black World* (previously, the *Negro Digest*). One of the most articulate and lively journals in America today, *Black World,* under editor Hoyt Fuller, has provided a platform for some of the best black writing of the present day. As a journal of arts and letters, it is outstanding, but it has also maintained a steady social criticism against the middle-class Negro who seeks to merge into the white power structure.

One of its most powerful strawmen is Chauncey Arringham Hildredth III, Esquire, a Negro lawyer in his forties who is allegedly embarrassed by the black identity movement. Two years ago there was a powerful rejoinder to this caricature by Wallace B. January of Washington, D.C. He pointed out that it is only the black people who destroy their leaders, those who have exhibited the qualities of "discipline, ability, fortitude, neatness and courage" [21] to face up to the white majority group alone, on its own terms, and win. In sharp contrast, he noted, Jews have always admired its members who have advanced to the top of the dominant culture. The comparison between blacks and Jews is constantly made by both blacks and whites in the inner city, partly because the internal migration of blacks has placed them in those sections of the inner city previously inhabited by Jews. As Fanon's philosophy professor told him, "Whenever you hear anyone abuse the Jews, pay attention, because he is talking about you." [22] Nonetheless I found very little anti-Semitism among black people, but plenty of anti-exploitationism.

There is a significant debate, and one which will be going on for a long time, between the black artists and intellectuals who interpret the aesthetics of the streets and who hear the black heart beat in the ghetto, and the socially mobile middle-class Negro, the black bourgeoisie.

Despite appearances, it is not an exclusively intrablack dialogue. It has powerful meaning for the future of the American culture and politics. William F. Buckley, Jr., among others, has been deeply moved by the organizational intelligence of the black urban voice, and he has suggested a black President in the year 1980. Buckley holds that the election of black public officials, precisely because they are black, holds a "considerable tonic for the white soul." [23] His proposal for 1980 is neither outlandish or bizarre. By 1976 it may well prove prophetic.

There are of course many who would disagree with Buckley, and many of these would be black. The more typical response to this presidential possibility, here in 1971, would be that of a black man who told me:

We are taught in school that anyone can become President in this country, we are taught to revere guys like — you know, "Give me liberty or give me death," — that Virginia cat that had slaves, Patrick Henry. We learned all this in the fourth and fifth grades but when a black man comes up and says the same thing, they say: "Now, wait a minute! We didn't mean you!"

So the issue at the present time is principally between the black middle class and their ghetto brothers. There is some evidence, as *Fortune* indicated in December 1969 that "Middle-class blacks are moving off the Middle." Nonetheless the class distinction between blacks is as real and deep as between any other ethnic group, black or white, perhaps deeper. Few indeed are the middle-class Negroes who have even a passing acquaintance with the local Black Nationalist leader, and the notion that they might unite in any northern Blacktown in common cause for the black race is so rare today as to be almost nonexistent. Tomorrow will be different.

✓Through the voices of *Blacktown, U.S.A.* the white reader will encounter black men and women, militant and moderate, that he has never met. He will encounter those who have never been in jail or on dope, never participated in a riot or marched for civil rights as well as those who have never been on welfare. He will find examples of those black Americans who "go to work every day, pay their taxes, root for the home team, worry about the high costs of living, shop for bargains, and go over the children's homework just like millions of other Americans." [24]

The voices of Blacktown have been muffled and distorted. They have been misconstrued and ignored. The only authentic sounds of black folks which have come straight, clean and whole into the consciousness of white America have been its music, jazz and the blues. White Americans do listen to the music of black men and women — all the while adapting and corrupting it a bit — but they have so far found it unnecessary to listen to the words of black people and to share their experiences.

There has been no dialogue between blacks and whites in America because they have never met.

The voices of Blacktown the reader will hear in this book are various, but not representative of all opinions, all the diversity of

45

character, talent, and opinion among black people. There are, for example, no proponents of the Back to Africa movement, no members of the Nation of Islam (the Black Muslims), no welfare mothers, teachers, store owners — though all of these exist in all of the Blacktowns of America. *Blacktown, U.S.A.* should be considered a sampler, a black miscellany of the rich and varied life-style of a northern urban folk. The reader may compare them with the stereotypes in his mind, the Blacktown of his imagination, and though he may find them in contrast less colorful, he will find them more real and more human.

What is finally remarkable about the voices in this volume is that they are so ordinary. I do not claim that this sample of black personalities has been selected from among hundreds of persons interviewed. On the contrary, I met these twenty-one people — fourteen men and six women, from eighteen years of age to one hundred — under the most casual of circumstances; some were met on the street and interviewed there. Only a handful of the persons I interviewed do not appear in this book. The point is that they are typical of black people everywhere, not unusual folks at all. At this moment in history, it is possible for any white person to come to know twenty-one black people as well as I have come to know those behind the profiles in *Blacktown, U.S.A.*

The circumstances of my meetings may be of some interest because they were for the most part casual and unexceptional. At least half of the people in the volume were encountered in my ordinary university activities, the other half were identified through the local black newspapers in various communities, especially Cleveland, Ohio. The localism of Cleveland does not change the theme of this book, *Blacktown, U.S.A.,* but merely enhances it. There are Blacktowns everywhere in America. There are urban plantations or colonies anywhere a large number of black people gather in the United States. The book could have been written in any one of thousands of Blacktowns in the United States, North or South. No unusual intelligence is demanded, no elaborate set of contacts or special introductions. All that is required is an interest in black people and what they have to say.

One caution to white people may be in order. There is only one thing that a genuine, conscious white racist hates more than a black person: a white person who consorts with them. The usual appellation is "nigger-lover." This point was brought home vividly to me some months ago when a friend, a white physics professor, was participating in a march against the central police station of a large midwestern city. He was the only white man in a small contingent of Black Nationalists, men and women. Despairing of the effectiveness of the demonstration, they decided to block access to the stairs of the police station, were promptly apprehended and booked for causing a disturbance. They were all duly released after posting bail. When their case came up before the local magistrate, each of the nationalists received some days in the workhouse — from six to sixty days. My white academic friend received no such sentence, but he was required to have several psychiatrist examinations to establish his sanity. He was then released.

The message was clear enough: black people receive punishment for their transgressions and white people who collaborate with blacks need their heads examined. A word to the wise.

On the other hand, the white man or woman entering Blacktown may expect no special consideration from the blacks, nor should he expect it. Many of those interviewed, as well as many who were not, regretted that another white liberal was on their trail. They pointed out that "at least with a Polish honkey or an Italian bigot, we black folks know where we stand. With you we just can't be sure."

Let me return to the circumstances of the meetings with the twenty-one individuals who comprise *Blacktown, U.S.A.* These are important because they help to establish the personality of each and indicate how various are the voices of Blacktown.

Harllel X was the first person interviewed and he was always gracious and expansive with me. He said he respected me because I have Irish forebears and the recent civil disturbances in Belfast suggested to him that I would understand the racial problem in America better than most. Like many others, he discerned that the Catholics in Northern Ireland were the niggers to the dominant

47

Protestant majority. It was Harllel who reminded me that the term nigger was used in the poor white section of Cleveland to indicate a failure, a faggot, a loser — regardless of color. Harllel himself is anything but a loser. He is an immensely attractive man, very effective with black or white audiences. His analysis of the roles of Martin Luther King, Muhammad Ali and Malcolm X is, so far as I know, unique.

In contrast, Francis Ward was always circumspect about my Irish past — and with good reason given his intimate knowledge of the Chicago Police Department. Francis Ward was more than a subject, he was also an excellent adviser and led me to understand some of the ideological differences between the various forms of nationalists. Black newsmen and black lawyers are the best interpreters of Black Nationalism and urban guerrilla warfare in America today, with the possible exception of black policemen like Gilbert Branch.

Detective Branch knows urban guerrilla warfare at firsthand though he denies that Philadelphia is as bad as Chicago in this respect. He knows Black Nationalism too and, like Harllel X, he believes that the policeman needs the support of the community more than any other single thing. It is for this reason perhaps that he finds it more difficult to be a policeman in his old neighborhood today than when he was a patrolman in his early years on the force.

In interviewing the women, the place of assignation was important. For example, Elizabeth Young and I made arrangements for lunch at a black restaurant and bar prior to the interview in a meeting room at the adjacent hotel. Our lunch was interrupted three or four times by black men who came by, they said, to pay their respects. Later she pointed out that they were checking up, just to make sure everything was all right. She also told me that had I been black with a white girl no one would have paid us the slightest heed.

Meeting Mary Conley was a wonderful accident. I saw her in Ed Bullins's play Clara's Old Man and knew I was in the presence of an authentic person. Mary Conley says that color makes absolutely no difference to her. Sometime after our interview she was tested

48

on this proposition. Several black, and Negrophilistic whites, were sure that I had been sent to harm and exploit her. She called me to say that they were misguided.

Mary Conley, and Harllel X, are exponents of the virtues of a ghetto life-style, a way of "coping" which black people have to defend themselves from a hostile environment. Harllel argues that this ability works in the white world too. In both these young and vibrant black people, one discerns a black *joie de vivre,* an openness to humanity that has not been affected by either Black Nationalism or the impoverished backgrounds from which they have both emerged to a richer and newer reality.

The older women, Zelma George and Ruth Watson, are remarkable contrasts in black womanhood. Each is a sophisticated and cultured person, and each demonstrates the point made most powerfully by Elizabeth Young that the black woman is more independent than the white woman. Though Elizabeth herself sometimes appears to hold conventional white middle-class standards of the male domination of the household, she is a very self-determined woman. Needless to say, neither Elizabeth Young, Zelma George or Ruth Watson would be much interested in the women's liberation movement. They have all been liberated a long time ago.

Annie Lee Walker, the oldest person interviewed in this volume, died a very long time ago, perhaps around the First World War. What remains today is a precious, protected wisp of a woman, almost oblivious to the present except when her grandchildren come around. She is a living memory, except that she moves with the agility of a forty-year-old person.

The other older people in this volume, J. Walter Wills, Sr. and the Reverend Joseph Eugene Solomon Ray are good friends, though Wills is twenty years older than Ray; Wills complained, as very old people do, that there aren't many people his age around anymore. Wills has been white about as long as Ray has been black but the years have a way of smoothing those things out. Today they are companionable old men who enjoy talking together with a considerable degree of understanding.

My association with young black people was different than with older blacks. The young were more certain of themselves and of the limitations of our relationship. They were better educated than their elders, more sensitive and more suspicious. Frequently I was asked: "Out of what bag are you comin', man?" The only answer they would accept was a stereotype: a professor, a liberal, a white man. Only older blacks would acknowledge that I could come into Blacktown as a person, as myself. They also seemed to sense why I needed to come. At these moments I was reminded of the endurance of black people, matched only by their magnificent patience. It was put most beautifully by a white friend, Peter Nabakov, who traveled recently to many urban ghettos, noting at the end: "They were *too much,* warm but elusive, helpful but wary, friendly but so, so far away, with a sadly amused kind of wisdom that, in different forms, I met in every black man or woman I encountered on my trip."

The young people in this volume are represented in the profiles, (Sababa Akil and Nondu El are both under twenty-one), and especially in the poetry which introduces various portions of the work. There are two poets over thirty, Mary Mason and Norman Jordan, who have a growing reputation in the Middle West and one poet, Langston Hughes, who is well known indeed. All the other poets are in their teens. Most of the poetry has never been published except in high school poetry magazines and in ghetto newspapers. Its power and variety, its perception and beauty, add a new dimension to Blacktown and I hope to the white man's appreciation of it.

The black professionals in this volume are an impressive group of men and women. They reminded one of the remark attributed to a black woman by Robert Storey, "Thank God for slavery!" Surely there are few black professionals in America today who regret that the slave trade brought black people to America. It is the same reaction one will occasionally find in northern Mexico when the campesino, looking across the border toward San Diego and Los Angeles, laments the fact that the Americans did not invade the whole of Mexico in 1846.

The younger black professionals in this volume, especially those in the section called "Black Professionals," are sensitive to the rapidity of change among the new young black generation. Not long ago a junior student at Phillips Exeter Academy, which Robert Storey attended, noted that "we are at Exeter to obtain knowledge of ourselves and when we become leaders we will derive our strength not from your (white) friendship or your brains or your money, but from ourselves." Robert Storey knows that the generation gap among black people is closing faster than among white people. And so does Ernie Green.

George Forbes knows it too and his perception of it is especially acute for a politician. As he reviewed his constituency — the older, moderate, hard-working parents and the younger, progressive, black-oriented children — I was reminded of Alice Johnson and her son, Nondu El (Lathan Donald). Forbes, and Elizabeth Young, warn that black parents will become radicalized as they perceive their children moving away from them under the influence of one or another form of Black Nationalism. As Alice Johnson reflected on her son's attachment to Ahmed El Ibn Said (Fred Evans), I discerned a regret that she did not meet Evans earlier and try for some rapprochement. This mother's sorrow and reflection may well be a paradigm for many other black families.

Ahmed El Ibn Said is also a paradigm, of the army veteran returning to the inner city after a stormy career in the service, seeking an outlet for his energies. As he awaits execution in the gas chambers of the Ohio State Penitentiary, Ahmed knows one thing well, he knows that fear is a kind of worship. He no longer fears the white man or the white man's image in himself, and his worship is only for Allah.

His young lieutenant, Nondu El, is remarkably wise in moral matters for one so young. His philosophical statements are rich in perception, however limited they may be by experience. As Alice Johnson suggests, it may have been Nondu El who led Ahmed, rather than the other way around.

Who is left? The nationalists. And who are the nationalists? In one way or another all the people in *Blacktown, U.S.A.* are Black Nationalists. In almost every profile, there is a strain of black or

51

Negro identity which the subject regards as the mark of a strong and proud people. The religious expression of this is contained in the profile of Rabbi David Hill.

Hill is a powerful personality with a sincerity which tempts both blacks and whites to regard him as a consummate con man. His local reputation is that of a gunslinging preacher who inflames black people against whites, especially if successful white business can be taken over for personal profit by Hill. The reality is otherwise. The David Hill in this book is a deeper and finer person than the white newspapers have yet discovered. And black newspapers, too, have yet to discover Rabbi David Hill. But they will because he won't be put down, especially when he turns to his radio audience of Methodists, Baptists and Catholics, chiding them gently by saying, "The only thing black in those churches is you!"

Sababa Akil is a young poet, a thinker, and craftsman, rather than a maker of revolutions. Yet he is important, especially to Harllel X, because he represents the young. He represents also some part of that spirit of W. E. B. Du Bois who, aged twenty-five, said: "I will in this second quarter century of my life, enter the dark forest of the unknown world for which I have so many years served my apprenticeship — the chart and compass the world furnishes me I have little faith in — yet, I have none better — I will seek till I find — and die." Since the interview I have learned that Sababa Akil is working with Imamu Amiri Baraka (LeRoi Jones) in Spirit House in Newark.

Sababa Akil and Nondu El may never have read James Joyce's *Portrait of the Artist as a Young Man,* but they know what Stephen Dedalus meant when he said: "I go forth to fashion in the smithy of my soul the uncreated conscience of my race."

Panther #1 and Panther #2 are members of the Black Panther Party for Self-Defense, but neither would grant permission to have his real name used in this book. This practice of anonymity by blacks goes deeply into the history of black people in America where, in some periods and in some regions, no individual names were assigned black people by their white masters; "boy" or "nigger" was in itself sufficient to gain their attention. Today, ironically, the strong young black male is deciding for himself to be nameless. Yet, whether voluntary or not, anonymity has been the lot of the American black for a very long time; Panther #1 and Panther #2 join a long line of black people. In addition, they are a foil to the cultural nationalists of the Afro Set and many other black organizations seeking historical and cultural roots in Africa.

James O. Cannady closes *Blacktown, U.S.A.* He is the appropriate figure because he leaves us in that uncertain state where American race relations are today. Cannady tried to live with white people. He tried to do everything white people demanded of black people. James O. Cannady is clean, industrious, a good family man, well-educated, courteous and friendly. But white people still don't like him and today he is rejected by his fellow blacks. Only in white America could one produce such a totally alienated man.

These are my last impressions of the twenty-one ordinary black men and women with whom I have had long and profitable discussions. Other impressions include the frozen scowls on the faces of the young bloods in a half dozen Black Nationalist storefronts, a contrast with the easy camaraderie I developed with black professionals. And there was the white male hostility, mixed with envy if she were attractive, when I was in a public place with a black woman; the prayerful shouts of the black church service; the after-hours lounges in the ghettos where the homosexuals congregate and where the wine list equals the best of the white restaurants; the "Mom and Pop" stores where most transactions are less than a dollar; the inevitable demand for funds upon entering the burned-out Black Panther headquarters following the latest police raid; finally, the marvelous psychedelics of light, color, sound and movement of a swinging Saturday night in Blacktown, followed by those peaceful Sunday mornings when black folks in their finery, and with their flair, walk slowly and solemnly to church.

These are the people and the places of Blacktown. The reader should now look at the profiles, read the poetry and meet the persons. The themes developed by the voices of Blacktown are many. There is no epilogue, no summing up of the main themes or lines of discussion. I would only remind the reader that the most interesting differences of opinion and attitude occur in that internal dialogue now going on both in the Blacktowns of America and in *Blacktown, U.S.A.* Listen to them carefully, white man, and you will learn something about yourself.

Some Objections

This, then, is a book by black people for white people, with a white editor as intermediary. It is incomplete in the sense that there were a number of persons interviewed who were not included in the final version. Moreover there were some blacks who refused to talk with me, others who resented my presence in Blacktown and disagreed with the purpose or usefulness of the book. And these were not only the so-called militants. They were also dedicated and selfless men and women who have concluded that black self-determination,

55

especially in the fields of publishing and the arts, now requires total independence from any tinge of white collaboration or white brainwashing.

They are the ones who refuse to accept the Malcolm X of the *Autobiography* (written in collaboration with Alex Haley), and who find Nat Turner's *Confessions* counterfeit because it was told to, and recorded by, a white man. Their judgment of William Styron's fictional account of the *Confessions* may easily be inferred. So also can one infer what they think of *Blacktown, U.S.A.*

And there were others who were simply tired — "bone tired" they said — of talking with the white man again. They were weary of his inevitable questions and of his apparent incapacity to learn — what they sometimes call the "Moynihan syndrome," i.e., another study of black folks by the white man. Some agreed to be interviewed "just one more time, but *only* one more time."

It may be that books like this may soon cease to exist in America. If this happens, it will mean that black people have stopped talking and white people have stopped listening. Many on both sides have already made their decision. And even among those who, with apparent goodwill, try to keep the dialogue going, there is increasing discouragement with results.

What these groups have not faced is what one black man — who preferred not to be included in this volume — called "intellectual dishonesty." And he added, "White folks sit down with black folks and they think, okay, I like you and you like me. Both of them are lying, so the whole relationship has been based on a lie." There is much truth in this observation.

Another perceptive black man stated that matter this way: "I am saying that just like it's my job to work with my brothers and sisters in such a way that they build and grow to their potential, you got a job with the white community. And both of us know that the way blacks or whites treat their own groups is a measure of how they treat each other."

There are other possible objections to this volume. The most serious has already been suggested. It is the charge that the work is vitiated by the fact that the black voices are not authentic, merely the reflections of a white man's mind and his culture.

56

This is a serious objection. If it is true that blacks and whites have never been in genuine dialogue, that much of what passes for discussion is based upon "intellectual dishonesty," that the black culture has been both ignored and exploited by whites, that whites are culturally deprived, it must follow that any verbal encounter between blacks and whites runs the risk, even the certainty, of cultural misunderstanding and a patronizing spirit.

The present volume does not avoid all of these pitfalls. And surely if a black man or woman had edited the interviews, a different volume would have emerged. To a black interviewer the subjects would have responded differently, and would have produced another portrait of themselves. But because the main purpose of *Blacktown, U.S.A.* is to reach a white readership, it is not inappropriate that the questioner was white nor that the responses were directed to, and edited by, a white person.

So far as the editing is concerned, it was done from the transcripts carefully typed from the taped interview. The transcripts required the usual deletions for irrelevancies and repetitious material, a concern for sequence, and uniformity of style. Omissions were infrequent, and there are no substantive changes except for an occasional transitional or explanatory phrase. One frequent problem was the inability of Negro typists to understand the sounds of ghetto residents. It was the same literacy, or oral, gap which obtains between many whites and blacks. Finally, no text can possibly reproduce the colorful sound and lively language of black folks rapping.

Another objection to a work offering the voices of Blacktown is that the black folks have once again conned the white man. Did they lie? If so, how much? One is tempted to answer: no more than was absolutely necessary.

Every interviewer faces the problem of the accuracy of the response, just as he faces the problem of the meaning and direction of his own questions. Let me reply by quoting two great interviewers, Robert Penn Warren and Studs Terkel. Warren dealt with mendacity by the simple remark: "Even a lie is a kind of truth." [25] So far as black–white relations in America are concerned, whatever lies black people tell white people reveal both a truth about blacks, and about whites.

And now Terkel.

Are they telling the truth? The question is as academic as the day Pilate asked it, his philosophy not quite washing out his guilt. It's the question Pa Joad asked of Preacher Casy, when the ragged man, in a transient camp, poured out his California agony.

Pa said, "S'pose he's tellin' the truth — that fella?" The preacher answered "He's tellin' the truth, awright. The truth for him. He wasn't makin' nothin' up." "How about us?" Tom demanded. "Is that the truth for us?" "I don't know," said Casy.

I suspect the preacher spoke for the people in this book, too. In their remembering are their truths.[26]

The most serious objection against this volume — that it is a white caricature of urban black people — must be placed against the alternatives. As polarization increases and as the white man finds fewer and fewer black people who will enter into conversation with him, the need for understanding increases. The serious consequence here is that many of those who are still willing to talk to Whitey are either brainwashed or are charlatans. Fortunately for America, the polarization and the noncommunication has not reached that point. But the storm warnings are up all along the way, and we are faced with the question: if black people won't help white people learn about Blacktown, who will? The more important question is: do white people want to learn?

It is a self-defeating process that faces us. Given the ignorance of white people concerning black Americans, there is need for understanding. But if the opportunity for that understanding is denied, whites will continue to deal with the inhabitants of the Blacktown of their minds, those fantasies and myths, those magical creatures who have only a little substance and no reality.

I repeat: one day in America books like *Blacktown, U.S.A.* may cease to exist. But let us say, as some have said, "just one more time." Perhaps the work of white editors and writers on the black experience will be justified if it moves white people to go beyond these interpretations and reach out directly to the black experience and the black culture itself. If they do, they will find, as this writer did, more than blacks in Blacktown. When the white man, first in this book then in person, enters Blacktown, he will also discover Whitetown — with all its myths, fantasies and creatures of imagination.

The most serious charge against this book is that it erects, once more, an image of black people created by whites, a white man's Blacktown. This would not surprise black people for, they keep telling us, we always create the house niggers with whom we can deal, and we continue to use them to control and oppress black people. When the black skin puts on the white mask, either by himself or with help of a white man, we have, once again, constructed a monolithic view of black people. But the deeper truth is that through his black constructs and puppets, the white man has been merely talking to himself.

Blacktown, U.S.A. avoids this criticism. There are black voices in this volume with whom the white American will feel comfortable and others that will threaten and disturb him. It is a most unrepresentative group of urban black folks, one which nonetheless represents the talent and charm, the intelligence and beauty and courage of an oppressed and unbowed people. They are not inhabitants of the white man's Blacktown, but of their own proud Black city.

TWO MOTHERS

MY MOTHER

She was my mother
her skins was smooth and soft like a robin's breast.
she was beautiful as a golden moon shining over the
mississippi on a warm summer night.
like the wind she wandered and was free in soul,
outside your lighted windows she looked for
food, your garbage, our dinner tonight,
escaping the whip.
tonight she will be my mother and not your nigger woman.
she will not warm your bed, you white bastard. What do
you know of love?

                           — wanda wilson
                             (Cleveland)

THE BALLAD OF NELLIE REED

Hey Nellie Reed,
I say you yesterday
High as a Georgia Pine,
Laughing and dancing.
Girl, you was rocking
The joint.
And tonight
You're laying in
An alley dead.
While
The ghost of
Your twenty-six
Year life (needing a fix)
Trembles in an
Empty wine bottle.

— Norman Jordan
(Cleveland)

REAL GOOD LOVER

I was born one morning, one hot, hot day
Don't ask me why I'm a lover, I was born that way.
The doctor told my mother I was smart
"One day your daughter will break some man's heart."
I grew and grew until I was in my teens,
Everywhere I went you can bet made the scene.
I'm like Mr. Otis Redding, I'm straight from Georgia Woods
They call me the lover, good old doctor mommy good.
I can do anything that can be done, anything you don't know
from me you can learn.
I really have it baby I've got what it takes.
If you aren't hip to my jive, I'll give you a break.
My name is Vivian and I've still some empty seats left.
I live at 809 North 16th Street.
I'm also like C. Clay, I always come out right,
no matter what the world might say.
I'm a real good lover, and there won't be another,
so don't miss one minute of the day cause I'm a real good
lover and I'm going to stay that way.

– Vivian
(Philadelphia)

LIFE

When I was young and foolish it was my great delight
To go to all night movies and stay out late at night.
It was at a dance I met him, he asked me for a dance.
I could tell he was a hoodlum by the way he wore his pants.
His shoes were neatly polished, his hair was neatly combed.
It was in my fathers hallway where I was let astray.
It was in my mothers bedroom where I was forced to yield
He lifted me up gently and held my dress real high.
He said do it my dearest darling or you will surely die.
The next morning when I awakened a note was by my side
It said my dearest darling, you will now have my child
For months and months I waited for the baby to be born.
It looked like its father in every shape and form.
So to all you hip chicks. Take this advice from me and
Never let a hoodlum get an inch above your knee.
He'll say your lovings well and when he's busted
Your cherries, he'll say:
              GO TO HELL!!!!!!

                                        — Anonymous
                                        (Philadelphia)

66

QUEENS

Queens, dark hued radiantly
  Black,
There is no dichotomy between
  us.
You are our immaculate concept.
It is to you we give the ultimate
of love, it is through you that we
perceive beauty.
Black Queens, Ebony Queens,
we love you.

— William Johnson
(Philadelphia)

THE COOL PEOPLE

Cool Black Nights
at home,
the place where
the cool black dudes
Roam.
Them hard-looking
    hard-talking
    hard-loving
Cool Black Dudes.
Them Ice-cold Soul Brothers
laying harder than any other,
Rapping on them sisters
    them fine looking
        fine walking
        fine loving
    them fine soul sisters.
These cool Black People
getting together on
those cool black nights
at home.
    Some work during the day

    slinging trash cans
    pushing brooms
    cooking food.
Some hustle all the time.
Some drink wine.
Some smoke reefer
    like you know,
    trying to get
    deeper!
There are those who leave
moaning and complaining,
Like saying soul is raining.
Us who stay
    We just lay 'cause
    they'll come home
    for them.
Cool black nights.
Cool black sights.
Cause its magic, jack
just to be Black
    COOL BLACK PEOPLE.

— Anonymous
(Philadelphia)

69

Elizabeth Young

Elizabeth Young is thirty-two, married to an engineer, the mother of three small children. She has been a rebel all her life, not "instant black" as she calls some of her Negro friends. Elizabeth Young is typical of the new black mother: emphatic, angry and articulate. It will be from families with mothers like her that the black family of the future will emerge.

You were saying just now that black folks consider themselves in two ways, individually and collectively. What do you mean by that?

Well, my thing is that black people in all generations — and I have grandmothers and great-grandmothers still living — have resented the white community collectively but individually they have always been black. Individually, they have had real good relationships with some white people, but collectively they resented the tyranny. You can understand that. And today, individually, black people have more courage than they had even, say a decade ago. This new-found courage of the black man is coming on.

The black woman, on the other hand, has always been painfully safe. She's never really had any problem in the United States or anywhere in the world. It's her man that she has always had to go to the front for. So now the black man is telling the black woman to stay home, that he is heading the household. No matter what he is, he is the head of his household. This is a fantastic feeling for a black woman and a brand new role for her. Her man works for the establishment depending on his age and how courageous he really is. The black man today is playing the role he has longed to play for so many years and frustrations are coming out in all kinds of ways.

The wars played a big part in all this. The black man got out of this silly United States. He got out of this country with all its prejudices and he went into another world where he was accepted as a man, and where it was legal to kill the enemy. He came back to another enemy, but it isn't legal to kill this one. If he would now have to take up arms against this enemy, he wouldn't think he was breaking the law because he didn't make that law. The law was made for white people.

So now he is head of his household and the most wonderful thing is that his children are respecting him. It has, however, presented a real problem for the black woman. It really has.

For generations and centuries the black woman has been the breadwinner of the family because the black man couldn't get a job. She washed dishes. She cleaned house. She was the breadwinner. She was the accountant. Since she made the biggest buck she was in charge. She went to work and commanded her own schedule. She did not have to ask her husband anything. She told him, and he had to accept this.

72

Can you imagine what kind of mess this put that poor man in? He had to accept it because he had to eat. And the biggest thing is that she did not respect her man. And of course if she did not respect her man, her children did not respect her man. They demasculated him really.

Most black women are real fighters, very aggressive women. They are an autonomy all by themselves. No matter how poor the house is, you don't invade it. Black mothers are the most protective mothers in the world. I don't care how poor they are, the black child gets more love than any child in the whole world. When there wasn't enough money to survive on, she prostituted herself to the white community. She did it out of sheer necessity. She did it and she hated it. It came down to a simple case of survival because we live in a capitalist society. The family had to eat.

Prostitution isn't in vogue anymore. There was a time when black women supported their families this way and their clientele was white. We've learned a lot about white folks by living in their bedrooms and kitchens. Black men never supported prostitution, they didn't have to. But prostitution isn't in vogue anymore.

I have a relative who lives in Florida and she had four children for a white man, and then she had four children for a black man. Now the four children for the white man — and remember the black man is still there and he knows that these four children are not his — are cared for by this white man with lodging, food and all the necessities of life. This white man provides for the total family unit. Now this relative of mine is an example of someone who could not make the transition, you see? She is now in an institution because when her black man emerged, she could not make the transition. She is an outstanding example of someone who could not get rid of the caste system that white people have passed down to us.

And this caste system exists in the North too. I have known many children who are products of this kind of situation. For ex- -ample, this kid got everything. When everybody else was riding bikes, he had a motorbike. When everybody else was riding motorbikes, he had a car. When everybody else had one car, he had two cars. When we went to public schools, they went to private schools.

The white community — we are no longer hung up on this sort of thing — called this kid a bastard, but white kids never got what this kid got. So this bastard child traveled, when poor white kids never left town. This black kid — and the other black children in the family — traveled by jet. And I'm not talking about Florida, Alabama, or South Carolina. I'm talking about right here, Cleveland, Ohio.

This kind of thing has been going on for a long time, yet even though the black woman has been doing these things — and, I must say, doing a fantastic job — she resented the fact that she *had* to do it. And always there was the good church there, you know the "good church," telling her what her role was. She had so many things to do and so few hours in the day and if she was working and couldn't afford to pay a sitter, her man stayed home and played the role of a wife. Can you imagine what that did to this man? Now that's just not the way our society should be constructed. Even in a polygamous society, if a man's got fifty wives, he is responsible for those women and they respond first to him, then to the rest of the world. Only in these United States does the black woman not respond first to her man.

But all of this is changing, like rapidly. What is now happening is that the white world is being made to respect the black man and the black woman is being made to respect her man. Since he can now make a decent buck, he can tell his wife to stay home. Of course, some women want to and others don't. Nobody likes to give up power. I don't care who you are. Nobody does, that's just human nature. But she is being forced to respect her man, and this creates a problem for her. Here is this woman raised in an environment where she has been prepared to go to work and where her husband couldn't buy for her. It was she who was supposed to make ends meet. Now this is no longer her role and it presents problems. But this is really what she has been living for.

All of a sudden, her hair is beautiful and she is ultrafeminine. Her children are something to be proud of, rather than to hide. If she is on a subsidy, she is not ashamed of the fact. Even if she is sharing a man, this man is the head of her household. And the man has masculine identity to the point where the children, when they look at the TV and see somebody with a natural haircut, say "There's my brother" or "There's my sister." Before they would say, "Why don't you fix up your hair like she has it, Momma?" All this makes for a good family composition.

I made this transition. I don't work. I stay home. It's not hard for me to stay home because of my philosophy. But for most people who have had a formal education (yes, I have a formal education), it is very hard to stay home because you are prepared to go to work. When I was a child, I asked my mother and then she'd ask my father maybe and then she went and got it. In my home, they ask mother for food, okay, but they ask their daddy for everything else. I don't even know when they ask him and when something shows up, he says, "Oh, the kids asked me for it." This gives me a good feeling, the fact that they have that kind of relationship with their father.

I'm really ecstatic about the fact that the black man is emerging because I see my children being prepared for the future. They will sit and talk with their father and he tells them exactly the way it is because he is a realist. Women aren't realists. They reserve the hope that things will not happen, but they always do happen. My husband says "a man's role is this and that." My son and I rarely even have a conversation because he is a man and there are certain things that he must do. My brother never had these kinds of conversations with his father. If he did, it would be, "This is the white man, and you stay in your place, boy!" My son doesn't have this kind of conversation.

But all of us know Negro men who let their women go off to work . . .

Well, as far as I'm concerned our people are all black. We all have our degrees of blackness, or our degrees of commitment, but we are all black. The white community makes us all black whether we want to be or not, and this is sometimes to our advantage.

Oh, I know there are dollar signs, and I know all the things that you can do with them. But if a black woman goes after them, she is competing with her husband and this makes for bad family structure. Some black people do combine careers and marriage, but I

75

don't think black people generally are quite ready for that yet. In fact, I don't know a black man who likes the idea of his wife working. He might tell her to go to work, he might need her to go to work, but basically he resents her going to work.

You know, since women have gotten their equality, they have become quite masculine, terribly masculine. And I'm not talking just about black people now. I'm talking about people. For example, if we have a budget and I'm putting in more in that budget than you are, then that makes me the commander of the budget. It's not supposed to be that way. I should be staying home. This makes me not only want my husband, it makes me need my husband. Everybody needs to be needed. There is only one law that I've ever heard in these United States with which I've agreed: "If a man provides lodging and food, and this is the best he can do, then the woman is supposed to be satisfied with this — everything else is extra." If he gives you your basics, then you are supposed to accept this and not push for more.

Do you think of yourself as an American?

Definitely, but you probably won't understand this if you are white. Black people have two cultures and most of us are now identifying with the black people around the world. But we are Americans. It's wild what you read in those nice papers about the black militants here at home. They say this and that about them, but the very people they define as militant are the most patriotic people I have ever encountered.

We love this country perhaps more than anybody else here because only we see this country being saved by giving us our share of the action. Now most of the time when we say "share of the action" white people think in terms of me visiting them, playing with their children, going to their churches and bars, joining their country clubs and having my daughters come out in their debutante parties. But these are not the things we are asking for.

We are asking for that collective thing I was talking about. Individually, we have never had any problems going up the ladder. Collectively, black people have never been totally accepted. Now let's face it. We are an ethnic group. We are the largest ethnic group in the United States. And that gives us a certain amount of power right there. But even though we are the largest ethnic group in this fantastic country, all other kinds of ethnic groups can go up the ladder but we can't collectively go up the ladder — even though we are all raised in the same environment.

For example, white people go to school and I go to school. Now it comes time to get our little jobs and get into the middle income bracket. But your middle income and mine are two different things. The more money you make, the further up the ladder you go. We're going up the same ladder, and let's say we have equal intelligence and equal everything, okay? But my middle income is less than yours and I go up more slowly.

If a white family moves into a nice little neighborhood nobody is going to scream. Nobody will ask how much they make, nobody will ask what their religion is — all that irrelevant garbage. But the minute the Youngs move into that neighborhood, the first question is "What does your husband do?" The next question is "How much does he make?" Then, "Do you go to church?" I'm not saying we want to move there, but we don't have a choice and that is what it's all about.

I'm not saying that if all the doors in the United States were equal that we wouldn't still live as a group because most ethnic people live in groups. Basically, people are more comfortable with their own kind. I'm a hard segregationist myself. Wallace and I agree one hundred percent on that. But my thing is that if the Youngs want to move into another neighborhood, they should have the choice. The fact is that we don't have the choice. My man can't say to his son, "You can be President," because in all honesty he can't be President. And he can't be senator or a leader of people, not of black people, green people or yellow people, but a leader of people. So what does he have to tell his son? "Find a way for your people. Find a way for your people."

In spite of these conditions, you still think of yourself as an American?

I am more American than any white person in this whole god-damn country. Their forefathers came here by choice. Remember that. I had no choice. My people came because they had to. They either came or died. And then after they got to this place, they created this country. What kind of culture does America have? What kind? We've got Negro songs, Negro writers, Negro this and Negro that. Anything a white man does, it's a European this and a European that. Everything that this country has produced culturally is black. The rest of it is imported from across the waters.

And because we have been underpaid for our work, we want reparations. Our biggest kick is that we weren't paid for the work we did. The Indians, because they were basically a peace-loving people, are due more reparations than we are. But I have no doubt that black people will get theirs. I don't even think on that anymore. We're going to get our share of the action, and I'm only hoping that greed doesn't set in once we get our share. We will not only get reparations from the churches, but from everybody.

And it won't be because of white guilt feelings. Let's get clear on that. White guilt feelings don't exist, because most whites say, "I didn't bring slaves over here, I didn't have anything to do with that." They will give you the whole garbage bit: "I've got more colored friends than you have, and I work with colored people and I do this and that with colored people; our kids go to school with them, share a car pool, and even go to church with them!" There are no such things as guilt feelings. People don't get guilty when it comes to money. You see, we are a country of causes. Suppose somebody gets burnt out, all of a sudden we forget what color they are. I do and you do. If there is a kid out there and he gets run over by a car, I don't care what color that kid is. I'm an adult individual, and a mother, and I'm going to that kid's aid. I may hate the mother like hell, but I'm going to help her kid. We're caught up in causes.

That's how it will work toward reparations, you know, like the Unitarians here.* This will catch on because other institutions are

* In November 1969, the congregation of the Unitarian Society of Cleveland voted to turn over their property — real estate and a large church building — to the Black Unitarian Universalist Caucus, plus operating expenses for a two-year period.

78

not going to let the Unitarians outdo them. We'll get caught up in this thing. It's prestige to say we gave to the poor blacks and all that, you know.

The reason I keep harping on the church is because black people in the past only had their churches to go to. This was the only place the slavekeepers couldn't go, where we could really be alone. They didn't dare enter those little shanties that the black people had for churches because they were whooping and hollering and creating such a ruckus. And of course there was plenty of strategy planned in those churches.

Then all of a sudden the slavekeepers permitted us to go to their higher institutions of learning. Okay, so I'm not saying this was such a good idea. And I can't say it was totally bad either. It created a thinking atmosphere. We became more objective and started really looking at things. It didn't bother us anymore that we didn't go to church. It didn't bother us whether we believed in a mystic God or not. New worlds were opened to us and we no longer needed the institutions of the church.

The church, unlike us, wasn't able to make the change. When they saw what was happening, they created a black Methodist and a white Methodist, a black Baptist and a white Baptist. All except the Catholics. At least they were honest and stayed separate. You got a few rebels there that try not to be separate but the good Pope, you know, says it is going to be separate. So it is.

Well, anyway, we found that the churches were not meeting our needs and we don't have any qualms about attacking white institutions. That is one thing we do well. We attack. We have learned that from the white man. He has taught us how to attack very well.

We are going to have confrontations, real confrontations. I don't know whether my country can deal with a real confrontation. In spite of the laws Congress has passed, in spite of the things the National Guard have at their disposal, and the police are equipped with, I don't know whether we can deal with a real confrontation. We've never had a real war on our own front, never! We have dealt with other countries quite well and they have been slaughtered. But not like you live across the street.

What about the Civil War?

The Civil War doesn't count because it didn't solve anything. The Civil War should never have happened. It should never even have happened. The textbook part of it is a bunch of garbage. It doesn't make any sense at all. I can't see Abe Lincoln being so liberal with a house full of slaves. It was a political issue, that's all. Did they execute any of the people down South who lost? No. They were heroes. What a fantastic job they did! This is all I ever read in the textbooks, all about the wonderful leadership that Lee gave. Oh, my goodness, he's a bigger hero than Lincoln.

The Civil War shouldn't have happened because it didn't make any real changes.

We were owned then, but since we knew we were owned, we didn't have any hope. Dangling hope has done big damage, big damage. When you hope, you know it's possible. Then the possibility never materializes. This is a disservice to anybody.

My one thing is that nobody in this country has ever gotten anything no matter what color they are, without a little blood being shed — or a whole lot of blood. We are caught up in blood. It's unfortunate, but it's the truth. We make our money on wars. We're caught up in blood.

Some people say now the revolution has quieted down. Even black people say it. The revolution ain't about to be quieted down. We say that because we were raised in a white society and have become intellectuals. Oh, we blacks are a land of intellectuals now and we do things on a sophisticated level. But it is just as barbaric as ever. The latest thing out now, rumorwise, is that since the Black Panther issue the establishment has opened warfare on the brothers. Hell, the Justice Department has been declaring open war on the brothers for years.

Right now the tension is so great the black people themselves are afraid to walk the streets. And they are afraid of black people and of white people, what with snipers just riding around shooting people for no reason at all. But black people are used to dying. We've been dying for centuries. Nobody got alarmed about it before, when we died for no reason. So I can't get really upset about us dying — if we don't die for nothing. If I or my husband can die so our sons will live in a better world, then that's what it is all about. It may be surprising to white folks, but we care enough about our young to die for them. So nobody even worries about it. If you die, you're dead. No real big thing. You are going to die anyway. It's a biological function.

Where were you born?

I was born in Madison County, Florida. I came to Cleveland when I was eight years old. My father had no education. I taught him how to write his name, after I learned to write mine. He came up North during the war, where the good jobs were. When I graduated from East Technical High School in 1955, our total income was about three thousand dollars a year. But I had had teachers, real teachers, black ones and white ones, men and women. They were the whole bit. Your one teacher was all the different agencies that we have now created. She was your social worker and your everything. And she didn't take interest only in the bright child but all of them.

One which stands out in my mind was a white teacher named Mrs. Violet. She was a hillbilly, with a real twang, the whole bit. She would ask us where there was a store in the community where she could buy turnip greens and collard greens. She had been raised on them. She was an English teacher. How I hated that woman, and with a mad passion! She made you produce and, of course, that would make you hate her. But there were several Mrs. Violets. In spite of all the regimentation, they made you think and make decisions for yourself.

I look at teachers now and think there might be one per school like I had. This is a real tragedy. I know the cost of living is up and one must eat. When I went to school, you could tell a teacher by their wardrobes. One teacher I had, a Mrs. Bell, wore this one dress all year — no matter what the season was. She was really interested in her students. She told me something that I'll never forget. She said, "Elizabeth, my biggest reward is producing a student like you." Then she said, "In spite of you." And she was right. I had lunch with her about a year ago and she told me that the joy in teaching is finding a child whom you can give direction, as opposed to them finding a negative direction. And then one day, she said, "You sit back and read the name of your student in the newspaper and permit yourself to say, 'I had a part in that.' "

We are no longer producing this kind of individual, the one more interested in producing students and less interested in teacher salaries. This is my biggest thing about the school system now. It is so caught up in buildings and facilities. We didn't even have a school library. We had a neighborhood library and the librarian — her name was Miss McGinney — knew all the kids. She knew the ones who couldn't read, the ones that wouldn't read, the ones that would never be able to read.

When I graduated from high school, I went looking for work. Since I had taken an academic course all the way through high school, I was not prepared to do a damn thing. I couldn't even type. Well, I'm walking downtown looking for work and I ran into Miss Hellerstein. She's a Jew and an assistant principal somewhere now. She says to me, "Elizabeth, how are you? Are you still fighting? Are you still a rebel?" I said, "Yes." Then she said, "When are you going to college?" I told her we can't afford for me to go to college. So about five teachers — three were men and two were women — decided that I was going to college. So they got together the money and sent me off to college.

Would you want to see black schools controlled by blacks?

Yes, for several reasons. Because of the background of black people, of their unending struggle, only another black man or woman can understand all the tragedies, and the rewards, of being black in the United States. Since schools are learning institutions, we must learn about ourselves. Our history book would probably look a lot different than yours, but we wouldn't have a separate unit of just black studies. That is really the silliest thing. These Mickey Mouse black studies programs are funnier than any other curriculum. They are really poor, like the musical appreciation course you take for one credit. Black studies should be integrated throughout the whole curriculum at all levels.

People read all kinds of negatives into black control of schools.

82

You get no reaction of course, when you talk about white control. It is perfectly all right for you to decide what your curriculum should be if you live in a Polish area. Nothing is made fun of the fact that you have Polish heroes, that your diet and your stores appeal to the Polish people, that you go to a Polish dentist, Polish physician and a Polish lawyer. But if we do this, we are openly criticized. And we have been so indoctrinated that we think our services are inferior. If you really want something done right, folks, go to the white man. This is a bunch of garbage.

I'm talking optimistically now as if there is time for us to have our own black thing. Actually I'm not sure we have that kind of time in this country. As this country exists now, I don't see it continuing for long. I see it collapsing, and not from outside forces. If you speak out today against something, you are labeled a communist or a socialist or some kind of negative. It never enters people's minds that something is being objectively considered. People just don't take enough interest in their government to know which way they are going. And until the black man is really free — in the essence of the word — then of course, the white man will never be free either.

What do you mean by that?

Well, in the first place, you are a white man and I am a black woman. We live in the same world, with all the transportation and news media. Today the world has become one big community. What affects me really affects you. When you think about it — and especially if you are a parent — what affects my child really affects your child. When the militants start burning, the white kids start rioting. It overlaps all the time.

Tension is high. Tension is extremely high. As long as I am a slave and you are a slavemaster you will never be free because you have certain ties to that slave. You see, you're still responsible for me. Before we were talking about guilt. That ain't guilt. It's a mixture of prestige and responsibility. They go together. Because you permitted the society to make me a second-rate citizen, you've got to channel your energy into keeping me a second-rate citizen. This is a full-time job. While you waste all that time and energy, you

83

could put it into something more constructive. But you whites will make it your business to keep me, as the saying goes, "in my place."

All white people?

Any white person over six years old is doing it, consciously or unconsciously. They may not be aware of it, but they are doing it because their environment influences them a great deal. When I say white, I say Polish, Irish and all the other kinds. When I say white I don't separate you. Now when you say black, the first thing you think is black woman. Think about it, just think about it. First, you think black woman, and then you think, black man. But when I say white, the first thing I think is white man. That goes back to the collective thing again, you see, and respecting you. You respect me fully only when my man is respected. The black woman, individually, has never had any problem. It is the white woman who has had the real problem.

I feel very sorry for the white woman, I really do. I don't feel sorry any longer for the black man because he is getting his. But because society put the white woman in the same bag with the black man, the white man was permitted to have his black mistresses and do anything he wanted. It was sanctioned by the community. The white woman, on the other hand, couldn't breathe. When she had a mammie, this mammie she took care of and raised these white kids. She had the main task. And this white woman couldn't do anything with the kids. They would go and ask the mammie and if she said they could do it, they could do it. They didn't even know their mother.

You will find strong ties between black housekeepers and white children in these families. They loved that woman to death. The mother was there, it was always their mother. But if the kids really want something, they go to the mammie. If she says they can have it, they can have it. That is strength. The white man said she had that kind of power in his house, and the white woman took whatever was left. And so I feel a great deal of sorrow, of pity, for the white woman.

And the ones I feel most pity for are the ones that marry black

84

men. I know several couples like this and the white women are really brutalized. The black husband just can't forget what white people collectively have done to him and he takes it out on his woman. And it ain't just him either. It is the sister, the aunts and the mother of the husband who give hell to that poor white woman. Some I know flaunt a black mistress at their wives, and shack up with white broads, too. They do it openly to hurt their wives. And the real reason I feel so sorry for these white women is they truly love their black husbands and can't leave them, even when they are catching hell and being brutalized every day.

White women generally have become very masculine at a time when black women are becoming ultrafeminine. You see, there is nothing in the world worse than a female lawyer or female doctor — all those jobs that command so many hours and take you out of your home. An eight to five job is one thing, but when you're really playing that masculine role and competing with men, you have to spend enormous amounts of time away from the home. So I see the white woman now in executive roles, all the while envying the black woman because she has this ridiculous thing about sex. She really thinks that only a black woman can satisfy the white man. And white men have thought this ridiculous nonsense too, and so have neglected their wives and homes. White men also envy black men because they think he has more sex potential. I think this is almost the whole thing between white men and black men, and it is silly. Biologically people are people.

Let me give you an example of how envious white women are. I went to a meeting a few weeks ago and there were about five or six white women over fifty there, me and four other black women. I was the only one who was ultrablack, the rest of them were still hung up on integration. They all had name tags on except me. Everybody knew who I was. They treated me as an enemy, they feared me. I don't mean fear from a physical standpoint as if I was going to attack them or anything. They sat there in complete awe of me and then, once again, I felt terribly sorry for these women. One gal came over and said, "You're Liz Williams (my maiden name), aren't you? I went to college with you. You haven't changed, have you?" I said, "No, I have just gotten older." Here was this gal, we

85

had lived in the same dormitory. She looked so enviously at me —
at the freedom I have as a woman, which she has never had even
in this country of ultrafreedom.

Part of her insecurity comes from sexual envy because we black
women have always made it with her man. She feels inadequate,
that you have somehow surpassed her. She believes all those myths.
And the funniest thing is when she or the white man tries to identify with us. For generations black people have danced one way
and white people another way. Now all of a sudden the white man
sings like the black man, dances like a black man and in everything
else, too.

It seems so contradictory to me. Here is the white man feeling
inferior to the black man, trying to imitate him, when it is the white
man who is the slavemaster keeping the black man in his place.

I don't see in my lifetime that we will overcome the situation
where black people will just be people and white people will just be
people. As long as there has been mankind, there has been a slave
and a slavemaster. Before the white man emerged, there were black
masters. While the white man was doing his thing in the Orient (he
never went on the African continent until recently), the black masters were doing their thing in Africa. And that black master was a
"doozy," in all honesty he was some kind of a cat, a real top dog.
He had more slaves than anybody. He had a real thing going before
the Christ bit.

Because of his tyrannical behavior, all his empires crumbled and
then the white man came on. But now the reverse is happening,
and it is the black man who is coming on, the role of slavemaster and slave will now be reversed. I see the white man being the
slave and the black man the slavemaster.

Now when the black man becomes the slavesmaster, he will be
as bad and as unfair as the white slavemaster has been to him. You
see our first thought is that if we hadn't been brought over here in
the beginning, all this lynching and stuff would never have occurred. Collectively, we hold all white people responsible because
they never really tried to improve on a bad situation. The black
man won't look at the people who are humanitarians; he won't
even think of them. He will think of that majority collective group

86

that perpetuated this mess, and he will deal with it. He will deal with it severely. Castro didn't do anything, folks! I mean that was just the prelude to the real thing.

Because the black man has been castrated — that is the only term I can use here — once he attains his true manhood, he will exercise it in every direction.

I only hope that when it does happen, as few lives are lost as possible. But I don't want to romanticize this and say there won't be any lives lost. I know there will be lives lost — white lives and black lives. There has to be. There has to be because of this new generation.

I have a nine-year-old son and he has now identified with a black organization and with the black race of people. Slowly it is coming. His father tells him he is as good as the next man and that he will excel because black people have to excel. They have no choice. When this generation comes on, the whole world is really going to have to come to grips with it. This generation is not being indoctrinated, as the papers say, by excommunicating the whole world. It is being taught to be a man. Whatever your convictions are, stand by them. If it means death, then die, but die a man. It is important to die a man. It is important for your woman, for your mother, for your sister that you die a man.

I have a little daughter who is a holy terror, but she doesn't fight her battles. She goes and gets her brothers. This is not a big change but it's the little changes that one sees. I see revolution after revolution happening in small units and large units. I see the students coming out of school now making some real changes, many more than my generation made.

But not all these children will have mothers like you . . .

Right, but they will have to get like me in order to relate to that child, or lose him. I know one woman, with a master's degree, very bright, who used to say to me when we were on committees, "Liz, behave yourself." Her oldest daughter is thirteen and she's got an Afro haircut. She is so black that the mother, who is a good mother, was in danger of losing this child. If I can't talk to my mother, then I'm going to find some adult I can talk to. What was this child looking for? She was looking for a black woman or black man to relate to. The mother, recognizing the danger, became black, I mean instant black.

In many situations, circumstances are making us black. We have no choice. If I don't relate to my children, then some undesirable elements will relate to them. I don't want that to happen because the only reason I became black was to protect them and to give them direction — as opposed to someone else giving it.

So you see I'm still being the protective mother like all black women have been.

Mary Conley

Mary Conley is also thirty-two, an actress and mother of a six-year-old boy. She has just finished a successful appearance in Ed Bullins's play, Clara's Old Man, *at Cleveland's famous interracial theater, Karamu House. Mary is brash and buxom with a happy heart and plenty of talent. She has played with some big names and will play with some bigger ones. Totally dedicated to the theater, she has made it her life.*

We talked on the stage of Karamu House and our voices had a

89

hollow ring in that peopleless place. Once we were interrupted by three little black boys who knocked on the stage door wanting to get in. Mary opened the door and one said, "Where do I go to be an actor?" Mary pointed to the director's office down the hall. When she returned, she said, "That is just how I got started here when I was eleven years old."

When I was a kid I never knew color. I never knew prejudice until I grew up. When I was a little girl we lived on the "Gold Coast" here on 105th Street and we weren't the only black children there. My girl friend was Jewish, the same age, and when we went out to buy ice cream she would always get chocolate and I would get vanilla. Then she would say, "Now you're vanilla and I'm chocolate." I'd say, "Naw, you got that wrong, I'm chocolate and you're vanilla." But it was never a thing that separated us. If grown people could be like kids. They don't see the ugly things. Life isn't ugly to them, they don't see that.

There were twenty-one kids in our family. Do I know their names? Not really. Let's see. There's Hattie, Robert, Andrew, Henry, Charles, Doretta, Tina, Maxine, Abby Jean. Oh my God there's quite a few! My parents were Mary Cook and Bishop Robert Conley of the United Abyssinian Spiritual Church of God in Christ. Before that, my dad worked in a packing house and before that he was a very good pimp. He pimped in the ghettos, with four or five girls, and was very good at it. I think that anybody who becomes part of God has first tried some of the world. This is what makes them switch around. When I was born he decided he was going to be a minister. Maybe I was his "gift from God" or something. I was the tenth one born.

I've known the time my father — who'd get his check once a month — would go over to the market two blocks from our house and pick up vegetables that were rotten on the sides. He'd cut off the rotten part and bring them back in a wagon and put them in the refrigerator. So, all we had to buy was meat.

It is this instinct in black people which comes from not having *anything* that enables them to cope with things that people who've

To The Queen
I could dance
with you
forever
Cheerfully
Jack Dagle.

"I never see color until someone shows it to me. And I don't believe God has a color. But I figure that if He made flowers different, He made people the same way."

never been in this situation can't do. It's a situation that you're born and raised in. No matter how high up you get — even if you become rich and you come from the ghetto — you always adjust because you started with nothing. So if you've got *something,* you can always make out.

I think the blacks are the only ones that can really take nothing and make something out of it within themselves.

I can remember when I was a child, when my mother died, my father took us to Telehoma, Tennessee. He kept us there until he arranged the funeral here in Cleveland. There were outhouses and my grandmother had maybe forty or fifty small little houses for men who worked the road. I'd have to go out in the morning and help put water in the little basins and things like this. It's a happy thing. I don't care what anybody says. To be in the ghettos — in the country or the city — is a situation which can be happy. When you're a child you say, "I wish I had a pretty dress for today." So, you have to go to the Goodwill and get a dress for Sunday. But it's a happy feeling. When you get older, you say, "Well, I can make do with this because I didn't used to have much."

Right now, for example, I have just two-fifty in my pocket.

My mother died when I was four and my father raised us. The people from the welfare agency told my father, "Why don't you put 'em in a home?" But my father said, "Well, they're mine and I'm gonna raise them." So we got on relief and he raised us . . . to the best of his ability. I had three stepmothers.

He was real fun-loving, nothing was really serious with him. He had a happy-go-lucky attitude and all of us have it too. If anything went wrong, he just said, "Well, tomorrow's gotta be a better day, 'cause today just ain't what it's supposed to be."

I used to call him "Pappy Jack" 'cause he was a big, tall, very good-looking man, about six foot three. And he moved us around like gypsies. If things weren't right, he'd clap his hands and say, "We're gonna move today." And we would. "I found a house over here," he'd say. And we never used a key. He'd lose them. We never locked a door and we were never robbed. We were the first kids on our block on relief that had a television. Every kid in the neighborhood would come and look at television in my father's house.

92

They'd come and eat, watch television, then shut the door and leave. Nobody ever stole anything.

I suppose I got my voice and sense of humor from my father. He used to sing with a spiritual group called the Wings over Jordan down South. He could really sing. The whole house would rock. In the morning he'd go into the kitchen and start singing. One by one each of us would get up in the morning, go take a bath and come down singing. It sounded like the Tabernacle Choir was in our house. Everyone in our family could sing and we would sing all the time, all the time.

I think that anybody really black is happy-go-lucky. Some people say they have an "I don't care thing," but that ain't true. It's more like, "I'm in this predicament and there's nothing I can do about it really. And if there is, I'll do it tomorrow." It's this attitude, you know, but while I'm doing my thing today, I'll do the very best I can.

Why isn't this true of poor white folks?

Because they don't have the background for it. They don't have our predicament, the hopelessness. We have the ghetto background, the background of taking five dollars and living off it for a week, feeding five kids with it, and having a different menu each day. Maybe it's neckbones and white potatoes, or maybe it's string beans and pig ears. It's the low income they are adjusted to. They are able to cope with things.

How did you get on with the stepmothers?

Not very well. I left home the first time when I was fourteen and lived in a rooming house with a Mrs. Smith. Then my father became ill and I came back home and went back to school. My stepmothers and I couldn't get along very well, and I wouldn't tell my father about anything they did because I felt that if he didn't know it, it didn't hurt him, you know. He'd find out things sometimes. I remember a lady we called Mom. She was Italian and lived across the street from us. She gave me many a whipping and sent me home, then my father would whip me again. He didn't even ask me what was wrong. If he saw me coming from the direction of her house, he knew she'd seen me doing something. Nowadays you can't do that. You can't hit other people's children. But this change only started five or six years ago. It may seem to others that today blacks have to do this and have to do that, but when I was a kid I never knew color.

This is the way I was raised and you can never take that away from me. I'm not saying there wasn't prejudice around my neck of the woods. We lived around all kinds of people, black and white. But it wasn't anything like today. Maybe we were kids and just didn't see it because kids have a sort of honest thing about life and a carefree thing. They don't see things that hurt adults. And things that hurt adults don't get to the kids either. There could have been things that I didn't see. Half the time now I don't see things unless they are really jammed down my throat, because I'm too busy doing my own thing.

When I was about sixteen I went to New York for a month and came back. My father sent for me. He told me, "Isabel (that's my nickname), you don't have good sense, so I'm going to have to look out for you." I was very hot-headed and fought a lot. I'd go to jail on the weekends, you know. I never could let anything slide. I had a chip on my shoulder because . . . I don't know . . . maybe because I didn't have a mother and things that other kids had. I was always big for my age so I fought a lot. My father would talk with me then. So when he told me to come back from New York, I came back. But I went back when I was nineteen and stayed five years. That was in 1959.

I moved to West 105th Street among Puerto Ricans, Italians, and blacks, like my neighborhood in Cleveland. I didn't know anybody but just wanted to see what it took to get there being on your own.

I really went to New York because I wanted to sing at the Baby Grand in Harlem. My father told me, "If you make it at the Baby Grand, baby, you've made it." So when I got there in New York, I wrote my Daddy and said, "Daddy, I just made it. I'm standing in front of the Baby Grand and I'm going to be somebody." He wrote back and said, "Please, honey, come home. You don't know what you're doing." But I said, "No, I've really got to do this," and I stayed there for five years.

I didn't really do anything in theater though. I worked at the garment center in New York and in a restaurant in Harlem. That's about it. I love New York and I'm going back there to stay, when my little boy gets big enough so he can accept life. Where I lived there were addicts, junkies, pushers. There were a lot of things and if you don't have a strong mind, some kind of guidance from home, you will do these things. I've been tempted a lot of times, but I said to myself: "Anything that tells me that you've *got* to have a certain amount of money in your pocket to survive, you know, for dope, well you just don't need it."

What did you do when you returned to Cleveland?

When I came back, I got pregnant. I do believe I did. Michael is now six, so I got pregnant the year after I came back. Married? No, I've never been married. I've never wanted to. I always wanted a lot of kids, but I never wanted to get married. That may be horrible to say, but I'm very truthful. I never wanted to get married because I didn't want anybody to tell me what to do. You know, if I go out till midnight, me and my son go to the bar and he gets a ginger ale. I take him with me, you know. I come home whenever I get ready, but I never want to get married.

I was a barmaid for a while. I like being a barmaid. I like anything that deals with a lot of people, because I like to have fun. That's what I like about the theater. You can watch. Out of my eye I can see people. I like to shock them. I like to see them laugh and when you're in a bar it's the same way as in a theater. You're always acting, you know, and having a lot of fun. I worked in a bar for about seven years and I loved it. I really did. I still do.

This show is the first one I've done at Karamu in the last two years. I've been going back and forth to play summer stock at Kenley Playhouse in Warren, Ohio. We also play in Columbus and Dayton. I did *The Women* with Gloria Swanson, Marilyn Maxwell and Dagmar. I got the biggest reviews in that one and it was my first show, too. There is one line in that play which, if I do say so myself, I did well: "The first man who can tell his wife he loves her

and another woman, too, is going to win the Nobel Peace Prize."
Then I did *Finian's Rainbow* with Barbara Eton, Rudy Toronto
and Don McKay. I did *Funny Girl* with Sherrie Lewis, Julius La-
Rosa, and Molly Picon who is just wonderful. She is so good, you
learn so much and she is seventy-seven years old. She can do the
Charleston, or anything better than I can. And I did *The Man Who
Came to Dinner* with Jack Cassidy, Joan Bennett, David Holliday
and Nate Barnett.

I've had some formal training with a German-Jewish fellow,
named Beno Franck, who is from Atlanta. You can't understand a
thing he says, and the first thing he'll call you when you do something he likes is a bitch. I'm very hot-headed and I started to fight
him one night for that. He said, "Why you bitch! Why didn't you
tell me you could do that part?" It's the only thing he says that you
can understand. But he's the best of my teachers. And he teaches
you the dirt, the ghetto part, before he teaches you the good part —
how to upstage, to act with your back, to say things and play with
the audience; things every actor should know.

I admire a lot of people in theater, like Molly Picon who is so
versatile. But would you believe it, one is a man — Burl Ives? I
love Burl Ives and Ethel Waters and Pearl Bailey too. Pearl Bailey
has a lot of "I don't care," or maybe it's more like "just let the
show go, baby." I like this sort of free thing. I don't like anything
that has to be real, real drama, you know. Could you imagine me
doing Shakespeare? I could never do this because it's not me and
something that's not me I could never put my whole self in. When I
do a part, I become that person. Every Thursday, Friday, Saturday
and Sunday nights, for example, I become a lesbian in *Clara's Old
Man*. Don't get me wrong. When I'm off stage, don't start no stuff
now. Bring on the men! But while I'm out there, I go right into that
part. You have to do this.

All my life I've been around. Anywhere in the ghetto, you can
see the kind of life we do in *Clara's Old Man*. They call them dykes
and punks. I've lived next door to them. And I observe what I see.
I'm a nosy person and I want to know why you're doing this or
that. Right now, I've got about four or five wineheads that see
me every Friday. They say, "Hi, Miss Isabel, how are you doin'?" I

say to them, "Did you get your wine today?" Then I go back in the alley with them and their wine — I don't drink it myself — and we sit right there on the curb and talk.

You don't have to go back into it, but you never forget. You never forget people. People have feelings and I don't care who they are, or how big they get. If these winos were to walk up to me on Broadway one day and say, "Hi, Isabel!," I'd say, "Hi, Baby, how you doing? You got your wine?" Don't ever forget people. You don't ever want to forget them because the people you forget as you go up a little bit, you will have to remember as you go down. You may just have to get something from them later. I love them. I love anybody who just takes life and don't worry about it.

I'm teaching my little boy the same thing. If you take what you got and thank God for it today, that's good. Be thankful if it is just some bread and water because you didn't have to have that. When you get so you sort of scorn God for what you are getting, you start getting less and you can't afford it, especially being black. No matter what I've got, or whatever I do, I'm always going to remember where I came from, and I'm going to love it. I love life in the ghetto.

Take *Clara's Old Man*. My "sister" brings home this refined dude and he's young, a teacher, and he's got finesse. I'm a lesbian, and a very rough one, and him just being there irks me. There's that part where I am trying to make Clara, my girl friend, look small in front of that dude without really giving away the secret because I feel that he should know. And I'm really hurt too because Clara hasn't told him that we are like man and woman, you know, we're going together. And the dude says something like, "When does Clara's old man get home?" And I say, "Clara's old man? Well, let me hip you, Daddy, Clara's old man is home right now!" I like that, it really tells a story. I don't like fantasy. It has to be something that really exists in life that I've experienced, or that I can find out about. Then I can really get into the part.

Another beautiful part is played by Norma Powell. Remember the old lady with the gin who drives her leg across the stage? She is great. If I didn't have my part, I'd like her part. It's no lead, but I wouldn't care. If I had to walk with that gimpy leg across that stage, I would do the best damn walk across they ever had at Karamu. I could be the least part, but just let me be there on stage.

Pappy Jack used to say, "If you're going to be a ditch digger, be the best damn ditch digger God ever put out with a shovel." He used to tell me all the time that whatever you are going to be — and I'm not going to tell you — but whatever it is be the very best. He used to say, "If you don't, I'm coming back to haunt you." And I haven't seen him lately, so I must be doing pretty good.

Do you think of the work of Ed Bullins and LeRoi Jones as "Black Theater"?

Yes, because the situations that happen in black ghettos just don't happen in white ones. If whites are born poor they can adjust and get out. They are liked. But the black man has to do more to get out and rise above that level. I know half of them don't try, saying "I'm doing okay. Why should I try to do better since I'm having fun?" They get a pint of wine and be happy-go-lucky, especially on Friday and Saturday nights which belong to black people.

I hear some of them saying they don't want to play an Uncle Tom part where you say, "Yes, m'am" and "No, m'am." But this is what they've been doing all these years. And they have developed their own happiness, their dancing and music — jazz, spirituals. Anything the white man knows about this music came from the black man down South picking cotton. He should be awfully proud of himself instead of wanting to get into a white situation. Develop that black thing you have because it is something nobody else has. You were born with rhythm and soul, so don't knock it. Develop it.

LeRoi Jones is an idol of mine. I love his work and the things he says in his work. You have to really look into it. It is deeper than *Clara's Old Man* or *Electronic Nigger,* so far as these plays by Bullins are concerned. LeRoi Jones is much more an "insight doer." I mean you really have to look into what he's doing and I've done his work too. One of the most powerful and best black poets I've known is Norman Jordan. His work is so good, and no one has really heard about it. We did *Cadillac Dream.* I played the mother.

It is a gorgeous play, really something. I don't know why his work isn't being done. I'd do it in a minute for nothing — and I'm an Equity player.

Did anyone ever call you a Tom for working with whites?

Who can call you a Tom for working? My God. If so, there's sure a lot of us Toms around, I can tell you that. There may be nationalists who will get after you for playing a maid's part or something, and they will say that is an Uncle Tom part. But I've been versatile, in fact I've never played a maid's part at Karamu.

I don't know too much about the nationalists and anything I don't know about I don't say much about. I don't support them because I've got to know what I'm doing. I can't go out there blind just because you are the same color I am, you know. Some of it is probably good, but nothing is good that is done by evil. Nothing is good when it is done by force. Nothing is good when you tell some-body they have to do this, like you have to let me move next to you. This is dictating to someone. For me, it has to be a thing where I am qualified to do this, no matter what my color. When I dictate to you, then this makes you start thinking, "Well, why do I have to let him, who in the hell is he?" If you want to really do something, get some education and meet the standards. And if you don't have any of this, the first thing you're gonna say is, "Well, I'm black, this is why I don't get the job."

You know there are some people who don't see your skin. They just see you as an individual. This is true. I never see color until someone shows it to me.

I don't relate to anything that hasn't got respect or a love thing going. Not that I'm talking about going around kissing. I'm talking about a godly thing. I believe in God. I don't believe there is any other thing that keeps me going but a God. And I don't believe God has a color. When you say that I'm wrong or you're wrong for being black or white, then you say God made the wrong thing. I don't think God ever does anything wrong. I just don't think he does. I figure that if he made flowers different, he made people the same way.

99

You can't just say, "I'm black, and I want this job." You've got to show some kind of initiative, some kind of know-how and education, in order to get a job. When you don't do this, then you're forcing people and then people rebel against force because this is America.

The only field I know where you can work with anybody, black or white, is acting. If you really have theater in your mind, you don't have any time for small things. Only small people think of small things. They don't care what color you are if you can learn. And I've worked with some of everybody in the theater. It's how you feel inside, and if you've got this bitterness you can't really get along with anybody, black or white.

In fact, anyone who wants to do anything so far as entertainment is concerned should start in the legitimate theater. When you start here, you can't retake it. They see it for what it is. So when you are good in this, you can be good in music, good in movies or television, good in anything. But you got to start here. This is your roots. And how can you beat it? This is better than going out in the alley with your switchblade, baby, because you can work up to try to be somebody when you get older. So, when I hear people say, "I don't have anything to do," they're wrong. I saw a kid on the bus on 105th Street and I said, "I'll tell you where to go. Come over here, baby." And when we got off the bus, I got on the phone and called his mother and said, "I've got your son at Karamu House. He has just gone into the art class. If you let him stop at 105th Street every day, I'll pick him up and take him." There is really no excuse anymore. There is no excuse at all.

Where do I see myself in five years? Well, I've got ten in one eye and nothing in the other. I see myself as being one of the greatest actresses in the world. I want to do something on Broadway. I want to do it so well that someone will say, "Well, I want to be like Mary Conley, *that* kind of actress." And I don't mean only the black situation but good in whatever show I do. Or maybe I'll be a singer in a nightclub. But it's got to be something dealing with people. If not, I'll die.

I love the theater. I really do. I like to see them laugh. It's a fantasy to them, another world. But to me it's real. I like to keep them laughing until the curtain goes down. I don't want them to leave. I don't want them to think about tomorrow. I want them to stay right there with me.

THE NATIONALISTS

BLACK WARRIOR

At night while
whitey sleeps
the heat of a
thousand African fires
burns across my chest

I hear the beat
of a war drum
dancing from a distant
land
dancing across a mighty
water
telling me to strike

Enchanted by this
wild call
I hurl a brick through
a store front window
and disappear.

— Norman Jordan
(Cleveland)

ANTHEM

Thy country's liberty
Worn down by slavery,
From thee we flee.

Land where our fathers cried
Land where the red man died
On plains and mountain side
From thee we flee.

– Anonymous
(Philadelphia)

COUPLET

Burning villages. That's politics.
Burning flags. That's unpatriotic.

— Anonymous
(Philadelphia)

VIOLENCE IN RE-VERSE

I wish I was an Alabama trooper
That's what I really want to be
'Cause if I was an Alabama trooper
I could kill a nigger lee-ga-lee

> — White High School Chant
> (Chicago)

Come on, Aunt Fannie,
    Come on, Sister Sue,
Kill a cracker! Kill a cracker!
    Oh! don't forget the Jew,
'Cause he's a cracker, too.

> — Black High School Chant
> (Philadelphia)

I AM A MAN

I am a man
And I will stand tall, white America.
And I will flex my muscles
And rear my children upon plenty,
Because this, this is the land of plenty.
And my sons will stand tall
With no scars on their backs.
And they will be strong, and proud, and wise
Because I, I will teach them.
And my daughters will be beautiful.
They will not carry the marks of the scullery maid
Upon their bodies or their minds.
And their children will grow
Taller and straighter and stronger.
And the beauty of my people
Shall become as the beauty of midnight diamonds.
And the shame of the past shall be forgotten.
Stand back, white man!
Look at me, white America!
Put down your whip and walk away now,
Because today, I am a man.

– Faith Thomas
(Cleveland)

Black Panther #1

This black revolutionary, minister of information for a midwest chapter of the Black Panther party, is tall with thinning hair. He is a difficult man to interview, saying little of his past and qualifying everything else as transitional or dialectical. He makes it clear that the positions noted here are not necessarily relevant to the present. Both ideology and tactics shift with the current exigencies of the struggle.

He is self-assured, with a deep calm and can become eloquent and impassioned when aroused. At these times, he exhibits an oratorical style which owes much to Eldridge Cleaver. Once he moved a white student radical to one side and took over the microphone to condemn a recent fire-bombing of the local Black Panther headquarters. The white newsmen forgot the white radical and listened to Panther #1.

Upon leaving, he told me that America needs "ten thousand Kent States" in order that white people will take up arms against the fascist and repressive regime of Nixon and Agnew. No number of murders of black people will turn America around. When blacks die, he said, it is, for whites, like going to church on Sunday morning — a ritual observance.

I was a college student when Deputy Minister of Defense Bobby Rush and Deputy Chairman Fred Hampton came to get me. Fred Hampton is now dead, murdered in bed by the Chicago pigs.* Evidently they had heard about my work. Now I take some courses in college but only ones that will help me, the organization and the people right here at home. I don't study things like Greek and Latin which won't do me any good unless I was planning to live in Greece or something like that. I only study technical courses and things that are going to help me become a better writer. I'm a journalist.

My field is political science but I'm not much interested in a degree, a piece of paper. I'm interested in what I can learn and what I can teach while I'm in college. Most of the time I am teaching more than I am learning, so I don't really relate to the piece of paper at all.

Who can join the Black Panther party?

The Black Panther party is a defense organization. It was organized by Huey P. Newton and cofounded by Bobby Seale. It is a black organization, and we have coalitions with white organizations

---

* On December 4, 1969, Fred Hampton and Mark Clark, both Black Panthers, were killed by the Chicago Police. Four others were wounded. Fred Hampton was deputy chairman of the Illinois Chapter of the Black Panther party. See Francis Ward interview on Hampton, p. 259.

and a working understanding with white organizations, like Mexican-Americans, Chinese-Americans, Puerto-Rican–Americans. We also have coalitions with young patriot organizations which are white but are not racist. We have sometimes to remind white people of things, like they should organize the white community and black people should organize the black community. When they get something that is workable, then we can have a working understanding or coalition for a specific purpose.

We work with any people who try to come forth to help somebody and who are willing to come forth, and recognize what America really stands for. People willing to recognize that America doesn't stand for the land of plenty and the home of the brave. There are such people. There are white people who recognize this and who are moving toward a personality like John Brown. They identify with the type of person who will bring about some changes so we can survive in this country. This is what's going on with white people.

We judge people by their practice, not by their color. This is the criteria of truth and we don't divorce ourselves from that. We believe in looking at and seeing our brother, our class brother. We see what he is doing. This is how we choose our friends, how we correct our friends and how we destroy our real enemy. It is not by the color of their skins but by their action. How they deal and feel.

We have brothers and sisters here from all walks of life. Some are from high economical backgrounds and some from low ones, and from different religious backgrounds too. This doesn't matter because once they come into the organization they adhere to the discipline of the party. We don't vacillate at all about our discipline which is very important in revolutionary organizations. So it doesn't matter about where you come from, or what kind of names you have, and stuff like that.

We are not concerned about nobody proving what they are to us. We adhere to whatever is necessary for our party and the people, black people and poor oppressed people period. We don't set up guidelines and all. We don't give a whole lot of drawn-out tests and stuff like this. We don't set up anything that is too elite, that the black community cannot identify with like some other organizations do. Mostly we want dedication and somebody that can take orders. Take them and still be critical and open-minded and who really want to serve the people. These are the basic things.

Separation? It doesn't mean anything to me period. It just means someone being divided, taking themselves away from something else. So we are not interested in separation or integration. We are basically interested in our liberation. If black people want separation, then we'll go along with black people because our party is about black people. But we say that separation at this time is premature here in this country. There is no separation in the black colony. We live in colonies. That is not separation. That is neocolonialism.

Our class brothers are groups like the Black P. Stone Nation, or the Cobra Stones and other black organizations.* We relate to them. We understand their plight is the same as ours. We are faced with the same enemy and the same repression. The same people are trying to indict them with all kinds of trumped up charges, like they are trying to indict the Black Panther party and black people period. We don't have any difference at all with the rest of the black organizations. In fact, we are coming closer and closer because of all the police repression that is being forced and put upon our organization.

When did you become Black?

I have been Black all my life, but I think you want to ask when did I become Black to the extent where I would dedicate my life to the liberation of people.

I have always been interested in doing whatever I can for black people and for poor, oppressed people. I never left the black community, what the sociologists call a ghetto, but that is a middle-class expression. We just call it the black community because it is like that all over the country, all over this city. There is no difference in my community. Freedom there ain't no different. They have just a little bit more, say, than I have. They just get a little bit more food, a little bit better house, a little better car. But as far as being totally liberated, there is no difference. Adam Clay-

* See Francis Ward interview, page 258.

ton Powell proved that. You can go so far, and be from such and such an economical background, but when you step out of your place and start exercising your freedom of speech or freedom of assembly, you just get knocked off. So there ain't no difference really.

We're black and oppressed and so we have to go on and try to liberate ourselves. We have been narcotized in the black community. We have been so doped up by the news media and all this miseducation till we cannot identify with ourself. But I think I've always bled when black people were hurt somewhere, no matter where they were at.

What does America mean to you?

America means to me just what the swastika meant to the Jewish people in the 1940's. It means to me what the rising sun of Japan meant. There are the true symbols of fascism. That is what is being perpetrated today. America means, it exemplifies, total repression to black people. It exemplifies the total repression of progressive people who are striving for basic needs in this country. It exemplifies total repression for those who stand up and confront the fascism in this country.

Genocide has become very real in America. It is a term that came through the Geneva Convention in Nuremberg and the trials right after the Second World War when Hitler and Eichmann had exterminated over six million Jews. It was declared a crime, an international crime, to take away a whole group or part of a group. It was declared a crime to kill off the leaders of a particular race or religion, or to take them or their kids and relocate them in a particular place.

This is the same thing that is going on in America. They are killing off leaders, like the twenty-eight members of the Black Panther party who are now dead; like the incarceration of two hundred members of our party. And it is not just the Black Panther party. They are killing people, black people period, like John and Michael Soto, Linda Andrews, and Mark Clark, Fred Hampton, Malcolm X and Martin Luther King. The Black Panther party is the particular target of genocide now but the main target is black people in general. This is the genocidal program now being waged by Nixon and Hoover. This is what is going on today in this country.

We are Revolutionary Nationalists. That is just a little different from Black Nationalists. However, Black Nationalists are our closest allies. The very key is liberation and we understand that Black Nationalists are brothers who are striving for their liberation just like we are. We don't have any disagreement with them. We just hope they will be a little more objective and study deeper so they can understand our party better.

Harllel X (Harllel Jones)

Harllel X is the prime minister of the Afro Set, a growing Black Nationalist organization in Cleveland, Ohio. He is about thirty, tall, handsome and athletic. He supports two wives and five children on $5,440 per year. He is a proud man, articulate with a broad ghettoese accent, much in demand as a speaker especially in white communities.

If you ask how many young people are members of the Afro Set, he quotes Malcolm X and says, "Those who tell don't know and those who know won't tell."

117

Where were you born and where did you grow up?

I was born and grew up in Cleveland, Ohio. My father was a busy man. He made babies. There were twelve of us. My father was a very moral man. I think in my early childhood I had more Christian philosophy than anyone in the neighborhood. At the age of about three we were put in Bible school every summer and we had to go each and every day and on Sunday we had to go to church. If we didn't go to church, we couldn't go to the show later on that day. He never allowed us to smoke and even today he don't allow us to smoke around him or my mother or the other kids, or drink either. He is real strong about some things.

After I became a Black man, he couldn't understand what had happened to his poor little son. He just thought that his son had some type of mental breakdown. He used to tell me, "I don't know what the hell is wrong with you. You went crazy or something? Why you talking all that stuff?" He would pick up the paper, my picture would be on the front page and would say Harllel X this and Harllel X that. He thought that I went crazy but not only him. Some of my co-workers did too when I worked for the city. Some of them would come up and say to me, "We know what you are talking about, but you gonna get messed up. You just don't say those things." They tried to hush me up, but we had to fight on. Today things have changed.

With my environment and home life, I picked up things from other youngsters, [and] especially after I left elementary school and went to high school. I changed neighborhoods but the neighborhood that I was raised in was a bourgeois, borderline area. It was in the eighteenth ward up on Eighty-first and Cedar. When I was coming up, whites were on Euclid and Carnegie and they were all over. Hough was white people's land. Cedar was just a border line. All the prominent Negroes lived in the ward. Merle McCurdy was the district attorney, Carl Stokes lived on Seventy-first, Claybourne George who has been head of the civil service ever since 1937. All the top attorneys, the Kelloggs, all of them lived on this street. They had a bourgeois thing going on during that time and the church I attended, Saint James AME was a bourgeois church

"You are dealin' with a man now!"

too, you see. After I left high school I was taken over to the old Kinsman area and over there the cats was rough. The cats from Quincy was hard core.

I remember my first experience when I was in the 7B and went in the toilet and saw these cats with a little cigarette and . . . "sniff, sniff." Drawing it in and . . . "sniff, sniff" I didn't know what they were doing. I went to talking to them and asked, "Hey, what are you doing?" This one was in my room and he was just sniffing. He said it was "weed" and do you want some? I just took it, sniffed it, and doing the same thing, saying this was weed. In other words that type of element we looked up to. We didn't really have anything to look up to as being Negroes. So the only ones we looked up to was the tough cat and the one that blew the weed and we just dug him. That environment let us to be like him or pattern after him in our own little way.

I had a knack for making a lot of friends and I made friends with the hard core instead of making friends on Cedar where I was raised at. I was in the area playing with the older boys and when they would say, "Let's do this and let's do that," I would always be the first to say, "I will do it." I remember the time when I went over there and there was this barn — looked like it was a two-story barn off Quincy. They told me that they wanted someone to fly an airplane, an old airplane that they had made up of a wooden crate with wings on it, they had a knapsack with a sheet in there and some tin cans that I was supposed to have talked into. They had it up on the peak where it was hooked and had a rope going around the other end.

I was suppose to fly. I was game and I jumped in and they cut it and it came off the roof and went up and went straight down and they told me to jump and I couldn't get out and then it broke up. I was a little afraid because I thought these were all older cats, I thought I had tore up their plane, so I laid there and they came running and saying, "We've killed him." What happened was when they came toward me I broke into a run and ran toward Cedar and stayed over there a couple of months.

I was running with this bunch, you know, and I wound up in the reform school. I was 'bout fifteen years old and I think I had been in jail maybe ten times then for all types of stuff. I could steal better than anybody else. I just wanted to do everything better than somebody else, but I didn't need these things because I came from a home that wasn't like this. And out of the twelve I was the only one that had been involved in anything like this — running with a street gang. Some of my own brothers, you know, that was a little older than me, they thought I was just a little hoodlum. And they thought all my friends was hoodlums and no good, see, but I learned a great lesson in being with them and doing time.

I learned mainly how to survive in this type of society that we live in, you know. I learned skills that I could use today. I'm not a square, you know. Anybody come up to me talking any kind of con game, or any type of game in the world, when he start it I can finish it for him. So in other words I'm glad I have this street knowledge which is a part of our philosophy. I know people and I know the street brother and I know what motivates him. I know what causes him to do what they do, see?

I see some of the youngsters doing some of the very same things that I did, you see, and I'm fortunate enough to set them down and tell them why they're doing it and what's motivating them to doing it. I can show them a different way to do something and it will be a whole lot more constructive and beneficial to them, you understand. Like if I see a person taking his first shot in the arm or smoking his first reefer, see, I just about can tell what motivated him to do this, you know. And I can also educate them on different drugs, different street hustlers, and things like this here too.

If I had nationalism when I was young, I probably never would have went to no penal institution, see, but I didn't have this. There wasn't no black talk but the youth today really have something to cling to. They don't have to smoke marijuana. What they can do is something useful for their people. They will have self-satisfaction in that alone.

Just like the pimp and the prostitute, you know, that's out there. You know, they're some of the best potential nationalists that we have coming up. They're dissatisfied in what they have, they don't want to work forty and fifty years and sit back in a rocking chair and own a old piece of house that pretty soon the man says "urban renewal's coming" and take that from 'em, you know. They want to have some type of prestige in life.

Some of the pimps and the dope addicts, and you know that Elijah Mohammed followers has a lot of them, they prove to be some of the best Muslims. Some of the prostitutes proved to be some of the best wives and some of the pimps proved to be some of the best educated people out, see? We believe in getting this talent.

If you go to a dice game you see a black man that's the house-man who maybe went to the eighth grade but yet when they ring them dice he's cutting them bets from all over the table, and throwing the dice back, getting the point, collecting these bets, paying off bets and stuff. The man can handle money. He can probably be working in a bank, you know, and if he was working in a bank he would be one of them type of tellers that when the money comes back, if anything, he'd have more than what went in. He's so fast and good with money. In other words this same fellow could be developed into a good bank teller. With a little more schooling this person could develop himself into a useful black man in our society. We could use his talent. A man, being a man, is gonna have to learn and want to do what he wants to do, not what we think is right for him to do. You can't tell him, "You go ahead and dig ditches or you go ahead and be a bank teller," you have to sorta pick out their qualifications and when you do, let this person be interested in their work and they will give their best performance in their job because they appreciate and like this type of work.

You see the Negro all of his life he never had a choice on what type of job he wanted to go into or what he wanted to do, see, he had the cast-off jobs. The whites can come up and say, "Well, what do you want to be when you grow up?" I want to be a policeman, I want to be a teacher, I want to be this or I want to be that or I want to be a big business executive or something like own a business. Black people couldn't do this here.

When did you first discover you were Black?

About eight years ago. It came about mostly in the civil rights movement in the early sixties. They were trying to sell black folks on eatin' in white folks' restaurants and sitting in the front of the bus. Stuff like this. I believed in integration then.

After I did some time, I came back and ventured into one of Elijah Mohammed's temples here and heard some of the teachings of the Muslim's philosophy — Yacub's history,* the way black people should act, the economic program the Muslims were carrying out. I remember everything that they told me. Everything.

A little later black folks began to get beat up by sheriffs, they were putting dogs on us and knocking our women down and disrespecting them. Everyday you turned on the television and saw a bunch of white folks beatin' blacks, women and children, while the so called Negro man was fighting for integration. I think at that time I came to the awareness that the majority of the people in this country were not really for integration. The whites were ready to kill black folks, to lynch and burn black folks. So at that time the only thing black folks could do was to get themselves together and instead of using the white man's toilet, get your own toilet.

If it was the will of white people to integrate we would have been integrated into the society already and there would be no need of me being a Black Nationalist today. He has shown us that he don't wanna integrate and he don't want us to separate either. He's in a bad dilemma. What he wanna do really is have his fingers on the twenty-five billion dollars that the black economy all over America is bringing in. He wants that, but he's not interested in black folks. What we're saying is that we will keep that twenty-five billion dollars among ourselves to build up our own community. And the exploitation that's going on in the black community, once it has stopped, the black community will build up by itself.

For too long we cried for civil rights and then we realized that this was a big hope. It didn't come from black people, it came from white people. We were told that white people had some type of rights that they could give us. We don't believe this anymore. We believe in human rights. We believe that we have human rights once we were born from a black woman.

So if we want any rights, the only type of rights we can ask for would be from other black people. We can't possibly go to the

* See Sababa Akil interview, footnote on p. 145.

white man and ask the white man for some type of rights because we know that he hasn't got our rights to give us. But he still thinks that he has.

The black man, in America, has for so long been trying to get over the philosophy of Black Nationalism to a lot of people and ethnic groups. Sometimes people wonder why speakers like me appear in almost a predominantly white audience to explain Black Nationalism. I'll tell you why. Black Nationalism is going to affect white lives just as it is going to affect the lives of my people. The things that I am saying, and the things that the Black Nationalists are saying, are the will of the majority of the American people.

Black Nationalism is an organization, a political party too. What we're really trying to do is to create black business, a black police force and a black city within a city or a nation within a nation. A lot of people say we can't do this. Why can't we? Universities and businesses have their own police departments but if we tried to get black policemen everybody would start hollering, "racism." And the racists are the ones who are going to call it racism. I have been branded as a racist but I know it is impossible for me to be a racist. I wouldn't be here today if it weren't for white people.

We have relied on the white man for four hundred years and he hasn't got us out of poverty. He hasn't cleaned up the crime in our community. We know the majority of the white people in America don't want black people to integrate. They don't want them to go to their schools, to their churches. They don't want them to live in their communities. The white man is so brainwashed that when he gets tired of his old home and he wants to sell it, he wants to decide the people he wants to sell it to. Since he is selling the home he is not living in it anymore, all he should be interested in is the money; but he is so racist he doesn't even want a black man to live in the house he once lived in.

We know at this time that black people are gonna have to sit down with one another and create their own businesses, and they gonna have to tell the white man to sit over there cause the white man has problems. If he could have done away with the problems of the black man, he would have been done away with them. But he can't. So we gonna have to rely on ourselves to do away with the

crimes in our community. All the prostitution that is out there —
all that I see and you see and possibly what the police sees — has
got to go.

I know there are a lot of white people that don't like this. They
can't realize why I'm here today, speaking the way I am. They think
I was their former slave and they are my former slavemaster.

We have never been slaves in this country but we were captured.
A slave doesn't work by his own free will; he doesn't have any
knowledge. You can believe it or not, but a lot of it was hidden and
didn't come out but it was there all the time. This is what the rebellion that came about during slavery time is all about. I guess that's
part of the mustard seed that has drifted down into this black man
who is here today.

One of the problems in America today is that the white man has
failed to realize that the black man has grown up to be a man. Most
of the time your white brothers call us boys, niggers and also Negroes. Today we call ourselves black men. And when you have to sit
down and wonder what is wrong with the black man today, you
have to understand that you are dealing with a black man and not a
little boy anymore. You can call him a boy if you wanna, but he is
a MAN.

The white man has actually brainwashed himself and not only
black people, but his own kind. For example, a lot of big businesses
want the Appalachian white to be ignorant, because an ignorant
man can't think for himself. A big businessman will stand back and
put his hands on the shoulders of the Appalachians and say what
good friends they are, and how bad black people are. Businessmen
are the power structure and we know that the power structure is
racist. So the poor whites have been brainwashed to think we had
tails, that we're no good, that we're lazy and all we wanted to do
was to sit up under a shady tree and eat some watermelon. They
believe this sincerely. Some have been so far back in the mountains, they don't even know that Richard Nixon is the President
now; some still think that Eisenhower is in the White House. I
know one thing about the Appalachian white though; he can clean
himself up, put on a shirt and tie, and he can cut his hair, and he

125

can go to some of your colleges and get a so-called education, and get him a job. A black man can't do that.

It was the white man who took the black man and told him he was nothing. Everything in his book, even the ugly duckling or the bad sheep (remember he was black), everything bad was black. And white kids read this. How would you like for your kids — if I was to educate your kids — to say the "ugly duckling" would be a white duck? You understand? The bad days would be white Mondays and instead of having Snow White you would have Ebony Black. How would you like that? This is what our kids learn, and your kids too. How would you like your youngsters to pick up a book called *Little Black Sambo,* and be told about a little boy who could run so fast that he ran around a tree until he made a tiger turn into butter and then he sat down and ate a stack of pancakes? That's why I won't sit down and eat in front of white folks.

I was once branded as an agitator. Some people said I was a socialist or communist. They said a lot of things. These things were said by white people. My politics are black, they are not red. I don't believe in taking no orders whether it is the white man here in America or the white man over there in Russia. I believe the black folks are going to have to get together among themselves and create their own "ism." Our "ism" is Black Nationalism. It's not capitalism, socialism, or communism. It's Black Nationalism. You put Black Nationalism in there and we'll have a choice to follow: something *good and black*.

How did the Afro Set get started?

First, we started a house on Superior Avenue called the JFK House. We used a little psychological effect and put "JFK" up there, meaning either Jomo Freedom Kenyatta or John Fitzgerald Kennedy. We were after the minds of the people and if JFK meant anything related to Africa at that time, it was no good. So a lot of Negroes came because they thought it was a John F. Kennedy house.

The purpose was to reach the youth of the area. You can't teach old dogs new tricks. Might as well take them young and work with them, see? Most older folks are set in their ways. A lot of them are scooped up on religion and a lot of them get married and can't fight for their rights because they might lose their jobs and homes and things like that, you see? Youth was the vanguard of the movement and they were not afraid to take chances, they wasn't afraid to fight for their rights. They intend to be a newer breed of black people that is coming up. They are more aware than their parents was and they want to correct the problem that was existing between an Afro-American in this country and the white world. We've got over a thousand young Black Nationalists coming up every year here in Cleveland.

Then the Afro Set got started about three years ago. It was after the riots that we had here. There was a lot of grand jury investigations, indictments and stuff like this here. They saw fit to rush the housing inspector into the JFK House and succeeded in closing the doors to it. They used the same old lies for health violation and condemned the whole building.

The Afro Set is strictly a Black Nationalist organization. I'm the prime minister of the Afro Set. I have seven ministers in command. We have educational ministers and believe in what we call the "scientific distribution of labor." What I am qualified to do best, that is what I am going to do. What my brothers and sisters can do best, that is what they are going to do.

We have programs going on all through the week. We have Swahili classes, current event classes, drum classes, jewelry making, pottery making, and then we have a lot of defense meetings. On Sunday night we have soul sessions.

The defense classes are conducted by the elite squad. They are more or less like the governing body and they have to keep themselves physically trim and obey strict rules and regulations. They go out and do physical workouts, like run a mile a day or something like this here, or push-ups. There's a lot of requirements that you have to go into to become a member of the elite squad. We have karate down there too, and judo also. In other words these elite squads learn to defend themselves against anything. And with weapons — guns, sticks, feet, anything.

If a criminal comes into your community and wants to take someone out and lynch them, you understand, then I think that what I said about the "scientific distribution of labor" applies. We got young black men that can stand up and repudiate them. If they wanna come with guns, we'll have guns to answer them with. All nations or groups will do the same thing. I'm not preaching any bloodshed, I'm just telling you today that the day when the white man can come into the black community to hurt black people is over. You will see because the younger generation is a little different from my generation and even your generation.

We have ministers also. We have three ministers in command. We have a minister of youth, of culture, of education. They do just about the same duties I do. They are floating ministers and float all over the city wherever there are Afro Sets to see that everything is functioning and the policies of the Afro Set are carried out. They get chosen by me on their ability, their dedication and their faith in the movement.

It's not too much of a democratic group. I do most of the decision making for the Afro Set. If there is a decision made by another minister which is wrong we will just go over it and correct it. We take votes at our regular meetings of all the Afro Sets on certain types of programs, allowing certain things to happen because we try to be a flexible type of organization and move with the time. What we did last year we can't do this year. We have a code of behavior and the Afro Set codes and the codes of Black Nationalism that all members have to follow, especially unity, collective work and responsibility, economics, education.

Our membership is from three weeks old all the way up to ninety years old. We have members in their fifties and we got babies in there about two or three weeks old that's in the Afro Set. We have children that's born under the Afro Set, by the kings and queens. The baby belongs to the Afro Set and the king provides for his queen at all times.

Then there's the code of physical behavior that we have, and the teaching, for example, "Ninety percent of the white world is not good and the other ten percent you can't trust." Every new member gets these forms, so they study and they are supposed to know these teachings. We don't allow the women to use contraceptives and we don't allow them to kill the fruit of a black man. In other words any type of abortion or taking pills to get rid of a baby under any circumstances. The worst evil that a Black Nationalist could commit is to have sexual relations with our opponent, our enemy. The Bandung world is different. That brings in Latin America, Asia, and Africa. They are different and they are invited to become members if they choose to become members. We have some mixed blood like Chinese-Black and things like this here. They are black too. They are members of the Bandung world, part of the family you see, anything that is not white is black. Of course, we have black people who are fair, and we have half-breeds with maybe white fathers and black mothers and they all live in the black community. But they are still black to us, too. Black isn't a color or skin pigmentation. It's a state of mind. Even white Americans can call themselves black, but not Black Nationalists. Black means that you think Black.

We want to bring Black awareness to our young black children. The majority of Negroes wanted to be white because all their lives they had been told: "If you are white, you alright; if you are brown, stick around; if you are black, stand back." And they believed that. They thought they were no good. They believed it was a bad omen to be black. We are trying to reverse this. We're trying to tell them to be proud of what they are, because they are not going to change their skin color. We can't hide our color or try to turn white, or put on those blond wigs that you're making and them great big red lips. All that white powder ain't gonna help us out. Some white man invented bleaching cream and told us to put it on a black skin and we would get a lot lighter. So we tell ourselves now to throw all that cream away. We know now that black is beautiful and that is not just a label but a state of mind. The only way black folks are gonna be able to do anything is to feel confident of themselves. We are black and today this is one of the things we're proud of. We're just as proud of ourselves today as being black as you are of being white.

We organize and teach our members while they are on their jobs or in school. We teach other people and set examples for the Negroes that are in these institutions. Like for instance our youth that are in schools, we teach them to be polite and kind to all teachers no matter what color they are, study their work and especially to get the basics of English and mathematics. The rest of the social studies and the history, they can just about disregard. We teach them to be outstanding students and set examples for other students in their room. We teach them that the students that are hollering and throwing things around and tearing things up are wrong. Our youngsters come up and tell them, "I don't think that is very black. You are acting like niggers or Negroes."

Do you believe in working at all with the present power structure?

Most of us don't believe in working with the power structure. For example, we have a black man named Carl B. Stokes who became mayor of this city. I was born and raised here in Cleveland and all I've seen is a white man in city hall and they never did anything. They never found a qualified white man then, so why are they lookin' to find a better one than Mayor Stokes today? If there's a better man, he hasn't been born. He does wonders for the city, not only for the city, but he put Cleveland more on the map than any other mayor. He's recognized when he goes out of town. He represents the people of Cleveland, not just the black community, but all of the people of Cleveland. He is not only a very good man but he is the most handsome mayor we ever had of Cleveland. I sure believe that black is beautiful and I think a lot of women think the same (and not only black women but white women, too).

I know that a lot of you out there, if he wasn't black, would be so proud of Mayor Stokes it would be a shame. But a lot of white folks here are racists. They don't want no black man to be the mayor of this city. This don't make me feel good as a black man. It makes me believe more and more that we must separate and break away because we cannot depend on the white man to do anything for us anymore. He got his games out there and he's full of them. He is not trying to get to the moon. Why does he want to get to the moon when he can't take care of this planet down here? Some people say he wants to go to the moon because he has no place else to go, having made a hell on earth. He don't know what to do with black people. As a matter fact the lives of black people in this country are lost.

Some think that if those "Negroes" don't like what we are doing in this country why don't they go back to Africa? We're not going back to Africa because nationalism means staying right here in America. The only ones that would be qualified to tell us to go back would be the red man and he's our brother. We know he's not going to tell us, for if he was going to tell anyone it would be the European man to go back over to Europe where he came from. If any of you got the idea of telling me to go back to Africa, I'll let you know what I'm gonna tell you: "You go back to Europe."

There's a lot of reasons why I don't want to integrate into white society. Anytime a society can allow four little black kids to get bombed and burned in Alabama, or night riders wearing hoods riding out to lynch human beings; anytime a society can take another human being and put chains on his feet and work him to death and then tell him he was no good, that he's a second-class citizen, well, it's wrong. The thing that white people gotta do is to go out and clean up their rotten society before they can tell black folks "let's integrate." I don't think we would wanna be as rude as the white man was here in America to any ethnic group.

One of the great hopes of the white man is to have us chasing after him every twenty years, moving into neighborhoods he has already left. Every twenty years black folks have been moving. What we're planning on doing now is staying here and building here. We don't believe in burning down communities, burning down homes and schools, cause we know eventually these schools will be controlled by black people.

If we keep running out to you we won't have nothing, so what we're gonna have to do is build up Hough, the black community, and we hope eventually to get the white policemen out of there, the white merchants and any other persons that's in the community trying to exploit the black people. This is our goal of bringing a nation within a nation. We feel that we can trust one another. We feel that we can not trust white people any longer. And if we fail, at least give us a chance to fail. You failed, now let us fail.

We believe that once we are on our own we will be like we once was, a proud African people. I know by our nature we are decent. I think if we can stay away from the white man and if we don't pick

131

up some of his characteristics, black folks will go back to being the peace-loving people they once was. Our job is teach black folks that the crimes they are commiiting against their own people are the crimes the white man wants us to commit on our own selves: the purse snatcher, the mugger, the rapist and the prostitute. These are white men's crimes.

Another thing are the white Johns that come out into our community. They want to "integrate" with our black women. Now I know that she is good and beautiful, but they need to stay out of our community. We don't go into their community lookin' for their women. One of the things that we know as Black Nationalists is that our women come first. We have to give respect to our women. Anytime outsiders come in our community disrespectin' our women, we need to run them out.

So we are only saying that we got to lead Whitey out of our community. If the white people want to do anything, they can go back to their own community and straighten it out. Stop those lynchin's and pull their sons and daughters out of Viet Nam so they can come and straighten out this problem out here in America, so people can live as human beings, not as dogs. They can go and grab George Wallace by the shoulder, and say, "Be cool, George." They can grab the Minutemen and tell them, "You might be pushing us in a war, brother." And please don't underestimate the black man who is willing to fight in his urban village. The white man should learn one great lesson from this war: every black man could be a potential Viet Cong in this country. He better start listening and better start looking at home, and he better pull his troops out of there. He better start rebuilding his cities.

What black leaders have had most influence on you?

There was a great necessity for Martin Luther King, Malcolm X and Muhammad Ali. All three of these people have served a great usefulness to black people. They worked under the hand of Allah, for his number one messenger, Elijah Mohammed, had been preaching for years, "Stay away from the white man, he don't want you, he don't love you. Get your own businesses." Before him it was Marcus Garvey who preached it, but the Negroes' eyes was blind. They couldn't see it. They couldn't believe that this Great White Father who fed them in the soup line didn't want them, see? They knew they were catching hell, but they didn't know where they were catching the hell from.

So what happened was all of a sudden a little man like Martin Luther King comes along. Martin Luther King came in that same bag, he said, "I'm a Christian, I'm a preacher," you understand? This is what the white boy had always said was the established leadership in the black community. He came as a Christian preacher, he came as a nonviolent man. The white boy said nonviolent is the way, so he came as a nonviolent man. So he went around, now knowing what he was doing, but he exposed the white man for what he was. He exposed him to millions of our people today. This made my work easy, it's making Elijah Mohammed's work easy, because the white man has been stripped down and become naked. Martin Luther King came peacefully and he said "I'm a Christian," and they threw him in jail. They didn't give a damn if he was a Christian, you understand? They twisted his arm, they put Mace on him, they beat his people, women and children, and black folks looked up and said, "O my God, this man is a beast, he's a dog, look what he's doing!" It woke people up, it woke them up. All the talk, all that preaching that the Muslims, and Black Nationalists like Marcus Garvey had taught, black people still refused to really start a mass movement. That was Martin Luther King's usefulness. He really exposed him better than anybody. Martin Luther King went down and showed them in their own bag. He came just the way they always told Negroes to come. And he was murdered by a white man.

Then came Malcolm X. Malcolm X was a ghetto brother, Malcolm X came from the ghetto. He shot narcotics, he sold it, he pimped, he did some of everything and went to the penitentiary. He went no further than the eighth grade, but he sat down with some of the top professors in the country and none of them could turn him around. He turned all them around, so in other words he showed black America that it don't matter what education you've got from the white folks, you understand? Here's a black man that came from the ghetto that's just like you. So he set up a hell of an image for black people.

Then came Muhammad Ali. Muhammad Ali said, "I'm the baddest thing on two feet." He said, "I'm the prettiest thing, ain't I pretty?" They hated his guts. They were burned up to see a big black, a former slave, marching around talking about how pretty he was and what he'll do, you understand? They said, "We're gonna get somebody, we're going to get a colored boy, we're going to get a Catholic boy, we gonna get a white boy to beat his damn brains out." They got Floyd Patterson and Muhammad Ali beat him bad. They then got big Ernie Terrell in the ring and Terrell went around talking about that he was going to whip him, "I'm going to whip one of those Muslims. His name is Cassius Clay." Muhammad Ali told him, "My name is Muhammad Ali." When they got in the ring, as you remember, Muhammad Ali started beating him and started asking "What's my name, what's my name?" Finally Terrell, a Negro, went down saying "Muhammad Ali." He made him call him "Muhammad Ali." In other words the physical strength of Muhammad Ali went around the world. He fought every opponent they brought. This was the physical strength that black America needed.

So, Muhammad Ali had the strength, Malcolm X had the brains, and Martin Luther King stripped the Man for what he was. These three people made a great contribution to black America. These are some of the things we teach the brothers and sisters. These are the parables that we teach our brothers and sisters about the modern day black man.

The new leader is a cross between Malcolm X and Muhammad Ali. Martin Luther King is gone. He did his usefulness and he did a damn good job of it. I wouldn't knock him but it's over with. His era is gone, but you see just where the white boy made his biggest mistake. Instead of him going along with Dr. Martin Luther King and telling him, "Don't strip me," he let Martin Luther King strip him for what he was. So he lost those church people, those Christians, those Negroes, those preachers, the nonviolent ones — they're through. You don't hear people talk about nonviolence no more.

A young black today stands up physically, you see, and says, "I'll challenge anybody." A police officer don't walk up to him and slap him in the mouth and call him a nigger without that young black showing his physical strength. In a lot of situations, they take guns from white police officers. During the riots, blacks just tore open their shirts and said "Go ahead and kill me." They didn't give a damn about dying any more. They just stood up like a man. The new black leader's mind works as sharp as Malcolm's. Years ago, you didn't find young blacks as sharp as what they are, especially the ghetto-type black. We got leaders now in every ghetto in the country, just like Harllel X, just as sharp. They can get on any radio or TV program and they can't get cut up, they can't be turned around. They are going to keep on striving forward.

We're products of Malcolm, you understand, and there are more of us that comes along, a new black generation. The white boy is going to have to finally wake up and say, "We are going to have to deal with a man now" and you don't use violence on a man. You sit down with him and negotiate, and the only thing the black is asking for is freedom, justice and equality.

"I'm not an American. I'm a victim of Americanism. I'm being held by Americans, lied to by them, tricked and exploited by Americans. I've been captured by Americans, you dig?"

Sababa Akil (Willie Tolbert)

Sababa Akil (Willie Tolbert) is one of fourteen children, born in the South. He is now twenty-one years old and the number two man, deputy prime minister and minister of education, in the Afro Set.

He is an expansive talker but controlled and serious. He is confident, quiet and disciplined. His Prime Minister, Harllel X, says "Ninety percent of white people are no good, and the other ten percent you can't trust." Sababa Akil says, "You can't trust the ninety percent who are no good either."

Do you think of yourself as an American?

No, I don't. And it's very, very simple why I'm not. Malcolm really did it when he said that being born in America don't make you an American. If you're sitting at a table with people dining and you have no food on your plate — you're not a diner, you dig? I'm not an American, I'm a victim of Americanism. I'm being held by Americans, lied to by them, tricked and exploited by Americans. I've been captured by Americans, you dig?

What do you mean?

Well, look what happened last summer. I made up my mind a long time ago, you understand, there wasn't about to be no army for me. So I received some papers last May and went down to see them. I didn't say I was a conscientious objector or anything like that. I just told them I was a Black Nationalist and I belonged to my people. I had my own flag and uniform, my own unit and commander, my own guns and drills . . . and I had my own enemy. And it ain't about America. I told them I wouldn't want to be associated with anything that stands for all the bullshit that goes on in this country.

So, they sent me into the security room and kept me there all day and next day they told me to come back. So next day I went down and there's trickery, you understand? They told me to follow them into a room and it wasn't the room where everyone was going to be inducted. It was a room with only one of the officers and when I stepped into the door this cat was reading some papers and I asked him what are you doing? Are you trying to induct me? And he said, "That's right! You're now inducted!"

So I raise hell, you know, and went through a whole lot of changes. They came up with two regular army cats, saying they were MP's and assigned to transport people to the airport and the plane leaves for Fort Campbell at twelve something. I said, "I ain't goin' nowhere." Then I went round the building and they sent some kind of investigators, probably one of them FBI cats, following me. I couldn't leave the building because one followed me and others were posted at the doors. So I went on back upstairs and saw a police sergeant who was Negro and he was talking about why don't you love America and all that here kind of stuff. He say you can't beat this whole country by yourself. I point out to him that the Viet Cong was doing it, you dig, in rice fields with tennis shoes. They are doing it every day, whopping your ass.

Well, they got a writ filed and I had to go to federal court the next morning. When I got down there, after contacting my attorney, I was thinking to myself as I walked in, "They must have found one of the FBI's ten most wanted men." You dig? And he must be one of the most violent, because they had all these cats here. There was about twenty-five security guards rigged up in the courtroom, and the federal judge, members of the subversive squad, guys from the detective bureau and from the FBI . . .

Well, they did a helluva railroad job. Soon as I entered the courtroom, I knew there wasn't going to be no justice. There is never no justice in the court. First the army got up and lied, you dig, and all of a sudden the judge read a statement that was phony, as phony as America itself. Then came a time when everyone takes a step forward suggesting you enlisted, and I take a step backward and declare myself a political prisoner. I said I'm not going to nobody's army and a colonel come up with a big ole brown envelope talkin' about "I'm your commanding officer." And I said, "You ain't shit, my prime minister is the only officer I know." He was an old cat and when I raised my voice, I seen his eyes start quivering and he was about to have a heart attack and stuff. He was the highest ranking cat on the set and I had blow'd his mind. I went through a helluva verbal thing with him and everytime I turned round, one of these federal marshals was on me. So I sit back down.

So two MP's jumped up from behind a door, searched me and handcuffed me and took me down to the basement, put me in one of those army vehicles and reported to the press I was on my way to Fort Campbell. But they took me to the county jail and left me there overnight. The next morning came and they transported me from there to Columbus and from Columbus to Fort Knox, and from there to Fort Campbell.

Once I was there they mimeographed copies of the press stories about me being a Black Nationalist leader and stuff, probably the FBI supplying them with this type of information. In Fort Campbell, they were saying, "So, this is one of Ho Chi Minh's boys!" There was a whole lot of racism on the set and I knew I must maintain my thing, you dig, keep my beliefs together. They tried to isolate me from the blacks, but it happened there was one brother from Cleveland. When he saw me handcuffed, hands and feet, and wearing my dashiki and everything, my black uniform, he knew who I was. When they locked me in a room, you dig, the brothers got to a window and I started running down what was going on and told him to go back and run it down to the rest of the brothers and stuff like this here. He went back and did this here.

Then they started moving me from point to point and I would see brothers standing around in circles, you dig? And they would say "Salaam" and stuff like this here and sayin' "Don't worry, everything is going to be alright." These cats was basically like the Cleveland police sergeant, you dig, ignorant to what's really happening. They tried to make it be a race thing telling me "I'm your brother." That showed they were really feeling my effect on the black brothers there.

This is a helluva story. They put me in a barracks that had only one black in it and all the rest white, about a hundred whites. I was getting all kinds of threats about we should shoot you, we should do this and going through all kinds of changes. So I didn't know at first they couldn't do it, they couldn't physically, you dig, lay a hand on me. After I found out, then like it wasn't even no thing. Like they wasn't even in the picture. They went out and got some regular little cat that had just been inducted to watch me. And some civilian whites came — you understand — up to the window where I'm confined and peek in. I figure it was probably a Klansman or something like this here. So I say, "I'll die trying to kill everyone of them I see."

So they start bugging me about getting up at some weird hour, like five o'clock. Like this wasn't none of my thing. I say I ain't in no army, I'm only here physically, you dig? When they moved on me, I grabbed a baseball bat. A sergeant wrote a thing where I attempted to use assault on him, and all kind of stuff. I didn't use the bat on them, because they were afraid even when they were circling me in the barracks.

The next day the MP's came and got me and put me in stockade. I thought it was goin' to be a weird thing, but when I got there I dug a brother. I heard him say, "Hunky, if you put your hands on me, I'm going to break your neck." I said, "Shit, I'm going to dig this here." So I fell in and organized the stockade and changed the different brothers names, giving them black names. We had some stockade rebellion, you know, and I ended up in the box, solitary confinement, you understand, for ten days, because they branded me the leader.

Round about this time they were thinking about letting me resign for the good of the service. It was a chapter ten discharge, undesirable, and I remember it had on it "SPN" and "246." I translated that to mean Special Problem Nigger number two four six, you dig? So they let me go a month, roughly twenty-eight days, after they kidnapped me and took me down to Fort Campbell. So I don't have no more worries about the draft, and I didn't fight for the slavemaster.

How long have you thought of white America as the slavemaster?

From the beginning. I was born in Clarksdale, Mississippi, in the heart of the Ku Klux Klan territory. I worked on a plantation, owned by white people in Clarksdale. My whole family picked cotton until, when I was six or seven, we moved to the North — except it was still the South. I view the South as being, as Malcolm says, "Everything south of Canada." It was like one of those fiction books where the mother leaves, goes up North trying to make a living for the rest of the family, then sends for them. We followed her up here after she got a job and got established in the community. We left the year Emmet Till got lynched in Mississippi.

I told my mother after we left the South that I would never again be a slave and I would never work in no factory. I never wanted to work in no job where you carry your little lunch pail for eight hours a day. This was never my thing.

In school I was a master student, but everything centered around being loyal to the slavemaster. After a while I found out, sometime in junior high, that education wasn't relevant to black people so it wasn't interesting to me anymore. They were always trying to teach us to say "Yes, sir," and "No, sir" to white people and if they did anything to you, just turn the other cheek. I remember the last time I was in the South, my brother and I went into a store and when one of the slavemaster's children spit at my brother, we collared him. This really upset the old people who didn't want to see us get lynched. In lots of older people in the South there is this fear thing. Me and other young people are born in the revolutionary cycle, the revolutionary age, and we can't understand the fear they have toward white people. We grew up quite rebellious.

What interested you in school?

I'm a poet. I started writing when I was about eleven or twelve years old. As I look over my early writing, it showed a search for something even though I didn't know what to call it at that time. It was a search for something that didn't exist among the people around me. I could write poetry, plays, essays or anything, you know. When everybody else was running to the library to get a report from a book, you dig, I would create my own story with a phony character and run it down to the classmates. Everybody would want to know where he could get that book, because it was a realistic story, you know.

So then like about the tenth or eleventh grade, an English teacher corrected a lot of my literature, but I see now that she was trying to get me to be a "status quo" writer, one of those Negro or lily-white writers. She felt the same way about literature as the average Negro or white person feels about it, that it should be kept in the same line as Edgar Allen Poe or some of those other cats, you dig. She asked me never to write poetry about what's going on around you. I didn't know what she meant. Like I was always writing that kind of poetry, but I never showed it to her. I wrote about the nightmare, the American experience, you dig, and put it in rather symbolic terms so I could get by with it in class. I was trying to project the message to the rest of the students. As time went on, I rejected doing even that because I felt that I will make these people accept a black man any way he is.

I read a lot, about slavery and books on the past and present, great Negroes and things like that. I knew I had been lied to somewhere and I wanted to find out where. Malcolm's *Autobiography* I read twice, and Norman Jordan's *Destination Ashes*. I had heard of a black poet living here in Cleveland and when I saw his poetry in a magazine, and a picture of Brother Norman, I knew that I wasn't the only one who thought like I did. Then I met him because he was living in the same area.

I organized students, too. Like, it's a weird thing, because that's where I had a whole lot of problems myself, with teachers and the administration of schools, them routine thinking bags. I've always viewed myself as a person helping to liberate some of them, helping them gain some kind of black feeling. If a student or friend of mine would get some static from his parents, I would give him lectures on ways to approach them, trying to free him from just being rebellious. Really I was before my time, you know, really now I wish I was in school, because everything has changed now. Then they thought I was insane.

I tried to organize the Afro-American society in our school, before it got started on college campuses. I took up printing. I was interested in printing because I knew that producing literature was a helluva thing. It was my thing, you know, and I drew up the form and went to the printshop and ran off forms about what was going on. I tried to tell the students we have a lot of power, you understand. I knew I had to relate to them since most of them dug dancing and most of them still do. We should have more dances, you dig, but we need to have black history before leaving junior high, too.

Hustling was never my thing. All through my whole life I have been sincere about what I have been doing, you dig. The majority of my life I've been searching for the truth, to pull the cover off this whole bullshit, you understand. Like when everybody would go to parties, I would go and after being there awhile you might find me standing in a corner creating a poem or something. And drinking wasn't my thing either. It always takes an experience to know this is not you, until finally you understand. It was a helluva thing being around people who did it all the time. People wondered and said, "Man, you be around all these people and don't drink." I'd say,

"That's right." It was a hard thing for them to understand, you know, especially when they had been indoctrinated as Negro. I've acquired knowledge of the outside world, you dig, just as an experiment. I studied it like you would study anything else. Like, why you drink, you dig? I analyzed. I would get drunk and have a hangover and stuff like this here, and after it was all over with, what had I accomplished? Nothing, you dig? Going to parties and dancing all night, then the next day I would be tired, physically, mentally, spiritually, you dig? What did you prosper? Nothing. So I said this is really not me, you understand. Drinking is not needed, and all this other negative stuff is not needed. I just canned it.

Why do the brothers and sisters call you "Maulana"?

It means "great teacher." I studied Swahili at Western Reserve University and teach it now to the Afro Set brothers and sisters. As a matter of fact I teach anything, you dig, that's relevant to black people. In almost every soul session we have at the Afro Set, I've rapped there and on a different topic. I give different teachings for the people and, you know, they started calling me Maulana. It started too, when I began making jewelry. I learned how to do it by myself, spending many, many hours. I would produce something and we would sell it wholesale to people coming from Pittsburgh, Akron, Philadelphia. After that I started teaching the brothers about pride and their black history, what was really relevant to black people.

On almost any topic I could teach the people. I try to qualify myself, because I knew, as a member of the Vanguard party in the Afro Set, that people in this position have to be qualified. The revolutionary principle is that people with unusual abilities have extremely heavy loads. I must be a person with unusual abilities, because I have an extremely heavy load, you dig? I was once the minister of culture, and once the minister of propaganda, and really brought the tradition, the African tradition, right here within the city to our brothers and sisters. I've satisfied myself, and the brothers and sisters, in holding these positions and being qualified to do these things. So I guess that's why they call me Maulana — all praise due to Allah.

144

And what are your teachings?

Well, I believe in Yacub's history.* I believe in the line of things, like color, and the farther away you get from black the more you become distorted in your righteousness toward your brother. Malcolm may have viewed some white Muslims favorably but only Allah knew what was really in their hearts, because the white man has been proven to be a master of deceit and a master of trickology. They are thieves, the master thieves, masters of liars, masters of everything in a negative sense. I know there never was a drunk, thief, robber or a rapist on the African continent, but we have them all here in America.

I read in history that the people who call themselves Jews were a nation of black people and were masters of everything they touched, business, mathematics, anything. And when the Caucasians came on the set, they admired these people so much they stole all their ideas, all their knowledge. They even stole the name of these people and called themselves Jews, Caucasianal Jews, that's what we have in this country. Our good black people wasn't in the habit of discriminating against anyone, so when the Caucasianal

* Mr. Yacub's history is described by Malcolm X in his *Autobiography* as the effort of the "big-head scientist" Mr. Yacub to upset the law of nature and to breed a nation of white people. According to Malcolm X, following the interpretation of the Nation of Islam, it took the 59,999 followers of Mr. Yacub, living on the Island of Patmos in Greece, eight hundred years to breed out the original black people, of whom Yacub, was one, and to create the brown people, the red people, the yellow people, and finally, the white people. These "blond, pale-skinned, cold-blue-eyed devils — savages, nude and shameless; hairy, like animals, walked on all fours and lived in trees" were born to kill and to break the peace of black people. When the black people realized their evil, they rounded them up, put them in chains and marched them from Arabia, where they had migrated, to the caves of Europe.

After two thousand years, Allah brought forth Moses to civilize this "devil race." The first group to be led out by Moses were the Jews. Yacub's bleached white race would rule the world for six thousand years, to the present time, when the original black race would return. Some of the original black people would be brought as slaves to North America in order to better understand the true nature of the white devil. Master W. D. Fard and Elijah Mohammed teach this message to black people in modern times through the Nation of Islam, the so-called Black Muslims. (See *Autobiography of Malcolm X*, Grove Press, Inc., 1966, pp. 165–166.)

Jew came on the set they accepted him. He looked odd in his color, you dig, but he had two arms, legs and a head, so they related to him as being upright, erect and walking like a man. So they intermarried, and then the white man stole our knowledge from us since he was always the master of deceit and trickology.

That is why Hitler did a thing on the Jews, because he knew that somewhere down the line they had some black blood in them. He was the kind of cat that wanted to create a master white race that had no contact with any other kind of people but white people. He saw that Jews were the masters of lying, and many other things, who had associated earlier with those black people who were sure enough masters, real masters of knowledge. Since Jews stole all their knowledge, Hitler knew that in no time at all, if he allowed these people some rope, they would probably take over everything, you dig. So he did a campaign against them, all six million of them, you know.

When black people study history, we find out that most other people who exist on this planet, we could be called their fathers, you dig. When we read in history about these cats called Hippocrates and Euclid, all these kinds of names, where they say they were fathers of medicine, and father of this and father of that, they are lying. We found out that the pope was a master of astrology and had to become the pope. But astrology is a black thing, a black science. Somewhere back in Africa, in one of the pyramids, there was built a shaft in it that every fifty thousand years would line up with some kind of star in the sky, you dig, and in order for them to build this pyramid they would have to have knowledge of the stars — fifty thousand years of knowing the stars. It was the white people, you understand, who stole that knowledge. That is why we aren't permitted to study astrology, why it is banned in schools.

So somewhere down the line the Jews associated with black people, like the Italians and almost everybody. Hannibal took many thousands of Africans on elephants over the mountains of Italy. White people couldn't get up there on their feet so he took the clumsiest animal in the world, the elephant, and went into Italy and occupied it for twenty or twenty-five years. That's why there are black Italians and that's why Italians have dark complexions and black hair. During World War II in Germany only a handful of black American soldiers occupied Germany for a limited time and they messed up the whole population. So you can imagine what ninety thousand Africans could do in Italy in twenty or twenty-five years, you dig? Same as the Irish, you understand. The Spanish Armada was defeated off the coast of Ireland, in the time of the Moors, and the Moors was black people.

That's why I say the same as Malcolm, don't none of these people ever get in my face talking about trying to discredit me or degrade me. I know my history and I know theirs. I know how to put them in their place, you dig? Our prime minister knows his history, and the brothers and sisters know theirs, so people can never confront us with the bullshit they confront the average Negro with.

Our prime minister teaches us that to defend something you haven't developed is invalid, you dig, and to develop something and not defend it is like not having it at all. So now we're in the process of developing. We are changing the thought patterns of those Negroes and whites who say we are destructive. We don't react to those statements that we're destructive, but we show the Negro that he can stand on his own two feet and succeed. For a long time, there's been this image that if we didn't include the Great White Father in anything we did, we would fail. So now we're relating to our own people. In the final analysis it's going to be the people who will rid themselves of the oppressor. We're now creating a people's army, for without an army you can be put back into slavery or led into concentration camps or suffer any kind of punishment.

You see, white people couldn't see the handwriting on the wall. Like Malcolm said a couple of years ago, America was in the unique position to have a revolution in this country without bloodshed. But white people blew it. America lied, promised and prolonged change. Now this change is coming about because the black man is standing up, stretching and finding out the truth about himself and the truth about the exploiter.

America might have committed genocide a long time, like they did with the red man, but they blew that too. They might still have it in mind, you dig, but I for one would never get into a concentration camp, and I know a lot of people who wouldn't. They are not

147

going to sit around and let white people commit genocide on black people. If they try to starve us to death, it would be foolish because everytime they would sit down to eat something, there would be blacks sitting in their doors and looking in their windows. If America don't submit, there won't be an America.

America is in no position to eliminate the black man and America knows it. And when I say black people, I'm talking about non-white people all over this planet. We black people have been sitting right here in the midst of all this bullshit, right here in the midst of this hypocrisy, right here in the central nervous system. It is the central nervous system that controls everything, you know, and without the central nervous system, the legs and arms can't function. Like the prime minister says, we're right down in the whale's belly.

Do you still write poetry?

I always write, you know. I write plays, poetry, articles. My thing is to inform and teach in any form, writing, speaking, any form to get to the people. Education is my thing: to educate the masses. I remember a statement that Napoleon ran down, "Three rival newspapers are more powerful than the mightiest army."

Black Panther #2

This Panther brother is an ex-GI and an unlikely looking revolutionary. He wears a black felt porkpie hat and the working clothes of a stevedore. His nappy hair sticks out at all angles from the hat and his gold wide-rimmed glasses and benign expression give him the amiable appearance of a construction worker on his day off. But Panther #2 works seven days a week for the National Committee to Combat Fascism.

When I asked him about his dress he seemed pleased that I had

149

noticed, and then told me why he wore such clothes: "To distinguish ourselves," he said, "from those 'nigger nationalists' with the Afro hang-ups." In his headquarters there is nothing which might be identified as Afro. It is a busy place with both black and white students passing in and out. Among the white students were several striking young blonde women who knew the codes and passwords necessary to gain entry to the office of the National Committee to Combat Fascism.

What is the relation between the National Committee to Combat Fascism and the Black Panther party?

We follow the ideology of the Black Panthers but we are also comprised of individuals who were mainly born and raised in this area. We are indigenous, but we try to follow the ten point program of the Black Panther party. Really, our purpose is to try to teach people and try to learn ourselves, the ten point program which is the social, political and military glue that makes this a self-perpetuating organization. We feel that it really manifests and exemplifies the needs of the black people in Babylon* today.

The Black Panther party was organized in October 1966 and from that day the repression of the power structure was intensified. Late in 1968 and early 1969 there was a purge in the Black Panther party and the ranks were closed. There was a national meeting in Oakland, California, and out of it came the NCCF as a united front against fascism. It was formed to provide a relationship with individuals who had not yet become revolutionary in thought toward the actual transformation of society from one of oppression to an enlightened society for all people. In relating to these individuals who had not yet come all the way, the Black Panther party wanted to include them within the ranks but yet exclude all the provocateurs, adventurers and opportunists. Since we work with everybody, we encounter some of these people who are really

---

* Babylon refers to the black colonies in America today, especially in the inner city. The ten point program of the Black Panther party will be found at the end of the interview.

undercover pigs. When they do their dastardly deeds, the Black Panther party is protected because they are not legally and technically members.

The committees of the NCCF consist of people that are ideologically members of the Black Panther party. That means we work with everybody, a large percentage of the people. And you know that we have quite a few "criminals" in the ghetto (I used quotation marks here because this is the kind of term used by the power structure to define certain members of our people). They say that you haven't been around until you're caught. You haven't done wrong until you're busted. This is the NCCF right there. In other words, there is no crime committed. If an undercover pig or some provocateur went through a lot of gyrations and gesticulations, it would come out that he is not a member of the Black Panther party.

And we have also community information services and neighborhood committees. I saw the list recently and it contains many recognized chapters and branches and national committees to combat fascism. They all have names and actual membership, but I wouldn't be at liberty to disclose them. The point is that the Black Panther party has functional organizations that are doing their political homework.

What brought you into the NCCF?

A while ago I ran into a political situation here in this city. We had the beginning of a Muslim mosque, you know, the Nation of Islam. I noticed the way the brothers rapped, they were rapping about things that to me seemed impossibilities. They were like the probabilities or dreams of the devil. That's the way to describe it. It was the first time I had occasion to rap with the brothers about the slavemaster, you know, this omnipotent administration. Anything they say is law and anything they do is right. The brothers were saying that this is the year of the doom of the slavemaster, the war of the megaton. That was in 1954 and it was like finding a chink in my armory.

Chairman Bobby Seale was in the air force. Were you in the service?

After high school in 1955 I joined the United States mercenary fascist pig army. I began to see the contradictions in the system, you know, the dual method of job assignment, of leisure dispensation, even of duty. I managed to achieve the highest job in the battalion, the highest one, above all the college graduates. I went from the top job in the battalion down to the lowest job in less time than it took all the honkies that went into the army with me to make PFC. I was demoted because of the racism, you know, this racism thing that is being perpetrated from all angles. We did have a few individuals that were not racists, one was Irish and the other was Greek. We were in the same squad, section and battery, we were all professional artillery men. These people were harassed and harangued just as badly as I was.

When I was demoted to the lowest rank and the harassment became so great, I did about three or four weeks in the stockade. When they let me out, I split. I went AWOL for a period of nine months. Then in 1957 I turned myself in on January 29. When I went down to turn myself in, they kept me outside talking over in the other room who was going to get credit for the bust. When you are on these metropolitan pig forces and you arrest somebody, they put a couple of stars next to your name.

I was sent to the stockade, a southern stockade, and then the contradictions really began to magnify themselves. In that stockade every black individual winds up the same way that I did when I went into the army. You may not start at the top but you definitely wind up at the bottom. In this stockade, every black individual winds up in the hole. I wound up there for eighteen days. So now I'm beginning to see there is a sharp line of demarcation drawn between those that are black and those that aren't black. The maximum physical limitation of time you can stay in the stockade is supposedly six months but we had five or six brothers — black brothers — that had been there two and three years. That is like doing two or three years in the city jail.

When I got out they gave me ten dollars and some old clothes but took away all my pay, benefits and a lot of my rights. They discharged me in racist Louisville, Kentucky, in 1958. I couldn't even use the bathroom in the racist bus station. My mind was expanding with this racism. I was wondering why those people that don't even know me dislike me. I had heard about Jim Crow and about lynchings, torture and brutality; I'd heard about segregation. But when you confront it face to face you become educated. You become a member of the Black Panther party. And if you don't actively participate in the programs of the party it is because you are either a coward or you feel some sort of obligation to a wife, children, mother or father.

I came back here and stayed awhile and then went to New York City, then Chicago and L.A., Detroit, Philadelphia, Mississippi, then Georgia and Florida. I just roamed the black experience for a total period of time.

I now look back at my army experience as part of the evolutionary process all black people go through. Even the sisters have to go through this, when they get pregnant and have children and go to hospitals. They shot them through the hospital in two or three days and the sister has to lay there sick in her pad with the baby, whereas some of these white people go into the hospitals three weeks before they have the baby and stay there months after having it. So all black people go through this process and I refer to it as being evolutionary and educational.

Were you bitter?

I was bitter with the fact I had to go into the army. I was bitter with the fact I had to go to school. I was bitter with the fact I had to live in America. I was bitter with the fact I had to be born in America.

Were there ideological reasons for joining the NCCF and the Black Panther party?

Yes, it was mostly the universality of the party line. It's not just the Marxist–Leninist ideology that we stress, we try to interpret it through the prism of our historical experience in Babylon. When I encountered this ideology, I noticed that it fit all the loose pieces

153

together for me. I knew the system was corrupt and illegitimate, and I was familiar with the Marxist–Leninist ideology and with the Chinese Communist party. I was familiar with the Viet Cong and the Al Fatah party. But the Black Panther party took this world-wide, universal ideology that mirrors all people within its grasp, it took this ideology and directly related it to our experience. And today our experience is in Babylon.

In my case there was nowhere else for me to go. I had been everywhere. I had searched with microscopes, telescopes, binoculars. I was looking and there it was: the Black Panther Party for Self-Defense. I saw that the first line of oppression in Babylon today is the gun. We know now that it is by the gun that our people have been denied our freedom. So here was an actual black organization stressing the need for self-defense as a people. We have been identified as separate, apart and distinct from the rest of the people in this country. So we must act as a people. We have to give everyone a gun. We have to hip everybody to their need to have a gun. This was definitely in line with my thoughts.

I had studied extensively the ideologies of other organizations and I saw that we were bringing Marxism–Leninism to a new level here in Babylon. Marxism–Leninism never dealt with racism, though it dealt with the class nature of the existence of all the people on the globe. It was Frantz Fanon that brought it into a Pan African context, a Third World context. Even Mao Tse Tung, Ho Chi Minh and these revolutionary people in Asia still didn't relate to the indigenous contexts that we have in Babylon today. In Babylon we have black, brown, yellow and white, whereas in China they have eight or nine hundred million Chinese people of the same extraction. Frantz Fanon, with his dialectic analyzation of Marxism–Leninism showed the relation to the Third World, specifically to black people.

I began to see that the Black Panther party really made this Marxism–Leninism universal and that it was an evolutionary process. You had Freidrich Engels and Karl Marx in the nineteenth century and in the early twentieth century Marcus Garvey. He was something of a Marxist–Leninist though he didn't espouse its ideology in writing or in verbal commitments.

How does the Black Panther party apply that Marxist-Leninist ideology in America today?

Well, specifically in Babylon today, it says that the state is merely the apparatus of the ruling class, an apparatus used to oppress those that are already oppressed, in other words, working-class people. And black people today are oppressed, even if they are black mayors or black congressmen. All black people today are in the working class. We don't have a black bourgeoisie. This is a sort of fixation some black people have. It is imaginary. We don't control the means of production, we don't control military forces, we don't control any land, so how can we be bourgeoisie? We are not part of the aristocracy, so we are definitely part of the working-class people.

You see, being black is not necessarily synonymous with poor, and poor is not necessarily synonymous with being black. But, you can't really separate being black from being poor. In the case of black people, even though we may become rich individually, we are still a colonized and oppressed people. We are still subject to any form that racism may take. It may take the form of a bombing, a lynching or a murder. Or it may take the form of some prejudicial treatment in a restaurant, a motel or an airline flight. Maybe there is one ticket left and a black millionaire shows up right alongside the white bourgeoisie. This is where the color of man's skin will count against him no matter how much money he has.

We are oppressed by the ruling class because we are poor and we are also oppressed by the racists because we are black. We are oppressed as members of the working class in general and black people in particular. In the Black Panther party we see that we are not only ghettoized people, we are not only contained nationally. We are also contained internationally. We are a colonized people, a people of a different national extraction, a people kidnapped from our homes. We are still definitely African descendants and so we refer to ourselves as black Afro-Americans. This means we are colonized by these white Anglo-Saxons, the white European ruling classes.

This worldwide struggle is definitely a class struggle. Since the inception of the world there has always been three classes: lower class, middle and upper class. Racism has been the invention of the ruling class to perpetuate the three class status into infinity. It must maintain racism to remain in power. Since the invention of the class system, and the invention of private property, we have had war. We have had race wars, religious wars, national wars. We have had all sorts of wars, but not internal class wars.

Every army is composed of working-class people. Every jail consists of working-class people. All the factories consist of working-class people. Right? So we say that when you take guns and kill the aggressor, you don't kill the aggressor because he is white, black, red, yellow or brown. You kill the aggressor because he is an aggressor, because he is trying to create inroads into the few remaining rights of an oppressed people for purposes of maintaining this class system. The aggressor is working for a ruling-class boss. In the past we have always taken a defenseless stand against our enemies. We haven't had the political perspectives necessary to act as one group of people, specifically as black people.

Black people in Babylon are definitely colonized and oppressed in an urban context. And their oppression is political. The highest form of contradiction is political contradiction. The highest form of political contradiction is political antagonism. The highest form of political antagonism is warfare. The highest form of warfare is urban guerrilla warfare.

How do you feel about coalitions with other peoples, other working-class people?

It is a matter of priorities. Before we can share in any of these functioning coalitions we have to have intrablack-people coalitions. We need to unify ourselves and solidify our own inherent strength. If we wait, we will be letting racism take its course and it is now on a one hundred percent genocidal course aimed at black people. What I mean is I could be across town trying to rap to some white man, some red man, some brown or yellow man while racism was here eradicating the colony.

We definitely do want to work with other people toward the total liberation of the working class of the whole world. But in America we cannot wait until the conscience of the working class is elevated to the consciousness of the black people. Last year we had some bourgeoisie type college students killed by the fascists and, in 1968, at the Democratic National Convention white people became aware of police brutality. But we have been aware of this since 1700.

It may take years before people will finally become aware of the contradiction between the pigs that patrol the ghettos and the colonies themselves. Even the Italians and the Hungarians and other communities will come to see that there is a contradiction between the people that comprise the community and the pigs that control the community. People will finally become aware but we can't wait. It is suicide for us to wait!

We must strengthen the black colony first. We have to educate black people to the political position in which we are in in Babylon today. We have to educate people to the strategic methods for dealing with the political situation. You see, black people are always the first ones oppressed when there is a new racist attitude or policy or program perpetuated by the ruling class.

The proletariat in the black colony is comprised of working-class people. And just as there are two divisions in the white proletariat there are two divisions in the black proletariat: those who work and those who don't. Some of those who don't work can't find jobs. These are the black lumpenproletariat. They are unable to get jobs because of some sort of physical, mental or social incapacity. Some of them don't want jobs, they are the people that have for so long been the dregs of the earth. We are trying to organize these people.

You see, the nonblack working class is mainly racist. But there are working-class Negro people who are also racist. Some of these people don't like the black lumpenproletariat. The ruling class of the power structure has managed to utilize the white working class, and the Negro working class, to perpetuate racism. It has managed to take the working class and move it in the form of armies, hard hats, prison guards, FBI and CIA agents. All these people belong to the working class and they are mainly white, mainly white racists. Here in America, and in the Union of South Africa, racism has

157

reached its highest form. Racism has got to be on the way out because it has no higher to go.

Eventually we hope to make class allies, but that is a further priority. Our first priority is to arm ourselves politically, to arm ourselves socially, to arm ourselves militaristically. We intend to keep educating, politicizing, socializing everybody to the contradictions until the people become aware of this rotten, corrupt, garbage-can system. And many of these contradictions are antagonistic.

Isn't this suicide?

For black people themselves it would be politically impossible to liberate the whole country. For this we would definitely need the help of Third World people and the working classes. But it is not impossible for black people alone to destroy this racist Babylon.

Huey P. Newton, minister of defense for the Black Panther party says it is better for us to commit revolutionary suicide that reactionary suicide. This is our choice. Eldridge Cleaver calls it the black people's atom bomb. We do have the power to disrupt and destroy the system. So we give everybody a choice. Do you want to have a power struggle or do you want us to take it into a race struggle? Before we accept genocide, the total annihilation of black people in Babylon, we will take Babylon to its destruction. This is revolutionary suicide.

Reactionary suicide is simply being killed for no political reason. Reactionary suicide is the condition under which we are now living. We have medical conditions that are despicable. We go to the cheapest hospital in this metropolitan area and it costs us ninety-five dollars per day; these are the city hospitals all over Babylon for Third World and working-class people. The other hospitals charge a hundred and fifty dollars per day, so you begin to see that the medical care is better for the rich or the ruling class.

Look at the educational system. It is despicable too. We learn nothing about black people. We learn nothing about the true nature of the society. We are compelled by the gun to go to school till we reach sixteen and then maybe we get a job making the minimum wage, a dollar sixty-five per hour. If an individual goes to school from age five to sixteen, this is eleven years out of an individual's life. He has been ripped off for eleven unproductive, uneducational years.

And when he comes out into the society he may be confronted with a jobless situation. We don't have jobs, therefore we can't buy medical care. We can't buy clothes. We can't buy housing. We can't buy more education. We can't buy the necessary things to survive here. What I am saying is that the power structure is not only committing overt acts of genocide against us but that covert acts are now being intensified.

We feel that we are now in a situation in Babylon where if we maintain our defenseless positions for three, four, or five more years, the power structure will have contained the black people, will have implemented its final solution to the "Negro problem." This is the actually sealing off of the colony and the isolation of all dissenters and militants in black America, herding these people into concentration camps, prisons and penitentiaries across the face of Babylon. This is happening today. Our penitentiaries are being loaded, bulging at the seams, with black brothers and sisters from the lumpenproletariat tradition of the black people.

This is reactionary suicide. We are subjecting ourselves to these conditions. We are not defending ourselves. We are confronted in the streets of Babylon with Magnum 357's, with .38's and .45's which the pigs carry. Sometimes the pig executes a brother on the spot for a crime that maybe should get a maximum of six months. Sometimes brothers are murdered in the streets for the perpetration, or alleged commission of a crime that is no crime at all. Fred Hampton was murdered in his apartment in Chicago. They raided his pad with fourteen pigs, fourteen vicious running dogs of the power structure, fourteen fatal masochists with submachine guns and shotguns.

Policemen who walk their beat and conduct themselves as gentlemen, we won't bother. Eventually we will want them out of the community when we start our program of decentralizing police. But we are not hostile against policemen as a group of people. We are hostile against the racist pigs that carry badges and guns and

159

utilize them as a tool of genocide against black people. Huey P. Newton says they should withdraw from the community and cease their wanton murder and brutality and torture of black people or suffer the wrath of the black people. And those blacks who are endorsed spokesmen for the pig power structure, Huey also says, should crawl back to the people and beg for a speedy reprieve or suffer a speedy and most timely execution at the hands of the people for the crime of treason — for the crime of being wrong too long.

Black people have been in every war since the revolutionary war. We say we have fought for causes wide and narrow, and for causes aloof and base. We say it is now time for black people to fight for their own cause, for their own guidance. If we have to move in this direction and if we are totally annihilated it is better for us than to be annihilated fighting in Viet Nam, Laos, in Cuba or South America, anywhere the white power structure tells the black soldier to go. Defending our right to total autonomy is our total liberation.

Do you regard the Black Panther party as a Black Nationalist organization?

Well it is definitely a form of nationalism, so long as you relate the Black Panther party to the geographic situation of black people in Babylon. You have to say that black people within the geographical confinement of this country have to be unified as one, so this is nationalism.

But we are on a political stage that is worldwide. So we have political, ideological and functional coalitions with our allies, the Al-Fatah, Al-Assifa, Eritrea, Zimbabwe, Viet Nam, Cuba, China and some other countries that are moving toward their total liberation. In this sense we are internationalist. We won't be able to transcend national boundaries and transform civil rights until we are brought to a new level of awareness with the Third World peoples who are moving toward class consciousness, not merely race consciousness. Malcolm X is the one who brought us to this level of awareness. We belong to the same class that the Viet Cong belongs.

Just as they are the vanguard party of the southern part of Viet Nam, we are the vanguard party of North America.

Al-Fatah is the name of the first surah, or chapter, of the Holy Quoran and the political and guerrilla organization was named after it. It is the liberation arm of the Palestinians opposing the Israelis and the allies of Israel. Al-Assifa is also named for a surah and is a political and military organization in the Arab world moving toward their total liberation in Jordan, Iran and Syria. And there is also Eritrea, those black Africans located in the northwestern part of Ethiopia and the Sudan. We have alliances also with the Zimbabwe, what the Europeans call Rhodesia. These people have spread into Rhodesia, Angola and even South Africa. They are more militarily activist every day.

These various forms of nationalism are linked internationally because they have a common struggle against a common oppressor. We all have a common monster, what can be described as an octopus. That octopus is worldwide racist imperialist capitalism. The belly or the head, of the octopus is in the Pentagon of the United States of Fascist Babylon. The reason we are at the last stage in this revolution is that the revolution in Babylon, where black people are, is in the head of the monster. We are in the head of a monster which is the most technologically and militaristically advanced nation on the face of the earth.

The tentacles of this octopus stretch across the globe into South America, into Asia, into Africa and all over North America — everywhere you have these racists who have taken their despicable capitalism, colonialism and imperialism, exploitation, murder, brutality, and torture. So anywhere you find these tentacles, you find some part of the people's army dealing with these racists at the highest level of political antagonisms: political conflict which is warfare.

Now there are other forms of nationalism, especially cultural nationalism. Right here in this city you have Afro groups linked with the organization of Ron Karenga, called US, in Los Angeles. We say that these people are cultural nationalists. They believe that power is in the sleeve of a dashiki rather than in the barrel of a gun.

161

We say that the Black Panther party is revolutionary nationalism, calling for a complete transformation of this society. We do not want to integrate into this system or be assimilated into it. We do not want to retract or to regress back into a culture that is maybe one million years old. We are obliged to no black history or black culture.

Culture itself plays a very minute part in our revolution. We feel that our culture has led us through our historical experience and we have managed to survive. We feel also that we have found ourselves in all sorts of negative situations and we feel that only those aspects of our culture which are political is part and parcel of our tradition. For example, we relate to Veasey, to Nat Turner, to Hannibal, to any black warrior. But our ability to dance and sing, to do the "Buck Dance," to wear kimonos, togas, tikis, dashikis is not important.

Culture is only good in that it is part of our experience as political tool, but not as a historical regression. You see, culture can be somewhat of a vulture which lives on that which is dead. It has to survive on carrion, on something already set in rigor mortis. We feel we have to create a revolutionary culture, a culture based on a gun, based on our total antagonism with the power structure.

All of our cultural ministers, for example, Emory Douglass, use their art in real political situations. Do you see that brother right there on the wall? It is a drawing of a young brother holding a gun. This brother signifies only one thing. See that hat he has on? It is only a cap. This man is not regimented. He doesn't have, say, a green or a red or a white uniform. He doesn't look like he is part of a paramilitary organization — if you take the gun away. But this man is definitely armed, he is armed sociologically, militaristically and politically. You know he is politically aware of the situation of black people today.

It is possible to bring unaware brothers and sisters to a stage of political awareness by using art and culture as a medium. You don't use the dashiki, the natural hairdo or any other form of dress. You use an instantaneous artistic medium which immediately defines the sociological and political situation, and brings the brothers to an awareness of what they must do politically to liberate themselves. This is what we mean by the positive aspects of our culture.

For example, take Fred Evans who took the name of Ahmed.* On July 23, 1968, in Cleveland, Ohio, he and some brothers fought the racist pigs. The real statistics were not reported by the mass media. There were thirty-three pigs killed and about one hundred twelve wounded. Twelve brothers were killed. I know because I was there at that time. Brother Ahmed was a cultural nationalist only in his social perspectives. He was a revolutionary nationalist in his political perspectives. He believed that the power structure should be moved on with guns and force. He found out that political power does not grow from the sleeve of a dashiki. But the whole thing is evolutionary. Black people first have to become aware of themselves as a people and from there they will become aware of their role on the world's stage. This is definitely an evolutionary process and the cultural nationalists are in a lower stage of political awareness. At the moment, though I can't judge them definitely, I would say they are reactionary, they are revisionists.

The Black Panther party uses the positive aspects of our culture and that is the difference between us and these other nationalists. In fact, we have quit referring to ourselves as nationalists at all. We are now revolutionary internationalists. The difference is that we have analyzed the situation in Babylon today using the prism of our historical experience in Babylon. We have found it necessary to try to transform this society from what it is now to a socialistic society, a society where every man, woman and child has the right to eat and sleep, the right to medical care, the right to education that exposes the true nature of the world we live in and the true nature of the people.

Huey P. Newton says that man is born with the right to live and the man who has the right to live must have the right to those things necessary to survive. There are five things: the right to food, clothing, shelter, medical care and education. These are the five rights of man.

* See interview with Ahmed El Ibn Said (Fred Evans), p. 317.

163

October 1966
BLACK PANTHER PARTY
PLATFORM AND PROGRAM
WHAT WE WANT
WHAT WE BELIEVE

The program is usually divided into one section of ten points entitled "What We Want" and then ten paragraphs explaining these points in a section entitled "What We Believe." For the sake of clarity, we have put each one of the ten points in "What We Want" immediately above its corresponding paragraph in "What We Believe."

1. We want freedom. We want power to determine the destiny of our black community.

We believe that black people will not be free until we are able to determine our destiny.

2. We want full employment for our people.

We believe that the federal government is responsible and obligated to give every man employment or a guaranteed income. We believe that if the white American businessmen will not give full employment, then the means of production should be taken from the businessmen and placed in the community so that the people of the community can organize and employ all of its people and give a high standard of living.

3. We want an end to the robbery by the white man of our black community.

We believe that this racist government has robbed us and now we are demanding the overdue debt of forty acres and two mules. Forty acres and two mules was promised one hundred years ago as restitution for slave labor and mass murder of black people. We accept the payment in currency which will be distributed to our many communities. The Germans are now aiding the Jews in Israel for the genocide of the Jewish people. The Germans murdered six million Jews. The American racist has taken part in the slaughter of over fifty million black people; therefore, we feel that this is a modest demand that we make.

4. We want decent housing, fit for shelter of human beings.

164

We believe that if the white landlords will not give decent housing to our black community, then the housing and the land should be made into cooperatives so that our community, with government aid, can build and make decent housing for its people.

5. We want education for our people that exposes the true nature of this decadent American society. We want education that teaches us our true history and our role in the present-day society.

We believe in an educational system that will give to our people a knowledge of self. If a man does not have knowledge of himself and his position in society and the world, then he has little chance to relate to anything else.

6. We want all black men to be exempt from military service.

We believe that black people should not be forced to fight in the military service to defend a racist government that does not protect us. We will not fight and kill other people of color in the world who, like black people, are being victimized by the white racist government of America. We will protect ourselves from the force and violence of the racist police and the racist military, by whatever means necessary.

7. We want an immediate end to police brutality and murder of black people.

We believe we can end police brutality in our black community by organizing black self-defense groups that are dedicated to defending our black community from racist police oppression and brutality. The Second Amendment to the Constitution of the United States gives a right to bear arms. We therefore believe that all black people should arm themselves for self-defense.

8. We want freedom for all black men held in federal, state, county and city prisons and jails.

We believe that all black people should be released from the many jails and prisons because they have not received a fair and impartial trial.

9. We want all black people when brought to trial to be tried in court by a jury of their peer group or people from their black communities, as defined by the Constitution of the United States.

We believe that the courts should follow the United States Constitution so that black people will receive fair trials. The Fourteenth Amendment of the U. S. Constitution gives a man a right to be tried by his peer group. A peer is a person from a similar economic, social, religious, geographical, environmental, historical and racial background. To do this the court will be forced to select a jury from the black community from which the black defendant came. We have been, and are being tried by all-white juries that have no understanding of the "average reasoning man" of the black community.

10. We want land, bread, housing, education, clothing, justice and peace. And as our major political objective, a United Nations-supervised plebiscite to be held throughout the black colony in which only black colonial subjects will be allowed to participate, for the purpose of determining the will of black people as to their national destiny.

When, in the course of human events, it becomes necessary for one people to dissolve the political bands which have connected them with another, and to assume, among the powers of the earth, the separate and equal station to which the laws of nature and nature's God entitle them, a decent respect to the opinions of mankind requires that they should declare the causes which impel them to the separation.

We hold these truths to be self-evident, that all men are created equal; that they are endowed by their Creator with certain unalienable rights; that among these are life, liberty, and the pursuit of happiness. That, to secure these rights, governments are instituted among men, deriving their just powers from the consent of the governed; that, whenever any form of government becomes destructive of these ends, it is the right of the people to alter or to abolish it, and to institute a new government, laying its foundation on such principles, and organizing its powers in such form, as to them shall seem most likely to effect their safety and happiness. Prudence, indeed, will dictate that governments long established should not be changed for light and transient causes; and, accordingly, all experience hath shown, that man-kind are more disposed to suffer, while evils are sufferable, than to right themselves by abolishing the forms to which they are accustomed. But, when a long train of abuses and usurpations, pursuing invariably the same object, evinces a design to reduce them under absolute despotism, it is their right, it is their duty, to throw off such government, and to provide new guards for their future security.

OLD FOLKS

NEGRO HISTORY

A ship,
    A chain,
        A distant land.
A whip,
    A pain,
        A white man's hand.
A sack,
    A field of cotton balls,
        The only thing Granpa recalls.

                     – Jimmie Sherman
                     (Watts)

THE PENNY PEOPLE

A penny is copper brown.
I am copper brown.
Pennies are copper brown.
My people are copper brown.
Abe "penny" Lincoln
Is copper brown.
He freed
The copper brown people.
He became
The copper brown
People's Prince.

— Robert Peppers
(Cleveland)

HEREIN I PROTEST

Out of a continent
Into the bondage
Slavery exists

Out of a reconstruction
Into the ghetto
Slavery exists

Out of a prejudiced alienation
Into the integration
Slavery exists

Out of an inequality
Into the democracy
Slavery exists.

— Selena Crump
(Cleveland)

SIGHT

A new colt is born to its mother;
It is beautiful.
A tulip raises its yellow head;
It is growing.
A robin returns to its nest;
It is singing.
Two lovers walk hand in hand;
They are happy.
An old man sits beneath an oak tree;
He is cold.
His hand holds a silver timepiece;
It has stopped.

— Paula Murphy
(Cleveland)

Annie Lee Walker

*Annie Lee Walker is a one-hundred-year-old mother of seven chil-
dren, two of whom died as infants, and three of whom have since
"passed." Her mother named her Annie and she added the Lee herself. The first, and greater, part of her life was lived in Selma, Alabama, with a "lovin'" husband, with whom she celebrated a golden
wedding anniversary two years before his death. Since then she has
lived in Cleveland, Ohio, with her youngest daughter, Josie Lee,
her husband and children. The other surviving child is William O.*

"The grandchildren visit me often and the kisses, oh goodness, the kisses."

*Walker, veteran Negro journalist and seventy-five-year-old editor
and publisher of Cleveland's* Call and Post.

*She is not a spry old lady, but her speech and early memories
are ready and quick. She insists she has been loved into living
longer by her children and grandchildren. Her memory is at its
best — clear and precise — on her earliest years growing up as a
young black girl, who nonetheless was light in color with long,
curly hair. As you listen, the later years seem almost uneventful
compared to the earliest ones.*

*Because — according to the classic tale — the courthouse in
Greensboro, Alabama, burned down some time ago, we cannot
be sure that Annie Lee Walker — or Mother Walker as she is now
called — is not older, or younger, than one hundred years. But
when people like Annie Lee move this close to a century, it is no
longer appropriate to count the days and the years. Annie Lee now
marks time by decades and epochs and by the ages.*

Yes, they visit me and the kisses, oh goodness, the kisses. Just
last Easter this house was just packed with grandchildren. They
come most every Sunday and for Easter my daughter has the
basket filled with eggs and we have dinner. They are jealous of
one another, and they don't want me to love one more than another. I have such wonderful grandchildren, and children. They
don't want me to move a chair. They say, "Mother Annie, you sit
right there and don't do a thing." My husband was like that too. I
had a lovin' husband and the children a lovin' father. We had a
café in Selma, Alabama. When he wanted to surprise me he asked
me, "Nona (he never called me 'Annie'), would you open for me
this morning?" So, I would get up at four A.M. and go down and
open for him and let him sleep. When I got home, I would find a
living-room set or a swing out on the porch, just any little thing. Or
I would get ready to go to church on Sunday morning and he would
say, "Nona, I don't like the dress you got on." Then he would go to
the closet and pull out a dress he had slipped into the house, unbe-
knownst to me. He would surprise me all the time.

We had a two-story brick house and when the café made a little money my husband would give it to me because I could save money. But I didn't put it in the bank. He would give a hundred dollars or so every week and I would tell my mother-in-law where I hid the money. And I told the lady who came every week to help me iron where I put the money, just in case anything happened to my mother-in-law. But I never told my husband because he wanted me to save it for him. I hid the money in a pot which I put in the garden under the flowers. When the time came to buy the house, I dug it up, counted out the money and paid cash. It was a beautiful big house with five bedrooms.

Were you born in Selma, Alabama?

No, Greensboro, Alabama, in Hale County. My mother had five children and I was the one in the middle. They have all passed now except one, a younger sister, who lives in Chicago. My mother was a slave and died when I was a young child. I don't remember her. My father was white. I never knew him. But I knew the father of my older sisters. His name was Boney Jones, he owned the plantation. But my father was different and my sister next had a different father. His name was Mr. Miller. He runned the grocery store. I would go there all the time and he would always give groceries to us.

My mother was from Galveston, Texas. I lived there in Texas until I was about six or seven when I went to Selma. After my mother died, my aunt took me in. She had two rooms and all of us stayed in those two rooms.

I didn't live there all the time. Usually I lived with white people who must have been slave owners because my aunt seemed to know them well. When I got to Selma they took me to a Miss Tollman and I worked for her. I was just a little girl so I would see after the baby. Miss Tollman had a little boy and he had a pony. We would ride the pony and I would rub the brass doorknobs. That was all I could do, just rub the brass doorknobs and ride the pony. The little boy's name was Cade, and he would ride the pony downtown and I would go along in the carriage with the family, then he would get in the carriage and I would ride the pony back. It was a Shetland pony.

Then one day she told me they were going away. She said she was going to some place where you go under the ground. She didn't ask me to go with her. I don't know what happened, but she left town and I was put with another white woman and stayed with her. She was named Miss Mary. Her husband was a drunkard and she was a beautiful woman. I stayed there with them in Selma until her mother got sick and she had to go to Taladega Springs for a special doctor. They carried me with them. Late at night they would send me down to the spring to get this healing water.

We stayed there all summer I know, and she fell in love with the doctor there. When we got back to Selma, her husband asked me about it. He said, "Now you can tell me anything, Annie. She ain't goin' to whip you. She better not whip you." So I told him that when me and the baby would be in the living room, they would make us go out and we would go walking in the woods. She made me go one way and then she and the man went another way. That was all I knew. I couldn't tell him any more than that.

I lived with a colored woman after that. She would whip me all the time. She didn't have but one bed and she had a husband and a child. I had to sleep at the foot of the bed. I used to stand at the fence at the gate and when my little cousins would go by carrying meals to their brothers that worked in the cotton mill, I would beg them to tell Malinda, my aunt, to please take me home. The next door neighbor saw me so often she went to my aunt and told her.

Run away? Yes, I thought about running away. But where would I go? I would just have been somewhere out in the world.

While I was with Malinda I went to school some. The Presbyterians had sent teachers from the North to teach in Selma, at the Knox Academy. It was free because they said since my aunt didn't have a husband, it would be all right. I enjoyed myself there but couldn't go everyday. I never got no higher than the second grade. Some time later my aunt had a woman who used to kind of coach me. You know, you would go to school to her at night when we get through with our work. She would teach us reading, that is why I can read and write as well as I do. She wasn't a teacher. She just taught us.

You see, nobody really cared, and since I was the brightest one in the family my cousins didn't like that. I was fair with straight hair, not kinky. They used to say I had the prettiest curls of anybody they had ever seen. When I lived with Miss Tollman I had a round comb that kept my hair back out of my face.

The colored people were meaner to me than the white folks. They didn't like me much. I remember we used to go berry picking and one day a train was coming down the track. I called to my cousin to get off the track and I called her a "slut." I didn't know what that was. So when I got home my aunt wore me out, but still she didn't tell me what it was. It wasn't until I was a grown woman that I found out. I read it somewhere. Many a day I wish'd I was dead.

I was a good looking woman in my younger days and the white men tried to get me, but I was too sharp for them. I runned. I was a good runner. One morning I was going to work and I had a good ways to go and it was dark there in the winter. There was an old shanty I had to pass every morning. This morning, there was somebody standing out there. They used to say, if it is a ghost and you bat your eyes, it will disappear. I bat my eyes and he was still standing there. He got just as close to me as you and said, "Oh yes, I got you this morning!" I went fast to the middle of the street and started running and didn't stop till I got to work.

We usually had no trouble though. Selma was a quiet place in the twenties and thirties. We didn't have no big trouble whatever. I do remember our pastor though who printed something in his church paper about the white people. The white people got hold of it because some colored folks carried it to them. I never knew what it said. They got after this man to kill him, our own pastor. The people there walked the streets day and night with guns, hoes, hatchets, anything they could get their hands on. My cousins slept under the bridge near the preacher's house to try to protect him. He lived right across the street from our house and I was afraid to go home. They got so close behind him that he had to get up in the tower of the Brown Chapel Church in Selma. They put a bonnet on him there and a Mother Hubbard dress, like he was a woman. That is the only way they got the man out.

How did you meet your husband?

Well, some white people lived near my aunt's house and they seemed to like me. So this lady, who had a husband and one child, got my aunt to let me come over to help her. When she moved uptown, she asked me to come and work for her. My aunt didn't want for me to go. She said, "Annie, I'm afraid you'll go astray." But I begged her to let me go. I was tired of hanging up wet clothes in the winter and taking them down all frozen. The white lady's name was Miss Turner and she paid my aunt six dollars a month for the work I did.

I met my husband when he was working in the grocery store and I was living with these white people. I think I was maybe eighteen or so. He came to the door to deliver the groceries. He asked about coming back to see me and I told him yes. He would come by and say he was just passing by my house and saw me and just wanted to drop in. His father was white, and he graduated from the high school. I learned about him later from my mother-in-law. She was a midwife in a nursing home and this white man took advantage of her. He dared her to tell about it, so she only told her mother when she got home. There wasn't much she could do anyway. So she had this one and later another one by her husband after she was married.

After we were married he got himself a saloon and later a café. We had the saloon a long time before we got the café. I would work for him. My mother-in-law kept the children and she was a good one to take care of them because she was a midwife and a nurse. She delivered all my children right at home. The café did better later on during the First World War. The train would pass through Selma and the soldiers would get out to eat. We had lunches ready for them. My oldest son, Alexander, served in the First World War.

We knew lots of white folks when we lived in Selma. It was an integrated community. The white people my son-in-law's mother worked for were white millionaires. Their daughter used to come and sit on my porch and rock my children. She would sit right down and rock them. My mother-in-law was also a seamstress and she sewed for them and designed clothes too. These people — their name was Hawthorne — were very fond of my husband's mother and all of us. People talk about the South but we had an integrated community. When we went to their house, we didn't go to the back door. We went to the front door and sat in the living room. We were treated just like anybody else because they were that type. In the South if you are good people, you are treated that way.

In ninety-nine years I have never experienced any racial discrimination against me. There are not many black people who can say that. Some of the best friends I have are white people. It is the colored who are the problem. I just don't know what to think of them, burning and killing their own. It is awful, awful.

Did you notice any change when you moved from Selma, Alabama, to Cleveland, Ohio?

No, none at all. I was just at home with my children and I stayed there. How they love me! That's why I've lived so long. All that huggin' and kissin'. I told my husband that if he died first I would never marry again. If I died first, I didn't want him to remarry again. He agreed to that. I said you should go live with your children because they were just crazy about him.

When he was dying, he called me in one night and said, "Nona, you are late tonight, why are you late?" I said, "I don't know why." Then I went to my room which was right next to his. Then he called me back and he said, "Nona, come in here a minute. I want to talk to you. You have been a good wife. You have been a good mother, and now God and your children are going to take care of you. I want your last days to be your best days."

He talked to me a long time till tears wrapped around my face, then he said, "Now go to bed and get some sleep." He said that because I had to get up the next morning and open the café. I opened the café and he died in January.

J. Walter Wills, Sr.

Walter Wills is the son of a white man and a black woman, both born into slavery in Kentucky. His father was the offspring of a white father and an Indian mother; his mother was the child of a white man and a black woman.

Except for a year which he spent as a young man in Saint Paul, Minnesota, he has lived all his life in the state of Ohio. He is now ninety-seven years old, with white hair and white skin — only the former was acquired in his advancing years.

In 1905 Walter Wills established the House of Wills, a mortuary company claiming to be the third largest in the United States. He estimates that he has personally directed burial services for forty thousand persons. Always active in community work, he has also developed a business philosophy and point of view which owes as much to American capitalism as to the shrewdness of Wills.

One of his admirers, John Bustamente, suggested last year that one can best pay honor to J. Walter Wills by believing, as he does, that today is the first day of the rest of one's life. Wills still begins each day as if it were one of his first rather than one of his last. But you know Walter Wills is old when he speaks. His voice sometimes slides into a bare whisper. When this happens, and if you lean forward, you will always hear something important.

Mr. Wills, you look very calm. How long have you been that way?

In 1911 I stopped on Central Avenue at about eleven o'clock in the day, stopped with both feet on the sidewalk and raising my hands up, swore I'd never worry again. I said that for a more peaceful living, for a better understanding, I promise that with the help of God — who is my refuge, strength and fortress — I shall make myself so strong that nothing in the world can disturb my peace of mind. I shall be too secure for worry, too noble for anger, too strong for fear, too courageous for doubt, too determined for failure, too confident for jealousy, too tolerant for prejudice, to full of God's love for hatred, too sincere for hypocrisy, too honest to take an unfair advantage, too generous to be a miser, too modest, too humble to be an egotist. I promised that I shall always live in the faith that the whole world is on my side, so long as I am true to the very best that is within me.

It happened in 1911 and I haven't changed my belief since then.

Tell me about your early life.

I was born in Yellow Springs, Green County, Ohio, on June 3, 1874 at six o'clock in the evening, so I am told. My father's name was Silas Wills, my mother's name, Anna Redmond. They were born in slavery and released when the Emancipation Proclamation

184

was declared. My father was a descendant of his master, which happens in cases, and when the war broke out he was drafted, but his father got him out after twenty-one days. My father was a positive individual. When he said a thing, that was it. He wasn't wishy-washy. They called him Uncle Si. All over he was known as Uncle Si. He was chairman of the trustee board in the church, and all the organizations called on him for decisions in everything they did. When he went to vote the first time, they denied him his vote and he sued them for five hundred dollars damage; he was respected for that. He had no Negro blood in him. His father was white and his mother was an Indian.

There were fifteen children of this union and I was the baby of the family. Six of the children — three sets of twins — died in infancy, and all my brothers and sisters have passed now. My mother and father met on the plantation. She had a white father too and her mother was black.

My sister, Nancy, was the only child born in slavery. Her master didn't want my father to take her away and he pleaded with him strenuously to have this girl remain, but my father wouldn't listen to that. So, they came up out of Winchester, Kentucky, and settled in Ohio on the Garrison farm. Mr. Garrison had a farm three miles out of Yellow Springs and they put my dad out on the tenant house and he took care of things. I was born there and my mother died when I was two years old. My stepmother raised me. She was a wonderful woman.

I remained there and attended Antioch College until 1899 when I arrived in Cleveland. The president, Daniel Albright Long, had come to our little home in Yellow Springs to talk with my father about sending me to Antioch College. My father told him (I was standing there listening) that he had raised a large family, and was in ill health, and that he had no money, but there was nothing he wouldn't do to see that this boy got an education. My stepmother was a practical nurse and she had brought up three children for Dr. Long. So, when my father passed away that fall, I talked to him and he said he had a scholarship for me. He told me I didn't even have to finish high school or stay in the house alone. "When you're ready to start," he said, "you can enter the preparatory course and live in the dormitory." That was in the early 1890's.

So after a year or two, I told my sister, Anna, who had been living with me and taking care of my dad's house, that she could go to Cleveland and live with another sister, Mary. Then the president came to me and said, "Now Walter, I have a couple here who want a single house. You can live in the dormitory where there will be no expense. You can have all your meals in the dining room, and I am going to get for you an agency of the White Star Laundering Company in Springfield. You can have the laundry done for all the boys; they will bring their shirts and collars to you. Pick them up on Monday, get them back on Friday. Keep them in your room until they call for them. You can pick up extra money." So I said, fine, went back to our house and decorated it, painted it and fixed it up special. The couple moved in and paid forty-five dollars a month rent. I told them to pay that to Antioch College, not to me.

Were you the first Negro to enter Antioch?

No, the second. The first was Alfred Hampton who became a Baptist minister. At Antioch there were no other black students then except for Walter Mason who married Bishop Arnett's daughter. Because he married her before graduating from Wilberforce, they wouldn't let him graduate. So he came to Antioch and took another year.

At Antioch I was never discriminated against, not once. I joined the Friday night social society, the literary society and was elected president of that. It was never brought to my attention that I was black.

How did you get into the mortuary business?

When I graduated I didn't have any money but I wanted to go to school some more. I wanted law, but really I wanted medicine. I wanted to be a doctor and they had planned my course at Antioch that way for me. When I got to Cleveland — my sisters were here — I thought it was going to be easy to get a scholarship at Western Reserve. But there was nothing. Hardly anything doing.

186

After a few days, a strike on the street cars broke out. I got a job as a streetcar conductor on Central Avenue. I had been reared in Yellow Springs, a small town, to show respect for the aged, and things the other conductors had not thought about. I was attracting attention from the people and from some individuals by the service I was giving. I was out on the job helping people off the car, taking the old ladies' baskets and sitting them on the sidewalk so they wouldn't have to carry them over, or if they were on the sidewalk, putting them on the car.

There was a boy I knew well, named William Gee, whose family lived in Yellow Springs. He didn't go to college but he was a good boy all right. He had been in Cleveland a year trying to run a funeral business with another man from Chicago. But they hadn't had one call. So Billy came to me and wanted me to go into the funeral business with him. I said, "No, I'm going to be a doctor." I just drove that streetcar, and later got into the insurance business.

Well, one day, Billy came to me and said, "Now listen, Buck," (Buck was my nickname), "Dr. Dodge is coming here tomorrow from Boston. He is the best in the country and is going to give us a lecture on anatomy. If you are going to be a doctor, fella, you want to hear that lecture. You want to hear it?" I said, "Hey Billy, that sounds pretty good. How am I going to hear it?" "I'll take you down, I'll take you down," he said. So he came and got me and we went down to a funeral parlor.

Dr. Dodge came out and was introduced and gave us a short talk. Then he stepped back and rolled out a cadaver with a white sheet over it. He put on his white coat and white gloves and walked over to the cadaver and pulled the sheet off. The man was green! So he gave us a lecture on how that had happened, what took place in the body that wound up with this green; all about liver disturbances, gallbladder and other things. Very thorough, good lecture. Then he said, "Now I am going to restore him to his natural complexion right before your very eyes. Now watch closely!" I watched. When he got through, the man looked just like he was asleep!

I turned to Billy and said, "Billy, I'm going with you in the funeral business. How much for half interest?" He said, "Oh, two hundred and fifty dollars." And I had all that money except two hundred and twenty-five. So I put my twenty-five dollars down and we went into the funeral business. This was the year that all funeral directors had to have a license. Neither Billy or I had one, but we went out anyway and became partners.

I had been studying music on the side, voice lessons and that sort of thing. At Antioch one of the members of my choir was a girl named Hazel Martin — who later became the first Negro principal in Cleveland. Her brother had just died and so he became our first call. It was our very first funeral and we were very careful about handling it. After the funeral was over, we went to Columbus and got our license. And because Billy hadn't spent as much time as I had in school, I arranged the seats so he could peek.

Did you meet any discrimination in those days?

Well, there were a few instances of it, but they were short lived. In 1909 I bought a house on Crawford Road. I had seen signs in the yard and had talked to the agents about it, but the man who owned it had an office in the Arcade Building. I called him and he told me to come down to see him, and not to talk with the agents so I wouldn't have to pay the commission. When I got there, he asked if I'd like some cigars. I said, "No thank you." Then he said, "Now, let's see, that property is up for eighty-two hundred and fifty. Let's make it an even eight thousand." I told him I had come prepared to buy it for seventy-seven hundred and fifty: "I'll make you out a check now and we can put it in escrow and it'll be all taken care of." He said, "I like the way you talk. I'm going to take you up on it. It's a deal." Well, that was Saturday. The first of the next week a white friend called to say that he had heard of a meeting in a doctor's office down near the house on Crawford Street. Some people had met with the owner and he was balled out for not keeping me from buying the house. Later that week, the owner called me down to his office and said, "Wills, I have no grievance against you whatsoever. I didn't know whether you were a white man or colored or what, and it didn't matter. I sold you the property, but I lost my friends." I asked him if he was sure they were his friends. "Are you sure?" I said. "Well," he said, "legally, of course, you and I have a right to buy and sell property to whomever we please, but my friends and I stand on a plane higher than the law, by God. We want to give you a thousand dollars not to take that property." So I said to him, "Sir, I'm going to show you today that I stand on a plane still higher than that. I'm not going to accept your thousand dollars. That property has been sold!" So we moved in and were very happy there.

Another time, much later — around 1925 — a Jewish real estate man came to me. We had been friends a long time and made deals. It seems that at this time he wanted to sell me a house on Chadbourne Road in Shaker Heights for only eleven thousand five hundred dollars. I told him that I didn't have that kind of money. "Why don't you keep it?" I said. And he told me, "I ain't going to keep it, but you got to buy it." I knew then what he was talking about, so I let him make the deal for me.

Right afterwards the chairman of the board of the Phyllis Wheatley Association, Charles Arter, who lived in Shaker Heights, called me to come to his office right away. So I got Miss Hunter who was superintendent of the Phyllis Wheatley Association and she came with me, crying on my arm, to see this gentleman downtown. We went into his office and he didn't let us get into his office before he yelled out, "Wills, I want an option on that property." I held Miss Hunter up, walked in and seated her. I said, "The property is not for sale." He said he didn't want to hear that kind of talk, because they were trying to raise money to build a Phyllis Wheatley home for working girls. He said if I moved to Shaker Heights, there would be resentment: "You are blocking the whole system." So I said, "All right, Charley, I've told you twice that the property is not for sale, but you've just got to have it. The price is now twenty-four thousand seven hundred and fifty dollars." "It's a holdup, a holdup," he said. I told him, "Calm yourself, young man, don't take it, don't take it. But, Charley, if you take that property, you got to pay twenty-four thousand seven hundred and fifty for it. Take it or leave it, it's up to you." Then I took the arm of Miss

Hunter and started out the door. He stopped me, called me back, and we signed the option.

In ten days I got the money and went out and bought a funeral home on Fifty-fifth Street, the old Kimber Funeral Home. I've always thanked that Jewish real estate man who used this means to get me a funeral home for my folks here in Cleveland.

What makes the House of Wills distinctive?

Well, we've always had a little glamor. It started first in Yellow Springs when I went to make a visit. An old friend told me his Dad had a team of black geldings, one three years and the other five. "Boy, you should see them," he said. So when I did, I went wild for them and bought them. They came in a freight car to Cleveland, and I sent them to a blacksmith because their feet had never hit pavement. Then I got the finest set of harnesses and took them down Central Avenue pulling the casket wagon. It was a glamorous sight. When they saw the first streetcar, they bolted over to the side. I got off the wagon seat and talked to them, patted them on the jaw and started out again. We did this four times and when the next streetcar came by, they didn't even see it. I kept them out till six o'clock just driving where the most traffic was.

But it isn't just this. Billy and I broke up over how to invest our money. His theory about it was that you should put as little as possible back into the business. I told him I was different and think you should put all you can beg or borrow back into it. I told him we should break up our partnership and run our businesses separate, that we wouldn't be friends if we stayed together. We dissolved it that day and I took on a new partner, my son, five years old, at home waiting for me.

Later we added new equipment, twelve-cylinder Cadillacs, a whole fleet of them. These things attracted attention and a lot of customers. And the funeral chapels are unique. We have four chapels in all, two in Egyptian architecture and one in Grecian; then upstairs there is a regular chapel. We have the best-looking equipment and the best of everything we can afford, organ and piano both, and we have a tape system for music. The music starts and plays while the folks are seeing the body.

At this point in the interview, I thought Mr. Wills looked tired and suggested we pause for a while. He said he was feeling fine and wanted to get on. I agreed, saying that I would ask him a series of questions which he should answer as spontaneously, and briefly, as possible. He said, "Let's go."

Since you have seen so much of death, do you have any particular thoughts about it?

I accept the Scripture just as it is. I have nothing to add or take from it.

As you look back, do you see an improvement in race relations?

Yes. When I came to Cleveland there were about five thousand of our people here and now there are over three hundred thousand. You can't look at television without seeing improvements in advertising. We are doing things we never did before. When we started the NAACP and the Urban League here we needed to fight racial discrimination in public places and seek equality. Every organization that has been formed to involve our folks, I've been part of it. Things are improving. Look at Mississippi. Those people are going to get tired of spending their money on separate schools. Then they'll integrate.

Do you see much integration in the United States today?

Yes, including intermarriage. For example, we had a half-black, half-white funeral. I have often mentioned that opposite colors attract the sexes.

What do you think the black people in the United States want today more than anything else?

Understanding.

From white people?

From wherever. Perhaps it will be helpful to come from the white man who can see the thing as it is, not as he wants it to be.

Not all the white folks will give them good understanding, and some of them are awfully bad, too. We've got to understand that improving the opportunities of millions of black people will help the entire nation. To hold them back is just wrong.

What are the particular contributions black people have to make to America?

Their own self-support. Everything they can do for themselves rather than have it done for them.

Do you believe in self-determination?

Yes, sir, but be determined on the right road.

What is the right road?

The right road is to get an education if you want one. Whatever you want, go and get it and pay for it. Don't beg for bread, don't beg for anything anymore. Assume your own responsibilities. The Negro must raise himself up to the point where the white man respects him completely.

This may be a white man's society he will have entered?

Yes, sir. The white man's society is all we have to imitate.

Do you think there is an Afro-American history and culture?

That won't help us now. That won't take care of 1970.

What do you think of the movement toward black identity?

We've got to find a way to show them they are misinformed, especially in their hatred of whites. That's the first thing.

Is this a justifiable hatred?

There is no justifiable hatred. What hate can develop into has no limit. They can destroy themselves.

192

Do you welcome black pride?

That is not a bad thing, nothing wrong with that. It is good to be proud, if you use it as an advantage to gain your step up. But if black people lose their value to the country by causing trouble, causing riots — all destructive things — they won't be wanted. That makes it bad for all of us.

Reverend Joseph Eu(gene)
Solomon Ray

The Illustrious Reverend Joseph Eu(gene) Solomon Ray, 32°, as
he likes to be called, is reluctant to admit his age. Judging from his
life story he is seventy years, more or less.

He is a cricket of a man — small, spry and bright — with the
quick step of one who knows where he is going. He enjoys the
pleasure produced by his thin, high-pitched voice; he readily re-
calls the past and easily projects the future.

He is versatile, having served as a minister, public relations man,

*porter, secretary, youth worker, church committeeman, newspaper-
man and orator. Reverend Ray says that "Through the years I have
been able to render a service where other people have not even attempted a ministry."*

*Currently he is planning a program for the restoration of the
ideals of Marcus Garvey in the 1970's. The Reverend Joseph Eu-
(gene) Solomon Ray has been black for as long as he can remember.*

When were you born?

I was born at 318 Minnesota Avenue, Kansas City, Kansas, in
the United States of America. I slipped in on January 27th at 2:30
A.M., on a Wednesday. I was born under the sign of Aquarius, the
same as Franklin D. Roosevelt. Did you know that every eighty-
four years we get an Aquarian in the White House? George Washington, Abraham Lincoln, Franklin D. Roosevelt. Every eighty-four
years we have an emergency and need an Aquarian. My father's
name was Elias and my mother's name was Holda Jane. We
answered to the slave name Ray despite the fact that my father was
the third generation from Ethiopia. His name was Godboldt. My
father's parents were born slaves in Arkansas. My mother was born
in Hannibal, Missouri.

My father was a musician, a vaudeville man. He played harp and
guitar, a fine artist. My mother was a concert soloist. The only
difference between them and me is I can't carry a tune — but I put
babies to sleep and I'm a good fellow to have around when anybody
is emotionally upset. When I talk to them they quiet down and
seem to be at ease. Many times throughout the United States I have
been presented to speak and the folks would be whispering until
they hear my whiny little voice. Then they listen.

My mother was reared in a fashion that she learned the King's
English and she taught me the very best. As a little child she talked
to me in adult ways. At age five I was on a church stage quoting the
second chapter of Matthew and singing *Twinkle, Twinkle, Little
Star*. Newspaper editors today say that I have a liquid form of writing, one word runs normally into the other making it very difficult

195

"If you're black, you b'long."

to cut anything out. And some folks say the same thing about my speaking. People who don't want to hear me, say, "Don't let him talk. For God's sake, don't let him talk!"

I was reared in church and took an active part in all church things. Following my conversion, they gave me the chaplaincy in all the departments of the church. I was nine when I was converted at a camp meeting in Belvedere Hollow in Kansas City. I was the first convert of the late Reverend Dr. Hearst. Reverend Hearst was a celebrated evangelist who devoted one part of the year to a revival and the other part of the year to having a barbecue. People would come from miles and miles around to get his barbecue and to hear him preach.

My mother was a liberal Baptist. A liberal Baptist is a person who has no prejudice against other denominations. She took me to a Methodist church across the street from the Baptist church where we usually went. She took me also to the Salvation Army, the Holy Rollers and various denominations. Because we crossed the street so often, people began to argue secretly about which church I really belonged to. This was because of my liberal mother's training.

My mother had one child before me that died at birth. My father gave me some half brothers and sisters. I was at the inquisitive age and wanted to know where children came from. My mother told me all about the angels and that other stuff. I asked her why did the physical contour of Mrs. Jewel change after the baby was born, and she said, "Well, now, if you don't believe me, you'll have to ask the Lord." And since I was a Bible student early in life, I did just that. I had a dream that I saw my father go into a room with a woman and shortly after that he came out and told me I had a half brother. He asked me what I wanted to name the boy and I said, "Henry."

The girl didn't know he was a married man, and a preacher at that. We had a little experience trying to catch up with him. He told me about the boy and told me not to tell my mother. But when she came home, I told her about the boy being born four blocks from where I was born, in the same hospital. Well, my mother took it pretty well but she got a divorce. The girl wanted her to know she didn't mean any harm, that she didn't know my father was married. The girl didn't know that ministers have the best girls in town. My mother took the girl to church and introduced her as her husband's wife. And the parishioners shouted, "What kind of a woman is this? What kind of religion have we here?"

Then Papa came home one day and the baby was crying. Papa took the baby and shook its insides loose. When the baby died, the girl brought the baby over to our house. I wrote the obituary and made all the arrangements for the funeral. I officiated because I'm the chaplain and, naturally, the big man. I was eleven or twelve years old.

In what other cities have you lived?

When I was in the seventh grade, my mother and I moved to Chicago. I worked in the office with the principal. When I graduated, I went out in the community and launched a petition to have the school board buy up the property from Forty-seventh and Dearborne down to Forty-sixth Street for a playground. During the summer I was employed by a Jewish family and, among other things, I picked up a little German. I felt right at home since my people came from the Jewish people's colony in Ethiopia. And for this reason I was able to contact folks in the neighborhood that spoke German in order to put over this petition.

Around this time there was a man by the name of Kaiser Wilhelm who was interested in teaching German in all schools throughout the world. He thought if people spoke his language they would respect his country. And people began to believe that if they went to Germany they would find the best in education and culture.

I then went to Wendell Phillips High School and I was an oddity at the time going to this mixed school. There were not many Negroes going there, but we had some very fine associates and classmates. A lot of black people came to Chicago around World War I, from Mississippi and Alabama. They asked the board of education for a colored school and the board of education said, "We can't give you a school. We've never had any separate schools here until you asked for it." That is the reason why Wendell Phillips today is a celebrated black school. Once in New York, the principal surprised me by telling me it was a black school. I was surprised because when I went there there were Jews and Catholics, paupers and millionaires — poor little old me and the millionaires just went hobnobbing together and having a wonderful time.

Later I moved to Milwaukee where I had an aunt, a very fine citizen, a missionary, respected by all the churches and the people at large. She was a much-married Capricorn woman. If a guy didn't do just what he was supposed to do, she'd put him out and get somebody else. When I went there to live with her, she sort of "hexed" me because she didn't want me up when she went to bed, yet she wanted me in when she was in. I decided from then on I didn't want any more Capricorn women.

But she was a missionary. She was a Mrs. AME * Church. She mixed with the Catholics and the Jews and the Seventh Day Adventists, the Goodwill Society and anybody that had to do with Jesus or Almighty God. It was her custom to entertain the minister or the preacher when he came to town, regardless of color or creed, and he had to have at least one meal in her house or she would be offended. And at the same time the prostitutes and jailbirds and cutthroats who died in the neighborhood expected her to be at their funeral. And when she wasn't, people thought she was sick.

Milwaukee was a very fine town and I was a member of Saint Paul's AME Church and sang in the choir. I went to a school of journalism on a scholarship and worked on a daily newspaper. I knew Abbott in Chicago when his little newspaper was on the back porch of his rooming house. Now it is a daily newspaper in Chicago.†

I stayed in Milwaukee for three or four years and then came back to Chicago. In 1919 they had the big race riot there and the police made a run on Providence Hospital, founded by Williams, a Negro, the man who performed the first heart operation in the world. The police let me ride with them on patrol because I had this newspaper pass and I went from one section of the city to another. I saw a Negro stand in the middle of State Street when the police motorcycle was coming right down the street and it split the man up and down — right between his eyes. It was one of those wrong-side-of-the-street things.

* African Methodist Episcopal
† The *Chicago Daily Defender* was founded by Robert Abbott in 1905.

200

Then in the twenties I came to this town, Cleveland. The UNIA * was just coming up here, at the Saint John's Church. I worked as a public relations man for Marcus Garvey's successor in the UNIA and I worked with the *Call and Post* † — always made it a habit to work for a newspaper and in public relations.

Many people don't know what public relations is. Many times when you try to talk to a man to help him at his job, he thinks you want the job. But if he wasn't a big man, and didn't have the job, you wouldn't have anything to write about. So, you give him something to write about, and you project him in such a fashion that the daily newspapers can't turn it down.

So with that background, I have been able through the years to render a service where other people have not even attempted a ministry. My own service and ministry owes a great deal to many people, but especially to the dreams of Marcus Garvey.

In what year did you meet Marcus Garvey?

It was my pleasure to have met him in Chicago in 1914, in the early advent of his second coming. Having gone to Wendell Phillips High School and mingled with the folks of various races and nationalities, and having served in several capacities in public life, I found that Garvey had something concrete and different. His ambition was not to chain people but to free them. There was no antagonism in his mind, though he was resentful that mulattoes in his country and in South Africa and other places got priority over the genuine blacks. It was his view that the white man was playing favorites with his sons.

When he came out with this different kind of ideology the NAACP and many other folks did not receive him because he was in opposition to their ideology. He taught the pure-blood line, you know. He said that you must marry your own kind, your own people. And you don't have to go out and steal and burn and demand from other people as long as you are hungry and can cook, as long as you are living on a farm and can hoe, as long as you earn

* The United Negro Improvement Association, the organization founded by Marcus Garvey.
† Cleveland's weekly black newspaper.

two dollars and can sew. You ought to have your own factory, your own hotel, your own bank, your own ships.

A lot of people are not acquainted with the fact that he bought several ships, not just one. But he didn't want to take Negroes back to Africa because there wasn't anything there they could do. You see, Africa until the advent of Mussolini was known as a dark, dark, dark continent. That was one of the biggest fallacies ever put in print or uttered publicly. But when Mussolini was preparing to go in and invade Ethiopia, they began to say in newspapers and magazines that our Africa is no longer the dark continent it used to be. The trick that Africa was backward was introduced by England in order that she might go in there and safeguard the diamond mines with a shotgun, and the gold mines and the rubber fields. It was one of those public relations stunts to permit the "Lord" to go in and take over the land from the people.

Garvey had the idea that we ought to have a philosophy of pure-bloods marrying your own and learning about yourself. It has been said that no nationality, no race or group of people rise higher than its knowledge of its own history and the culture of its women. In all the Bibles you read, you find some restriction because it is the woman that nurtures the child and plants in the mind of the child her attitudes and characteristics. So Garvey's theory was having his own school, just as he had been trained in the parochial schools sponsored by the Church of England in the West Indies. These schools were very effective means of propagating an idea that the English people should carry out their theory in Africa of the superiority of the white man. Garvey wanted the same thing with a different ideology.

I agreed with him because I was a third-generation offspring from the Jewish colony in Ethiopia. I had seen pictures and read the Bible. In Revelations, we believe it was said that Jesus was to be a black man with kinky hair, and a man named Solomon said he was black but comely. All we needed to know was a little more about ourselves and be a little more independent, more aggressive.

About this time I joined the one church in the world established as a nonviolent protest for black people by Richard Allen. About the time the United States was looking for their Constitution, I found that the African Methodist Episcopal Church was teaching the same thing. Though Richard Allen did preach in white churches, he taught the people of his own race that they ought to do something for themselves. He educated his family and his people in the community of his race. Wherever there was a new African Methodist Episcopal venture, they organized a school first. That is the reason for Wilberforce University, Allen University and others who are teaching the African language, to send their new bishops to Africa to get their feet on the ground and to know exactly what it is all about.

Garvey tried his best to incorporate the AME Church but he did not succeed. The bishops believed in the separation of church and state, and even though they accepted honors from him as chaplains and other offices in the UNIA, they did not permit this church to become a state church. The AME Church and the UNIA have the same independent philosophy — they welcome anybody that will join in with them.

My last contact with Garvey was when he was in the Tombs* and this thing we call prayer worked. I called nine people together for nine days and gave them the same prayer, right here at 2200 East Fortieth Street. The members came and we prayed that the Lord would give Garvey the option of freedom. Now the option of freedom meant that he would have died in the Tombs because he was not accustomed to being incarcerated. He was a man who traveled extensively. When you are handicapped you die, you know, and people came back with their reports that he looked so badly, and we prayed more. And on the ninth day, the U. S. Government asked him: "Do you want to serve out your time or be deported?" Of course he accepted deportation.

What do you think of the Black Nationalism of today?

Some colored people have just found out that they're not colored anymore. But the idea of being black has never been a difficulty for me. It always seemed to me to be a very fine thing.

Garvey's movement has been and is being duplicated. Well, maybe not duplicated, but imitated by groups who are using the

* The city prison in New York City.

red, black and green colors in various combinations. Eventually when you talk to them, they'll say something about Garvey because it is Garvey's movement. It is just like Jesus who prophesied: folks would come along and imitate me but don't go out to see Jesus because I won't be him.

Most of the civil rights leaders are Garveyites in the sense that they try to embrace his philosophy. The father of Malcolm X was a Garveyite. And this thing we call Muslims, this man * is not preaching Garveyism but he is using a similar technique in telling the people they should learn for themselves, they should do for themselves, wherever they go they should pay their bills.

We are looking forward to absolute vindication in the 1970's. There will be a resurrection of Garveyism. It will be properly understood that he was doing the same thing the Irish did. The Irish had a provisional government which was organized in New York City, and they took their president from there to Ireland, you see. The UNIA is a symbolic provisional government. In 1921, all the black nations of the world sent representatives to New York City to sign a Declaration of Independence declaring themselves to accept the red, black and green flag, and philosophy that was presented by Marcus Garvey. They said, among other things, that wherever you have a large amount of black people, there should be black representation. In other words, when you've got enough of them, you should have a black policeman, a black councilman, black school teachers and a black mayor.

We have over in Africa the Biblical leader, Haile Selassie. If you read your Bible, you know that Ethiopia is the Biblical name for blacks. Garvey's program sings and speaks and quotes Ethiopia. Garvey said that he would not redeem Africa, that Africa would rise up and redeem herself. People now are gaining more respect for the type of philosophy he offered. They understand it wasn't his purpose to send ignorant people to Africa.

We don't believe you have to tell the U.S. to give us a piece of the U.S. We think that the flag of Old Glory is a sacred thing. We respect it and we respect all for which it stands. The custom is that

---

* Elijah Mohammed, the Messenger of Allah, head of the Nation of Islam in the United States, the so-called Black Muslims.

whatever country you are in, you respect that country's flag first, and then you have your red, black and green flag. But you need the red, black and green flag in the United Nations, you need a country behind it. In the same fashion you can be an Irishman or a Jew or a Frenchman in the United States. You live here but you have sworn allegiance to another country. You were born in another country, but you still live in the U.S. and you are still protected by your home country's flag and government. If anything happens to you, all you do is tell your people or your ambassador. You go to the embassy.

We buried a boy last Tuesday and the claim is that he was shot in the face by the policeman when his hands were up in the air, walking toward the policeman. Well, he could have been vindicated and represented, regardless of whether he was a robber or what he was. He could have been vindicated. Garvey said that if you are black you belong. You are not a saint or a Methodist, but black. If you are black you belong.

Garvey wanted the people to have a God first, one God, and one aim which was a homeland in Africa. Just like the Jews are doing. Oh, yes, we want to live in Africa. We want to live anywhere in the world, but anywhere we live we want to live under our own flag.

So we are Black Nationalists in the sense that it sets up a homeland program. This was Garvey's idea, but Garvey was able to do and say whatever he did because he was an Englishman. He couldn't be shot in the U.S. or in Cuba because he was under the English flag. He taught the black man that when you have your own government and flag, you will be protected wherever you are.

TWO BLACK WOMEN
AND A NEWSPAPERMAN

MY WORLD

The smell of stale food lingering thick in the hot garbage-filled hallways.

The cry of babies wailing loudly for . . . for many reasons.

The sound of children laughing, crying, playing on the dirty streets below.

The girls with their mini-skirts, sweet talk, beautiful dreams, high hopes and swollen stomachs.

The boys with their wide afros, bright dashikis and false ideals of Black pride, sitting in the alleys, standing on the street corners, cutting school, going a lot of places . . . going nowhere.

This is my world.

The police with their big talk and their high and mighty ways . . . hypocritical.

The landlords with their two-way smiles, sweaty brows, beady eyes and open hands . . . cunning and greedy.

The teachers always complaining, watching, grinning, pretending to be interested, coming to school at eight o'clock because it's their job, driving quickly away, looking straight ahead at 3:30 p.m. . . . . afraid.

The preachers with their loud voices, holy talk of sin, evil, corruption, forgiving the world of today, glorifying and praising the supposed world of tomorrow . . . pious.

The social workers with their prying questions and no answers, chewed off pencils, $50 briefcases, walking stiffly up the street with eyes unseeing, ears unhearing, hearts unfeeling, saying "I want to help you" . . . thinking "I don't give a damn."

My world bleak, cold, crude, cruel, uncertain, uncaring, unknowing, unkind.

My world filled with hypocritical, cunning, greedy, afraid, pious, don't give a damn people.

This is my world. Will it ever change?

– Yolandia Hurtt
(Cleveland)

SOUL IS

Soul is a Black soda cracker.
Soul is Black walls in the White House.
Soul is a candy bar named Rap Brown, product of
    Wallace Industry.
Soul is Black Christmas.
Soul is Black St. Nick for little White kids.
Soul is a White Aunt Jemima on the pancake box.
Soul is G. Wallace pickin' cotton in them ol'
    cotton fields.
Soul is ordering greens, chittlings, and corn bread
    at the Ritz.
Soul is having the rats walk out of Harlem saying·
    that it's too dirty to live in.
Soul is the Black House.

— Earl Torain
(Cleveland)

FEEDING THE LIONS

They come into
our neighborhood
with the sun
an army of
social workers
carrying briefcases
filled with lies
and stupid grins

Passing out relief
checks
and food stamps
hustling from one
apartment to another
so they can fill
their quota
and get back out
before dark.

— Norman Jordan
(Cleveland)

RESTLESS LADY

> Now that my soul is feasted
> I shall never be free
> pray take me where you wander
> take me to the East & the West & the North
> count me among your throngs of lovers
> and should you weary of my presence
> Bid me farewell in Miami.

— Mary Mason
(Cleveland)

SOCIETY

My brother is cool.
My sister is boss.
My father is bad.
My mother a whore.
I am together.
You are uptight.
Is this society?
Then it's not right.

— L.P.R.
(Philadelphia)

THE HOLDUP MAN

No coal in the furnace, no shoes on my feet.
No cash in my pocket, no good food to eat.
No reason for living, not going to die.
No more of your giving, no tears to cry.
No room for your pity, no way to get worse.
No time to feel sorry, just give me your purse!

— Jonathan (Beaver) Lowe
(Philadelphia)

I AM SOMEBODY

I am
SOMEBODY.

I may be poor
But I am
SOMEBODY.

I may be on welfare
But I am
SOMEBODY.

I may be in jail
But I am
SOMEBODY.

I may be on grass
But I am
SOMEBODY.

I may have done wrong
But I am
SOMEBODY.

I am
SOMEBODY.

— A church chant
(Chicago)

"If you must use a term, then I prefer Negro with a capital 'N.'"

Zelma George

Zelma George is the executive director of the Cleveland Job Corps Center for Women. The young women lack marketable skills; they are from impoverished backgrounds, both black and white, seventeen to twenty-one years of age. Dr. George is a sixty-five-year-old cultivated black woman, large in every sense. Possessed of a beautiful voice, she once sang the lead in Menotti's The Medium.

She has a great capacity for laughing and for loving. Her perceptions about poverty are keen and her commitment to people total.

219

In her long and distinguished career she has been a concert singer, professor, social worker, diplomat, dean and administrator, research fellow, judge for the Miss America contest, lecturer and writer.

You were telling me about the award you received two years ago at the University of Chicago . . .

Oh yes, that was one of the great, great moments in my life. When the Alumni Association wrote to tell me that I had been chosen as the Alumnus of the Year I wanted very much to accept it. I was totally unprepared for it and flattered beyond description, but I did not write them right away to tell them that because I was debating with myself whether I dare write the kind of letter I felt impelled to write. Several weeks later, when I was in Seattle, Washington someone called me to ask if I were going to accept the award. I was, of course, very embarrassed and apologetic and told them so and that they would get my letter in a few days.

First of all I wanted to assure them of my gratitude for the faith and esteem the citation expresses and the illustrious company in which it places me. My four-year experience at the university constitutes one of the most important single influences in my life. It was for me a way of life and out of it I have found so much that has helped me fashion an exciting, busy, pluralistic life-style.

The citation had special personal significance for another reason: it symbolizes a tremendous good growth that has taken place in the university itself, and I gave a few personal experiences as a student and a human being to illustrate that point. The first one had to do with the fact that Negroes were not allowed to live in the dormitories on the campus when I was there, and I told how my father and I would make application for my admission each quarter. I would be refused each time without consideration simply because I am a Negro. Our appearance each quarter constituted our own personal brand of confrontation, protest a la the 1920s. I must tell you that there were quarters when, if they had said that I was accepted, we would not have had the money for the board and room! But we could not let the situation go unchallenged.

I recalled too, trying to get into the choir year after year, each time being refused for the same reason. When I finally appealed to the chaplain it was explained to me that the reason for the denial was based on the judgment that my presence in the choir would be as disturbing to the worship atmosphere of the university services as the limp of a lame person would be in the processional. My father was the minister of a very large Baptist church in Chicago and I was the organist. I wanted very much to be in that choir at the university because it represented the only way I could gain my freedom from my family and my pre-college Sunday schedule in my father's church as "the Minister's daughter" and therefore, you can see the double disappointment in their refusal. It was not because I did not qualify. I remember well one time when I responded again to the announcement of "choir tryouts" and I seemed so disappointed at being turned down, the director told me my voice was "too good for the choir" — it would be like putting Galli-Curci in the choir! She was one of the great voices of my youth.

I also told them in the letter that I refer to my right knee affectionately as "my interracial knee." It was injured in a basketball incident at the university and corrective gymnastics led me to the swimming pool. From that very first day in the Ida Noyes Hall pool I have another experience which illustrates a completely different set of consequences. In order to understand this incident, you must know that at that time every woman graduate of the university was required to be able to swim the length of the swimming pool before graduation. Negro women presented a statement from the YWCA certifying them. They just did not take swimming classes.

When I arrived at that first swimming class and handed the teacher my class card, she told me as she did all the others, that I could immediately get into the pool at the shallow end, play around a bit and get used to the water. When I stepped into the pool, all those already in, got out. One young woman went boldly to the teacher and said loudly, "I do not swim with niggers!" The teacher who was checking the cards, looked the young woman straight in the eye and almost without stopping what she was doing, said: "Swimming is an elective." This student had no alternative but to leave. She simply could not bear to return to that pool. Every one of the others started slipping back into the pool, one at a time, like little seals, and for the University of Chicago, the issue was resolved forever and I was privileged to participate in and to represent the university in many swimming events.

There was still another reason why I wanted to spell this out a bit and welcomed its publication in the magazine, and I said so in the letter. It is important that today's blacks and their non-black contemporaries know that they did not invent the concept of protest. They have a long tradition of protest and there have been some changes made on which they can build.

Many Negroes have worked for many years at problem-solving in this area of race relations on the basis of great personal conviction and courage when we did not have the support of a movement in doing it. Many of us were either the first or the only Negro in many of these situations and often we had to prove ourselves as human beings with the capacity to achieve. The progress was slow, but there was evidence all about us that a new day was a-borning.

The year after I was graduated, a Negro woman was taken into the choir and the next year another opened the door of the dormitories. Many other developments make me glad that I have lived so long. I think there are times when it is exceedingly important to "read the minutes of the last few meetings."

There is one other thing I want to say about my University of Chicago experience and that is that although much of what really constitutes a university was not fully available to Negro students — even to those among us who were aggressively seeking the full experience — I cannot fail to remember and be grateful for the help I had in trying to make the most out of what was for many Negroes a frustrating experience.

Why wasn't it frustrating for you?

I am a religious person and I have always sought divine guidance and strength in everything I do. I had religious parents and a very happy family life. My father taught us that God is love. He is the father of all mankind and therefore his children should be one. God is no respecter of persons; we are all equal in his sight. You see, both parents had college educations and were people who were involved in helping people define and achieve "the good life" for themselves. My father was president of a boarding school when I was born. It was the Hearne Academy in Hearne, Texas, a church-related school designed to teach Negro children from families who were dissatisfied with the quality of education the public schools provided for Negroes and who could afford to send them away to school. This was his first job. He and my mother met at Bishop College in Texas, and after graduating, mother taught school while he went on for graduate work in theology. They were married after a seven-year engagement, and I was born fifteen months later as the first of six children.

My father soon decided he was getting too few Negroes and of too limited a selection and so he went into the active ministry in the Baptist Church. He wanted to reach the entire family — and he did.

I had two remarkable parents and a very rich home life about which I hope to write some day. I certainly had a lot of support from my family. My mother still lives at age ninety-two, is active and a very great force in all our lives.

There was also support from a few individual teachers in the university. The most outstanding influence in my undergraduate life was Dr. Robert E. Park from whom I took Sociology 1 when the Park and Burgess famous textbook was in mimeographed draft form. I also took the first course given in a white university about the Negro. It was Sociology 43, "The Negro in America," taught by Dr. Park. This was Black Studies a la 1923!

And there were pioneering efforts by organizations. I had the privilege of being a part of the group that organized and led the first interracial YWCA on any college campus, at the University of Chicago in 1922. This group provided opportunities for women students to get to know one another and talk about the problems in informal groups.

Were there other Negroes at the University of Chicago?

Oh yes, there were quite a few Negroes in both graduate and undergraduate schools at the University of Chicago, and they were part of a larger group from the complex of colleges in and near Chicago, including Northwestern University in Evanston. We organized an Intercollegiate Club, with a membership of over two hundred of which I was the president for two years. We sponsored program opportunities for student talent, presented outstanding speakers, occasionally on the campuses, conducted forums and debates and along with the Greek letter sororities and fraternities, provided the social life for Negro students from which they were completely barred in the colleges and universities thereabout. It is impossible for me to adequately describe the feeling of rejection and injustice which I experienced every year when they would elaborately decorate the gymnasium and make the swimming pool of Ida Noyes Hall into a scenic lake with tables around it, in preparation for the big Prom. You would watch this process for days and hear the excited talk about dresses and dates and fun and know that not once had it even occurred to anyone that the Negro student was not included in this experience — they had not even been considered which is worse than being denied or rejected. We were simply ignored.

Tell me something more about your parents.

My father was born in Dallas County, Texas, and my mother in Ennis, Texas — about thirty-odd miles apart, but they did not meet until they went to Bishop College, a Baptist school which has moved recently to Dallas from Marshall. After graduation my mother returned to Ennis to teach while my father pursued his divinity graduate work at Virginia Union University, Richmond. He later studied under Shailer Matthews and Edgar J. Goodspeed at the University of Chicago Divinity School.

He pastored in Dallas, Hot Springs, Arkansas and Topeka, Kansas, where I finished high school, before we moved to Chicago. He died in 1925 at the age of forty-seven — in his prime as a leader — of cancer, the year after I was graduated from the university. His illness was sudden and he died at the Mayo Clinic Hospital in Rochester, but it was not until the post mortem which my mother requested, that we knew what was wrong.

We moved to Chicago in 1920 where masses of Negroes had been transported to that area by industry, looking for labor during World War I. My father's name was well known in the South, and they flocked to him and his church looking for guidance and help in making the transition to urban living. He preached a practical, relevant gospel, organized an "institutional church" with all kinds of services to the new citizens and to youth. When he set up tennis courts next door to the church, and converted the large Sunday School room with equipment for basketball, and had a baseball team, several of his deacons transferred to other churches in protest against these "worldly" activities.

Whenever any of the national Negro leaders came into whatever city we lived, and especially Chicago, they came directly to our home and church. They were sure of a good audience and the sale of their books, pamphlets, etc., especially if it related to Negro history.

Education was very important to my father and the need for a good education was taken for granted by all of us. I had four sisters and one brother and there had never been a question about whether or not they would go to college, only where.

Every one of them did finish college and has made good families of their own.

My mother, for the last twenty-five years before her retirement, was Coordinator of Religious Activities on the campus of the Tennessee State University in Nashville. A few years ago, a student center was dedicated in her honor and named for her; all of her six children and their spouses were present. Everyone present who was old enough was entitled to wear at least a bachelor's robe, with two doctor's and three master's degrees among them. It was an inspiring thing to experience for we had not realized this until the committee wrote to ask how many robes to order.

A minister's family fulfilled his dream even though I was the only one who had graduated when he died. At forty-seven years and with a growing family, he did not leave us with financial security, but he did leave a beautiful home with a mortgage, over five thousand books and six children. I did not marry until they had all finished college. It seemed the right thing to do since I had been able to finish without any financial problems before he died.

He was a remarkable man in many ways. Perhaps he didn't know African history as well as he knew classical history, but he

225

knew the contemporaries who were making history such as Booker T. Washington, Du Bois, J. Weldon Johnson, William Pickens, Walter White and many more.

We always had these people for dinner, and my parents always included the entire family when there was company, for the table conversation. Only the adults went into the living room after dinner for the really important discussions. My father started including me in this adult group when I was a senior in high school, and then I would be in the front row in the church when they would speak. This was a thrilling experience for me every time.

What were your father's ideas about integration?

This was not a term we used in his time but his basic belief and practice indicated that he knew this was inevitable. I think he would hope the Negro could enter this process from a position of personal strength instead of weakness. It is difficult, if not impossible, to successfully "integrate into." This is a two-way process which results in a new condition.

I know when I went to the University of Chicago, he took me the first few days and we would sit in the car or on the campus during those beautiful early fall days and talk about this brand-new, powerful experience. As he observed an overwhelmingly larger number of white students than Negroes, he said to me one day that whatever there was in this university that I felt I needed, I should get it. I was entitled to it and had paid for it. I should not hesitate because I would be the only Negro there and I should not walk into the experience like a scared dog "with his tail between his legs and his head down" but he said, "Walk in there like a bulldog — confident, with no need to intimidate, but prepared to fight for what you want, if necessary."

We talked about this often as I ran into problems and I must say this was not an easy assignment but it was one that helped me many times to fortify myself when threatened psychologically or otherwise. I think this is a part of the concept of integration — not just desegregation but integration.

I am sure my father did not believe in separateness although he preached "pride in your heritage" and in your opportunity to "contribute to the heritage pot." He said, "Maybe I can't brag about my ancestors, but I am an ancestor! Look at my children!"

What would he have said if you had brought home a white man as your bridegroom?

Oh I think he'd be more concerned if I brought a Catholic or a Jew or a Moslem or Buddhist. I am glad that I came along during a time when you could choose a wide variety of friends for whatever reason you might have to want them in your home and not be so limited in the things to do. We made our own music. My parents would not permit a victrola. Our friends often brought their instruments or we sang a lot. We had a lot of family games such as dominoes, checkers, chess, and we shared them and there was always exciting conversation. And there was food and in our big kitchen — we often made fudge or homemade ice cream and other goodies, sharing the chores. My father's library was on the third floor and he was an exciting man for them to meet either in his library or as he joined us in whatever else we might be doing, from music to eating! So, the color of the man wasn't nearly so important as what he could contribute to the evening's fun. Because we had such an interesting home there was never a dearth of visitors. My mother was a perfect organizer and this was a tremendous help in keeping things moving — preventing the plans of the evening from collapsing. I don't think we ever gave her enough credit for our "successful" occasions at home.

I think, nevertheless, if I had reached the serious stage looking toward matrimony with any of my friends with radically different backgrounds, in religion and/or color, or culture, my parents would have made sure I was conscious of all the possible consequences so I could decide whether or not our love was strong enough to match them. He did just that with a Negro I thought I was in love with and he felt would present certain problems later.

Why did you go to a northern institution like Chicago?

My father left it up to me to select my college, but I completely agreed with him that the peoples of the United States had to move closer and closer together. Already people were working and going

227

to school together more and more. He said, "There is more segregation on Sunday mornings at eleven o'clock than any other hour of the week." He felt, therefore, that more and more of the leadership of the several ethnic groups must be educated together so that they can be prepared to work together.

My father reminded us that he brought us out of the South where the schools for Negroes were poor, to areas of good public school education but he asked all of us to promise to return to give at least five years of service to Negroes left in the South who couldn't leave. Each of his children has fulfilled this pledge. I worked as Dean of Women at the Tennessee State University for five years and have done other kinds of sharing in the South on several occasions.

So I got my Ph.B. at the University of Chicago with a major in sociology and a minor in psychology. I did two quarters' graduate work in the School of Social Service Administration. I did my master's in personnel administration at New York University. I worked at the University of Southern California on my doctorate in sociology and got it from New York University. I was a Rockefeller Research Fellow for two years.

Then I worked a year as caseworker for a family welfare agency in Evanston, Illinois. I was then eligible to take the exam for probation officer of the Juvenile Court. I passed it and was appointed immediately and worked in the Juvenile Court for five years. From there I went to be dean of women and left there for Los Angeles where I organized and was the first director of the Avalon Community Center. From there I went to do the research project for the Rockefeller Foundation. From there I came to Cleveland as the wife of Clayborn George, an attorney.

I had leisure for the first time in my life and before I knew it I was on almost every board in town and found it necessary to reassess my activities and cut down on a few.

You use the term "Negro," not "black." Why?

Well, you must know that I am working for the day when nobody will need to use either term in referring to me, or people like me. If you must use one, then I prefer Negro with a capital "N." I define a black as a Negro who has just recently discovered his history — and, that he doesn't know it. He's ashamed of this and so he wants to learn about it off by himself right away, quick. I've been through that stage. I was brought up on it and I taught a course at the Tennessee State University in Negro History. I witnessed much of it being made and was privileged to sit in on the discussions of many of the history makers. I went through the personal period of embarrassment as I studied the "research" findings regarding the incapacity, immorality, laziness, stupidity, happy-go-lucky, criminal predilections of the Negro. I found my answers and I know who I am and what I want to be, where I intend to go and how I intend to get there. I will not be dragged through that again. And, I arrived where I am without having to swing the pendulum too far to the other extreme.

Nevertheless, I know that the present "all black is beautiful" slogan is an extremely useful myth and I am anxious to help anybody I can get *through* it. It is a means, not an end.

The important concept we have to deal with is the individual — the infinite uniqueness, the dignity and worth of the *one*. This is at the crux of Christianity and democracy.

Ruth Watson

Ruth Watson will be sixty-five in three years but she is not likely to depend on social security. By that time she will probably have a doctor's degree in social work from Wayne State University in Detroit. A high school dropout from Atlanta, Georgia, she went north to Harlem at eighteen, around 1926, dancing her way to success and her first regular income. Since that time she has always had money coming in regularly.

She is an elegant woman, strong willed and attractive. Her first

230

beauty shop, in Los Angeles, was called Lady Ebony. She is still a
Lady Ebony.

Our conversation began as she perused a book of photography
by James Van Der Zee, the seventy-three-year-old black photog-
rapher whose contribution to the Museum of Modern Art's "Har-
lem On My Mind" exhibit was widely hailed. Some of Mr. Van
Der Zee's photographs include show people of the twenties who
helped to make the Harlem Renaissance of that period.

Oh, my God, I was never that hefty. But these are sure the glori-
fied show girl days. I didn't know we were posing in the nude back
then. I'm looking at clothes now to date these pictures. I never
wore high top shoes like these girls have on, but the generation just
ahead of me did. These clothes look more like my mother wore.

This looks like Bo Jangles. It *is* Bo Jangles. And see here? I
can't hardly believe that one of the Mills Brothers was ever that
young, though I saw them when they were quite young. There are
many people here I recognize. I just might find myself here.

I think I told you that in 1928 I worked for Lou Lesley in
Blackbirds, it was called *The Blackbirds of 1928.* It wasn't my first
experience at dancing but it was the first black chorus line, everybody was black.

Before that I had worked at Connie's Theatre Nightclub at
132nd Street and Seventh Avenue. A friend of mine worked there
and she told me to come in and rehearse. At first I couldn't dance
at all. I didn't realize that every step had a name.

We did the time step, then "Falling off the Log," "Over the
Top," and "In the Trenches." You were told that on a certain beat
you would "Fall off the Log," then "In the Trenches," and I finally
got it down pat. And sometimes we started dances popularized by
some celebrity, like the "Black Bottom." I came along during the
"Black Bottom" and the "Charleston." You really didn't have to
be talented to do them. But the unique thing about my working is
that they had never had anybody black as me before. All chorus
girls had been fair.

One of my friends was Billie Yarbough, the girl who played the maid in the first edition of *The Man Who Came to Dinner*. She worked one end of the line at Connie's and I worked the other. Billie was my color. We knew then, even more than now, that if you were the blackest you had to be the best. So we worked for a long time in the line together and we just did our own thing. I won't say we made a name for ourselves but everybody in New York knew us as the two black girls on the end of the line. It was fun.

Now here's a picture of Florence Mills, the star of *Blackbirds*. She was never a chorus girl. She was called a soubrette, sort of the star of the chorus girls. Actually she was in the first edition of *Blackbirds* in 1927 and I worked with her in 1928. She was even blacker than me. Lou Lesley never made money until she came along.

Florence Mills was the star and Mantan Moreland did the comedy along with Buddy Mills. Lou Lesley wrote it and produced it, but really it wasn't anything you wrote. You just got a show together by getting some dancing girls, and some comics, and putting the show on the road. It was, to my knowledge, the first time there had been a completely black chorus on Broadway.

Florence Mills was the most fantastic black woman I have ever seen in show business. The only person I'd compare her with would be Diana Ross of the Supremes. She wasn't pretty by any means and had little bird legs, very skinny. But she had such personality, she just bubbled, and the ability to sell a song, and dance in front of the chorus line. She was a beautiful person to watch. She passed on in 1929, the same year as Valentino, and we haven't had anyone to replace Florence Mills in that length of time.

Mantan Moreland was my best friend. He couldn't read or write and I used to write letters for him. He is still around. He played in the Charley Chan series. I saw him last week on the Late Show. Mantan was his real name. He came from Monroe, Louisiana. He had a partner, Emmett Anthony, and the two of them were to me the funniest men who ever lived. They were even funnier off stage than on.

They didn't do blackface and this was in the time when there was a lot of blackface. I never did like the cork on, and then all that white stuff on your lips. I guess to sell their act most black comedians did put on the cork except for these two. But if you were already black, why put cork on? I guess we were just emerging at that time.

Here's a typical pose of the day. It's Marcus Garvey. I hadn't noticed him before. He's in the back seat of a Packard, lots of brass on it, dressed up in one of his big hats. Usually this popular pose for taking pictures included two well-dressed women in the front seat, as if they were driving the car.

And here is Reverend Matthews of the Moorish Jews of New York. There has been a temple there for years. Lots of black people haven't seen the Moorish Jews, but if you live long enough in New York you see everything in the way of religion. You name it and New York would have it. This was especially true in this time when we were really trying to find ourselves, really trying to identify. We became part of all kinds of cults.

This man here is Daddy Reese but he's recent. Father Divine was during my time. I remember the fifteen-cent meals we used to get at his place. Back in those days nobody had any money and we were glad that Father Divine existed so we could go to the mission and eat, all you could, for fifteen cents. The food was delicious and a full-course dinner: dessert, salad, soup, and everything. Whether you wanted to be part of what he was doing or not, you walked in, said, "Peace," and got your stomach full. You didn't mind saying Peace for fifteen cents to get your stomach full. You had nothing to lose.

Here is a church I remember; it is now Adam Clayton Powell's Abyssinian Baptist Church. It was his father's church in those days. Right across the street was a YWCA and when I left home from Atlanta, I got a room there. The first Sunday I decided I would go to church. I got up bright and early and went across the street, found a seat and sat down. I had been in that seat about ten minutes when a great big, fat lady came over and said, "You're sitting in my seat. I have been sitting in that seat for the last twenty-five years." I thought this was horrible. Here I was a young person, and in church. She should have been very happy for me to be there. So she chased me out of that seat and she meant *move,* don't hang around! I got out of that seat and never went back to the Abyssinian Baptist Church again. And ever since, when I go in a Baptist church, or any church like that, I think about that woman on that Sunday morning. What kind of Christian was she? She didn't want me to come in and enjoy her old church, so I just sort of lost interest at that point.

She didn't really chase me out of religion because I never had to go to church to feel that sort of thing. The church I enjoy the most is Unity. They don't preach but lecture. Spirituals don't move me. I like to feel I never had that feeling of having to belong to a religious body or group of people who worship one day a week to feel at oneness with God. When I was young, of course, I grew up with religion. We went to a Baptist church on Auburn Avenue in Atlanta, called the Wheat Street Baptist Church. To my knowledge, there have only been four ministers in that church in over a hundred years. It is one of Atlanta's largest, and a beautiful church. What I remember most about that church is that we used to have a candy called "pulley candy," and you could buy, say a pound for a nickel. So we sold pulley candy for about a year to send our minister, Reverend Bryant, to Jerusalem.

It's funny what you remember, but when Reverend Bryant came back from Jerusalem, after having gone there with the money we sent him on, he charged you fifteen cents to come to church and hear all about his trip to Jerusalem.

Now here is a picture of Jack Johnson. You would always remember him for the tam o'shanter he is wearing. And this may be Bo Jangles again. Bo Jangles was in class all by himself, like one of the untouchables. So was Ethel Waters. They were respected by everybody in show business. They really had a talent, something to sell. You recognized it and wanted to be like them. It was in the Lafayette Theatre on Seventh Avenue that I first saw Ethel Waters. I had never seen a black star before, and the height of every chorus girl's ambition was to work at the Lafayette Theatre. I worked there finally, doing *Running Wild*. I danced my heart out and made sixty-five dollars a week.

Show business was big then and I was very fortunate. The Whitman Sisters were around and since they were from my hometown, there were times when they took me home when I couldn't get a job. I lived in Harlem with an aunt and I usually had work. For about ten years there were plenty of shows. There was Miller and Lyles who had shows and any number of people. Mrs. Marcus Garvey rehearsed for about six months for a show that never opened up; her daughter was in the chorus line with me.

Sixty-five dollars was a lot of money but you know silk stockings cost a dollar fifty a pair in those days, especially the ones with clocks on them. I only liked the ones with clocks. And the clubs were big. The Cotton Club was in a class all by itself. But I didn't know any black girls to go to the Cotton Club to work until it went downtown about 1932, and then they hired some brown-skinned girls. Most black people didn't go to the Cotton Club while it was uptown — around 147th Street. Duke Ellington became famous at the Cotton Club but he was not available to black people at all. Most black people never got a chance to see him.

There were others, of course. Cab Calloway came along in the early thirties and he was at the Savoy, but it was not a show band and known nationally until they started going into the Apollo Theatre. Louis Armstrong was around but I don't recall where he was working.

These fellows in these pictures look like gangsters and probably were. These were prohibition days and I remember fellows like Mad Dog Cole, and the fellow who ran Connie's Club was named Connie Zimmerman. He had some connections with them because every so often gangsters would come to the club together. They would lock the doors and not let anyone else in after the first show. They would spend enough money to make up for the loss of any other customers that didn't come in. They would come for the last show and you might have to dance until five in the morning. They would throw money at you because it didn't mean anything. Maybe if you had a little song they liked, they gave you twenty-five or fifty dollars. But I was afraid of them because of what I read in the papers. It was a job and you had to work.

I had a friend who dated a fellow from gangsterdom. She was my best friend, and she and he were going real strong. Then she was found with her mother, aunt, and baby, murdered. She was a beautiful girl and had been dancing since she was fourteen. Her mother used to bring her to work. They never knew who did it, but everybody in Harlem knew what happened. She just got carried away. Everybody liked pretty clothes and these flapper clothes were beautiful and expensive. The dresses were very long in back and short in the front, and your hats came down over your head like a pail. In their greed or desire, some of the girls got off on the wrong track because of those beautiful clothes.

How long were you in show business?

Over ten years. I stayed as long as I could. When you get thirty-two you just don't stay the same. You're getting a little paunchy and your legs are getting bandy. You can stay in a nightclub, but to me it was really a job. My life was a little different from most girls. I didn't drink and carouse. It was like any other day's work. I went to work and left and went back home about three in the morning. For the first couple of years I didn't know anybody. And the people were a little older than you. I remember one fellow called Snake Hips Tucker who did a pelvic sort of thing like Elvis Presley; he was kind of kooky and I was scared of him. But most were so ignorant that they couldn't give you any information and being young you had nothing to offer them. I was quiet and for a long time I didn't even have a boyfriend.

Then I met a fellow who felt I was headed, not necessarily in the wrong direction, but in no direction at all. I didn't have any direction. I started dating him. He was a Jewish fellow who had got stuck at home with his mother when his father died. Everybody in the family had married and left home, so he was caught there. So long as his mother lived, he couldn't get married. He dated me for eleven years and during that time — let me think of all the things I went to school to learn: cosmetology, millinery, tailoring, floral design, just anything. He insisted on one thing: I had to go to school or work. I had a job at a store on 125th Street — Bloomstein's. I worked on the first floor selling pillows and made eighteen dollars a week. This was quite a comedown from sixty-five, but even eighteen a week during the Depression was better than sixty-five during Prohibition. I even had a girl come to my apartment twice a week to clean and I paid her seven dollars and carfare.

It wasn't unusual back in those days. You didn't go with a guy if he didn't pay the rent and buy the clothes. Perhaps women are much more self-supporting today, I don't know. I didn't call this shacking up because to me shacking up with a guy means he lives there. I had a date with this fellow every Saturday night. He'd sleep over. Then he would go back to his mother on Sunday evening around seven P.M. after Major Bowes Hour. We listened to Major Bowes on the radio and then he'd go home. He would call me later, around eleven, to keep me from going out anywhere else, you know. He'd check back. But it was too late for me to go out. I was a sleepy head. Then on Wednesday nights I would see him again and other than that we'd talk on the phone every night.

I feel that he was the guiding factor in my life. His name was Phillip. He steered me into a lot of things, like if you're going to have one dress have a good one, one good black dress. And he gave me extra money and would say, "This is money to put in the bank." I had never saved before. I got started putting a little bit of whatever I made in the bank and learning to buy a good thing. My values, I think, came really more from this person than my background.

I never thought of him as Jewish or white or anything but only a person. He may have thought about me differently. Let me put it this way; all of my girlfriends who dated black guys got hit across the head once in a while. They'd get slapped around and have a little heartbreak. But I had eleven years of perfect bliss with a white man. I never got slapped once. He was twelve years older than me and we were just compatible in every sense of the word.

Marry? Well, he wouldn't have married me even if he hadn't had a mother. He wasn't about to marry me because I was black. I didn't mean the same thing to him that he meant to me. His mother wouldn't let him marry anyone really. Before me, he had had a southern white girl and when his mother would hear my voice, she would say to him, "You really like those southern girls." We'd laugh about it and he would say, "If my mother knew you were a Negro, she would have a heart attack." Alone he would call me "his nigger." We had a joke that he could say nigger to me and it wouldn't bother me. He would say, "Aren't you my nigger?" And I would say, "Yea, Yea." He was a good guy and he didn't say it to hurt me.

I lived happily in New York until about 1935 when I went to California with Phillip. He took me along on a business trip. He was a perfume exporter and sold to big companies like R. H. Macy. I liked it there so when he went back I stayed in Los Angeles. He dismantled the apartment for me and shipped my things and I went to a school of cosmetology in Los Angeles, Henrietta's Beauty Academy, for two years. Phillip sent me a check every month just like an annuity, so I had no problem.

A friend of mine had a beauty shop across from the academy and I served her customers while her saleslady was ill. The customers liked me so much that I started to think about building my own shop. By the time the saleslady came back, I had enough customers of my own to work every day and make money with my own clientele. You had to work every day because this was in the late thirties and early forties and things were rotten. There was no money. All California had was sunshine and oranges. I was very comfortable but I knew I was playing a dangerous game by leaving Phillip in New York and living in California. He came out every winter and stayed about three months and then I could come to New York any time I wanted to.

In 1936 I opened a shop in Los Angeles. There was no such thing as *Ebony* magazine, and I came up with the name, Lady Ebony. Phillip had taught me that you don't just stand around all day and work with your hands. You never make money from labor. You put products in and sell them, and you make money without tiring yourself out. So I got a cosmetics firm to label some cosmetics for me with a Lady Ebony design and sold them in my shop. I had very good skin and an abundance of hair and was, well, pretty good-looking. I was able to sell the cosmetics because I said I used them. Everybody wanted to use what I used. Then the Second World War came in 1941.

In September of that year I got a letter from my ex-husband. I may have forgotten to say that I married briefly, for three months, while I was living with Phillip. It didn't work out. He was a nice fellow but a mama's boy. He had no father. We grew up next door to each other in Atlanta. His mother was never around, a very unattractive woman, black as the ace of spades. He was a handsome fellow and didn't look white, but you knew his father had never been a Negro. He was exactly my color but with different hair, very, very refined features.

In this letter, he said he loved me, always would and would I remarry him. I said, "Yes." He was then stationed in New Jersey. I called Phillip in New York and told him. Phillip had always told me he wished I would meet a nice guy and get married. He felt he had never seen a black man or "Negro" as he would have put it, good enough for me.

Whenever we had friends over on Saturday night, my black male friends always talked down to their white women and he resented this. I didn't know all the psychology I know today. He probably had a hangup too and must have hated black men. We used to talk about black men and white women. I would say, "Well, if you can go out with me, why should you care?" And he would reply, "Yes, but I have to give you money or you wouldn't have me. Those black men are getting money from the white girls. Why can't they give the money?"

I think now that white men do like black women. And most white men, whether Jew or Gentile, see a sexual connotation wherever the black male is concerned.

So far as Phillip was concerned, I hadn't looked for anybody because I wasn't interested. In fact, I didn't have any contact for most of those eleven years with black people. I had some few friends from my home. He always knew when I had been with them because they were so loud and profane. He didn't like profanity and he could tell everytime I had been with these people because I'd say a few "damns" myself.

So I went to Lakehurst, New Jersey, and my husband and I were married again in the Cathedral of the Air. I stayed in New York about a month, and the day after we were married Phillip took my husband and me to dinner. He liked my husband who was a very nice fellow. So we said good-bye and after that I only had one letter from him when I got back to Los Angeles. He told me some things he thought I should know about the way I should conduct my life.

239

He said something like, "I've taught you to walk now, and I want you to walk without me." Really it was the best experience of my life. He was just a beautiful person.

You'll find that there are really very few men in my life. I'm sort of a one-man woman. Men used to say to other fellows that they were wasting their time with me because "that woman is only interested in one man, the one she is with." They were kind of right.

Where did you go from there? You're about forty at this time?

Right, about forty. My husband left me on December 20, 1945, when the war was over. I flipped my lid. I went to Atlanta to look for him because I knew he had gone back home to his mother. I had relatives there too and I needed them, especially a cousin who had leaned on me all her life. So I stayed a couple of months with her, looking for my husband. I really wanted him back and it was too far to sneak into Atlanta from California to find this guy. I loved him and I couldn't eat or sleep.

I looked everywhere, even down in Florida. Finally I saw him in Birmingham. He was a musician and played in a band there. He said, "Ruth, please don't kill me." I'm kind of surprised I didn't because I had gotten to that stage. I was really mad. Well, he promised he would take me home and we would go back to Atlanta together. I waited for him the next day but he never came back. That was the last I ever saw of him.

I spent some time in Atlanta then and got to know my family a bit. I'm an only child. I saw my aunt, really my great-aunt, who had let me live with her when I was a chorus girl in Harlem. I had just been fascinated by this woman. She wore beautiful clothes and I was enchanted by people who wore pretty clothes and who were pretty people. She was the only woman in the block where we lived who was unmarried and she was beautiful and everybody talked about her. I'd go to the store for her because she had such beautiful lingerie. She would wash it and hang it on the line, you know. I told everybody, "When I grow up, I'm gonna be like her," and my mother would say, "I hope not." She wasn't really a lady of the evening, but some gentlemen used to come by later at night. She was a most attractive woman and very, very reserved. Whatever she did, nobody really knew. They thought they did, but they weren't sure because she kept to herself. But she was very nice and spoke to everybody.

Of course, she was old when I visited Atlanta in 1945. So was my grandmother who had been born and reared in Atlanta. She used to tell about what the slave owners used to do to them and how her mother had toppled an overseer into a huge vat of hot sorghum. But I think she was justifying my temper. When I was young, I had an awful temper.

Atlanta prepares you for anywhere in the world, anywhere. Atlanta is without a doubt the best proving ground for living of any place you will ever go. It prepared me for Harlem. You get to know all kinds of people. At eleven I knew all the con men around the country. They came in the spring from all over and did their conning in Louisiana, Alabama, and all over the southern circuit. They stayed in a rooming house near my mother's place. They must have been nice people because they liked the kids and we used to sit on her porch and get to know them.

Naturally after hearing all this, I knew the games — like the Pigeon Drop — so well that nobody could pull them on me in New York. We had a red-light district in Atlanta and we knew the names of the most famous prostitutes. One was known as Chilly Wind, she was legend in our town. Kids in Atlanta are very sophisticated. We had sections like Dark Town, Buttermilk Bottom, Tan Yard Bottom, Lightning, then the West Side and Summer Hill. If you lived in Tan Yard Bottom, you were supposed to carry a knife and if you lived in Lightning, you were a very tough character. Black Bottom had all kinds of people, and it was special because it was close to Peach Tree Church where all the elites who were Baptists went to church.

We didn't really have a drug scene like today but there were people we called, not drug addicts, but dope fiends. They took laudanum which is an opium derivative. It was heated in a spoon; these are things the cooks knew how to do. This is why black people say that we know white people better than they know us. Back in those days white people didn't give a damn what you knew about them because black people were nothing. They didn't care what

241

you saw, so when they were using things like laudanum, the cooks saw it and would come back and tell it. White people were careless, they couldn't care less about what a black knew about them. But we found out and would tell. Our prostitutes did the same thing. We know you better than you know us.

Black people had to survive, and they learned early how to do it. If you had kids you would have to get somebody in to help you take care of them, anybody. We had probably fewer incidents of miscegenation in those days, but we had many more mulattoes than today. It was most unusual to see two black people get married because your mother would tell you, "Don't you go and marry anybody black and bring me all those nappy-headed babies." In those days our standard of beauty was somebody who could pass. But today I'm happy to see two blacks get married and be proud of their offspring, not hide them for shame that people will see them.

I've had my problems with white folks, too. Once I was riding through Grosse Point, Michigan, with a white fellow and his law partner and his wife. The houses were very nice and the lady said to her husband, "Drive down that street. I want to show Ruth a house I've always loved." We drove past and it was a beautiful, long, just glorious house — English Tudor. She held my hand and said, "If I ever get that house, I'll let you come and cook for me." Now I can laugh at that, but at the time I didn't. Here is me who hasn't made a bed three times in my damn life. I just don't do housework, somebody else has always done it. And here is this woman inviting me in to cook for her . . .

How do you feel about white folks today? Do they make you angry?

They don't make me angry. They make me sick. I'm sick of them. I'm not angry. I don't hate them, but I am actually sick up to my teeth with their sickness. They have no rationale. I asked some of my students at Wayne State the other day why they didn't like me and several said, "Because you're black." Now you've got to have a better reason than that. You can't dislike me just because I'm black. I live just the way they do, only perhaps better and all they can think of is, "because you're black." White people are sick.

Anybody who can waste energy hating and restricting anything or anybody would have to be sick because when you do that you have no energy for anything else. My own thrust for material things — you know I serve my chitterlin's on the best china and with sterling silver — has made me lose a lot of the feeling that some other black people might have. I have been so damn busy trying to get myself together that I really haven't had too much time to think about white people. I've had to learn all kinds of strategies to beat them out of whatever I could beat them out of. I have had everything material under the sun that I wanted. And some of it I didn't pay for. But I got it. They let you have it. But what about all the other black people who don't have this kind of "coping strategy," as I like to call it? So I'm not really too concerned with the white man because I know deep down, he is going to get his. I'm not necessarily saying that black people will sock it to him because I think we're stagnant now. We have done all we're going to do.

Stagnant?

Yes. So far as revolution is concerned, black people are stagnant. I don't really think we're going to set towns afire anymore. I think we've found out now that there's other ways of getting some things done. When I say stagnant, I mean in the terms that would upset white people. The only thing that upsets white people has been the fires in the ghetto. Nothing bothered them till we started to burn up Detroit.

Even intermarrying won't upset them. Just because their daughter marries a black man or their son marries a black woman, they are not going to jump off buildings. In the first place, white people love mulatto Negroes too well and always have. I know that intermarriage is going to be the only solution, but in the meanwhile we're not going to be able to do anything except through legislation. That will happen when more black people get political power. Legislation be damned so long as we've got the white structure we have. But as we move more black people into areas of power, then our legislation can be meaningful.

This has been a long time in coming. But now our time has come. Now we have to make known our intentions — whether or not we are willing to accept the old way of life or whether we

243

should let people know we want a change. I don't see it as anything we can stop or as anything we really started. I don't think you could find anybody who would tell you at what moment the awakening came. It is just at the point now when history has to be made.

Can the young black people wait for legislation?

They're not really waiting. Just you listen to those police calls. They tell me more than just some criminals out on the street. There are too many of them out there doing the same thing. It's true they are robbing blacks. Some of them have not yet graduated to the white scene. But they are taking everything they can from white people, just as soon as they can get their hands on it. This is reprisal for the past. Or maybe reparation. You got it and it is mine. They call it "Ge' a 'chere" which means "Give it to me." These police calls tell me that the young black waits until nightfall and then says, "Whitey has it and now I'm going out and take it." Around here the folks used to steal chickens, but we have stopped the chicken bit. Now we rob banks. Of course, each one will try to get it together in his own way.

The thing that has frightened white people more than anything else happened to be the riots, but I don't think we're going that route anymore. The only route we can go is to get more black people in places of power so that if there is legislation we have somebody there who can be our voice. Other than that we don't have a leg to stand on. In the meanwhile there are those police calls.

Where do you see yourself in five years?

Growing. I have to grow a little every year. Every year has to be just a little better than the year before. I don't think a material reversal would upset me, but if I ever got to the place where I felt life held nothing else for me and I'm not going to grow another inch, I would be very unhappy.

In three years I'll go down to social security and get — not what I have coming (nobody ever gets that) — but what they are willing to give me. I hope to have the doctorate by that time just to prove

244

to someone who is forty that he can make it. If he looks around and says, "Damn, she made it at sixty! Now I know I can do it," then I'll be satisfied. And I would like to be a dean in a southern college, maybe in Atlanta. You see, I know why white people have tried to run us out of the South, just to have all that good climate for themselves.

You see, there is not too much else I want to do. I feel that I have had a good full life. I've done everything I ever wanted to do, everything I dreamed as a little child in Atlanta. All the games I played as a little girl have come true. When I was little, I was a dancer and danced in the back yard and saw myself on the stage. I made it. Then I wanted to be a teacher and I've made that. I've been in the right places at the right time. When you go out to do a thing, you do it well and you come back saying, "I didn't know I could do that." Now my friends expect this of me.

Being a Capricornian, I've always been in charge. You remember I said I was a "one-man woman"? There's no contradiction. I need a man to lean on, a strong and quiet man. You can lean on them if you want to. They will let you carry as much of the load as you wish to make you happy. It's not that they can't carry it but they let you do it — and they are always there in case you need help. I have to have a man who lets me do my thing.

My mother never had any experience and had never been any-place. I'm sure glad they didn't have pills in my mama's time because I'm so happy she let me get here. It has been a beautiful experience. Children? I don't know if children would have changed the course of my life very much. I don't think so. I feel that my life has been so structured that I didn't necessarily have to have children to have a full life. I know I am a woman. I don't need children to prove it. I'm all female.

And I think I have a formula. I have young friends who want to be like me, just like I wanted to be like my aunt who had the very bad reputation and the pretty lingerie. They think I am a secure person. So I say to them, "You work at it and dream about it and then you can make it happen." Beyond that, you can't go. I've played a game forever. And everything I played has come to pass. I've done everything so I feel I've been very fortunate to live this long. Hell, life worked for me and I made it happen. I said, "Well, this is what I want to do and this is what I did."

Here I am coming from Atlanta, and having been born within two blocks of Martin Luther King and know his mother. Everything has happened in my life. So I'm not impressed by any of it. I read about it and listen and feel that this is this man's time. Like King or Kennedy. Everybody has a time. Every era gives you somebody else. I can't say I have really been impressed by any of it. I don't know why. I just couldn't tell you.

Francis Ward

Francis Ward is a working journalist with a gimpy right leg. Now assigned to the midwestern bureau of the Los Angeles Times, *he is thirty-five. The polio-damaged leg does not prevent him from moving swiftly and efficiently through the scores of hours he puts in on a major news story. He sometimes complains that he has more analysis and background than appear in the columns of the newspapers which print his by-line. Watching him move through a city and its people, you believe it.*

247

He speaks rapidly, his questions are incisive, his manner direct and intense. He is an expert at locating hard to find people, following up leads others might ignore. His notes are voluminous.

Unlike most newsmen, he neither drinks nor smokes. If he has a vice, it is eating. He is the father of five children. His wife was director (1969–70) of the Afro-American Cultural Program at the University of Illinois. With an Afro haircut and a beard, he cuts a striking figure as he walks through Central Police Headquarters in Chicago.

I joined the Students for a Democratic Society (SDS) when I was in graduate school at Syracuse in 1959. Of course, it was not then what it is today. It is an understatement to say that SDS is far more militant now. In 1959 it was nothing more than another version of the Young Democrats. They were staunch leaders in nonviolence, law, the system, or however you want to put it.

I didn't do any work on the student paper at Syracuse, just concentrated on the three semesters to get that journalism degree and get the hell out. Before Syracuse, I went to Morehouse College in Atlanta, where I was born.

Afterwards there was the problem of getting work. The master's degree from Syracuse was not much of an entrée into the field. Most of the people graduating with me got jobs but I didn't. The reason in my case was lack of experience and because I was black. More particularly because I was black. I remember writing many letters to the major dailies in the North explaining that I had my degree and some experience with a black daily, the Atlanta *Daily World*. For a year I was a proofreader and part-time reporter for the *World*. They always wrote back and said the only openings they had were for copyboys. That was about the standard reply, especially after they interviewed me.

In New York, they had six dailies at the time; I checked out every one and followed up ads in the *Editor and Publisher*. Everything.

So I went to work for the SDS at their main headquarters in New York around mid-1961 for about two years. I did a little office

"Deep down in his heart, the white liberal tells himself, 'I'll kind of leave the policeman alone and I won't bother him about brutality, particularly since the brutality isn't against us.'"

work there, ran some errands. I was no slick policymaker, but I do remember doing one rather lengthy paper which they used at the 1961 convention of the National Student Association. It was a paper on right-wing groups. I did some extensive research on the Young Americans for Freedom, which is the conservative answer to whatever the New Left has. It was formed in 1960 on the Connecticut estate of William F. Buckley, Jr's mother.

At this time the SDS was beginning to take what people regarded as a leftward turn. There were some in the group, including Tom Hayden, who were beginning to flirt with a group of young communists who were really far-left socialists. And there was another group called the W.E.B. Du Bois Club which was pro-communist. The SDS flirtation with young communists disturbed some of the old timers in the League for Industrial Democracy. A lot of people don't know that the SDS started out as the young wing of the League for Industrial Democracy, a socialist group in New York. They had offices on different floors of a building located at a hundred and twelve East Nineteenth Street in lower Manhattan. The LID members were old time socialists and some labor people who had fought the battles of the thirties and forties. They were scared as hell of any kind of involvement with the communists.

The most galling, frustrating, nightmarish job I ever had was also during that time. I worked for the New York City Department of Welfare. I don't see how anybody could ever stay on that job for the six months I did. I was a caseworker, an investigator, the one who had direct contact with the clients. You know the ones. The guy who makes the home visits and talks with the people. You're the one to whom welfare applicants come when they apply for relief.

I was assigned to the South Bronx where I lived, a very urban area. It used to be Jewish, Irish, Italian. At that time there were pockets of predominately Irish and some Jewish people, but more and more it was passing over to blacks and Puerto Ricans. My case load was about seventy-five to eighty cases, about fifty of them ADC mothers. I formed some crystal clear and definite attitudes on the welfare problem which haven't changed a bit. Number one, there is a prevailing myth that people on welfare cheat. I don't believe that, and the more I worked in the department the less I believed it. If more people had a choice, they wouldn't be on welfare. Sure, there are some that probably get some money they don't deserve, but that is quite consistent with the American ethic. I think anybody who can will cheat for a few extra dollars, and I don't see why we should expect welfare people to do any differently than a banker, a real estate man, or a newspaperman. If he can hustle him a few extra dollars, he's gonna do it. So will the welfare client.

You see, because it is tax money that is supporting them, we place higher standards. It is appalling, ignorant and outrageous to assume that a welfare mother has extra children to get extra money. At that time in New York City, the assistance level was about nineteen dollars a month for an extra kid, for food, clothing and incidentals. The rent money never went up. A woman stayed in the same apartment. So that means all she got was an increment, a supplement for the welfare of this child. About nineteen dollars a month. It is preposterous to assume that women go out and have a bunch of babies to get nineteen extra dollars.

What was your first newspaper job?

Jet magazine. I started in January of 1965 and remained there until February 1967 when I moved over to the staff of *Ebony*. In 1966 I covered the Hough rebellion for *Jet* by phone. I didn't come to Cleveland.

Why do you call it a rebellion?

I regard explosions not as riots but as rebellions against the oppression that blacks have suffered as a result of being penned up in big city ghettos and being totally powerless. Politically, they are better defined as rebellions than as riots.

The Cleveland story in Hough was depressing. There was a couple leaving their apartment and they had packed their baby and a twelve-year-old nephew in a car and were trying to leave the scene of a burning building. En route to the home of the wife's mother, the car was stopped by the Cleveland police. Some questions were asked through the window and then, somehow, the

251

man's foot accidentally slipped on the accelerator and the car moved forward. As it did, the police simply let loose and riddled the car. There were more than fifty bullets fired directly into the car. Miraculously, nobody was killed but all four occupants were injured. The woman's right eye was shot out and the baby had severe brain damage. The husband was seriously wounded. The family's name was Towne. The case is still in litigation.

When I went to *Ebony,* I also made some trips. I remember going to Houston to cover the Muhammad Ali–Ernie Terrell fight. But the trip I regard as the best was made in the spring of 1967 doing what *Ebony* called its Baseball Roundup. I enoyed it tremendously because I'm something of a sports fan. It gave me a chance to meet a lot of black baseball players.

The story itself was a sop, probably the easiest story I ever had to do. I remember the lead we chose for the story that year. It was on black catchers. Elston Howard, John Roseborough, and I did some rather extensive research into old-time baseball players. One of these days I'm going to sit down and do some real in-depth research for a long essay or short book on the old Negro National League and the Negro American League.

The teams in these leagues were every bit the equal of the white major league teams. The whites may have had an edge in numbers, but in terms of any individual player, the blacks could match the whites in every department. Once, in 1953, Harry Carey, the old Cardinal broadcaster, said in the middle of a game, "Gee whiz, those guys from the colored league can sure bunt, run, throw and hit."

I remember the names. There were the Kansas City Monarchs, the Cleveland Buckeyes, the New York Black Yankees, the New York Cubans, the Newark Eagles, the Baltimore Elite Giants, the Homestead Grays, who played some games in Washington, D.C., and some in Pittsburgh. In Atlanta, my hometown, they didn't actually have a big league team, but since the white team was called the Atlanta Crackers, the Negro team was called the Atlanta Black Crackers. Would you believe it? The Grays consistently produced the champions and the best ballplayers. That was the team Josh Gibson played with. He was to the Negro Leagues what Babe

Ruth was to white baseball, and he was every bit as good a hitter.

Josh Gibson suffered a mental breakdown and committed suicide. I think it was in the late forties. He jumped out a window. Some of his close friends alleged the reason he did it was because of his frustration in not being able to break into white baseball. Everybody knew he was good enough but nobody ever gave him a chance. There may have been other reasons for the breakdown, but I haven't researched it enough to know for sure.

The white and black leagues played after the regular season. They were barnstormers. The blacks won some games and the whites won some. The barnstormers were the very best from both leagues. Bob Feller went on these trips sometimes and Dizzy Dean used to barnstorm some games against Satchel Paige. Paige would hold his own. Bob Feller was notorious for his antipathy against blacks. He was never friendly toward them, and made comments about how inferior they were even after they joined the white major league teams. He always downgraded the abilities of Larry Doby, who was with the Cleveland Indians in 1948, and Jackie Robinson who was with the old Brooklyn Dodgers. He never accepted blacks as equal ballplayers despite the great exploits of Doby, Robinson, Roy Campanella, Don Newcombe, Dan Bankhead and Sam Jethro.

Robinson played with the Kansas City Monarchs and he was certainly not the best ballplayer on their roster. He was chosen primarily because he was a college graduate and because of his temperament. Branch Rickey felt that Robinson wouldn't be so quick to pull out his razor if he got into a fight with a white ballplayer. He was a good ballplayer, but not the best on the Monarchs at the time. After Robinson broke the color line, a lot of other black ballplayers followed.

One reason the black newspapers were big at that time was they carried stories on black baseball. Of course none of this was read by the white readers. They didn't know it existed. The black papers — the Chicago *Defender,* the Pittsburgh *Courier,* the Baltimore *Afro-American,* the New York *Amsterdam News,* the Cleveland *Call and Post,* the Kansas City *Times,* the Atlanta *World,* the Birmingham *World,* the Memphis *World* — all these papers consistently carried accounts of the games. You can't imagine the popularity of Negro baseball unless you talk to some of the people who were there, or to some of the old-time players. It drew tremendous crowds.

How would you rate black and white newspapers today?

The quality is better in the *best* white press. That's why I'm convinced I can probably do more over a long period of time with the Los Angeles *Times* than, say, the Los Angeles *Sentinel.* I'm sorry to have to say that, but I think it is true. The best white press probably does a better job than the best black press.

But I want to be careful about this because most white newspapers still don't do very much on blacks. Some do. The major well-known papers do, and some have begun to make a stab at improvement. I mean papers like the *Christian Science Monitor,* the New York *Times,* the Chicago *Sun-Times,* the Chicago *Daily News,* the Los Angeles *Times,* the San Francisco *Chronicle,* the Baltimore *Sun,* the Washington *Post,* the Atlanta *Constitution,* the Miami *Herald,* the Minneapolis *Tribune,* the Des Moines *Register,* the St. Louis *Post-Dispatch.* These papers have improved in quality and quantity in writing about blacks. But I stress there is still not anything like what it ought to be.

Some of the writing is done by black reporters and some by whites. But no newspaper, including my own, has turned loose a black reporter to let him do what he ought to do as a black reporter. And that is simply to write as often as he can about the community and its problems, its prospects, its people and history. No newspaper, black or white, has turned loose a reporter to do that.

You can see this in the problems I had in being hired. I first applied to the Chicago *Daily News* for a job. I talked to the city editor who was an Irishman, very courteous and cordial, but he gave me the run around for a week. I had four interviews with this guy. Finally, in my last interview, somehow the question of my eyes came up. I told him I used reading glasses for a very minor eye problem that I have. My eyes don't coordinate well without glasses. And he said, "Oh, they don't?" He seemed gratified. I could see the relief breaking across his face. So, he said he would call me. Well, I didn't wait. I could see the handwriting on the wall. The next day I went down and talked with the people at the Chicago *Sun-Times*. A week passed and they hired me. After I started with the *Sun-Times*, the city editor of the *Daily News* sent me a letter saying he didn't think I could work for the *News* because of my eye problem. I still have that letter. One of these days I'm going to frame it as one of my personal mementos to American equality and decency.

At the *Sun-Times* they made it clear they didn't want a black reporter who would cover only stories about blacks. They wanted a general assignment reporter, capable of covering any story. I don't quarrel with that necessarily, though in actual practice most of the stories I did turned out to be black stories. Not all though. I don't really mind that, but I think the black reporter gets short changed oftentimes, especially on a major interpretative story about blacks. They give it to some white reporter, on the pretext that they can't have black reporers doing only black stories. And they always have an out too if it is a school boycott, a demonstration or explosion. They send me, or another black reporter, on the assumption that we can get the story better. Yet when it comes time to write, to do an interpretive story, they call on another guy, a white reporter, because he is alleged to be more qualified, experienced or whatnot.

I objected to this practice. It is one reason why I left the *Sun-Times*. I thought they were taking advantage of the black reporter, and doing what was beneficial to the newspaper. I even think, and I don't want to sound arrogant, that some of the pressure I generated — along with some others — has resulted in some changes at the management level.

Let me give you an example. I was particularly interested in stories about the police when I was working at the *Sun-Times*. There is a unit in the Chicago Police Department that calls itself the GIU, the Gang Intelligence Unit. It is an elite force of about two-hundred men whose job is supposed to be keeping surveillance on, gathering evidence against, youth gang members which will be used in their prosecution. The GIU has in fact become an arm of the "Red Squad," though Chicago policemen will indignantly tell you you ought to call it the "Subversive Unit." Every big city police force has a Red Squad. The one in Chicago is very notorious. It spies on, and harasses the hell out of Black Panthers, SDS members, the peace people, and anyone else the police consider a leftist.

I recall several times asking to do stories on the GIU and being turned down. So I wrote a long memo to the editor of the *Sun-Times,* explaining how a story on the GIU could be developed. I never got a response. But after I left the *Sun-Times,* there were several articles on the GIU which I thought were rather good. No such story appeared when I was there. So I think that maybe some of the ideas I argued for sunk into the conscience of management after I left. Or, maybe some of the management's own white friends might have said it's time for the *Sun-Times* to do this kind of story.

When you get to black newspapers, none of them are consistently good. Some are pretty good, some are mediocre and some are very bad. There are a couple of newspapers which show promise, one is the Milwaukee *Courier,* another the San Francisco *Sun.* The *Sun* has a good reputation because of its publisher, Dr. Carlton Goodlet. Goodlet is very militant, with money, and he has long been a defender of leftists of all stripes.

Is there a free press for black people in America today?

No. There is no free press for anybody, black or white. And I don't mean in terms of direct political censorship or control, as you might find in a totalitarian country. There is a form of control in this country, but it is indirect and very subtle, sinister really. It is exercised by people who come almost entirely from the middle or upper classes. When they come to manage a newspaper, they bring these same middle- and upper-class values. This is why in the economic aspects of newspaper publishing there are built-in biases. Ownership comes from one economic strata.

It is no secret that every publisher may lean in one direction for a particular cause or for a particular people and against other causes and against other people. Editors and publishers are frequently persuaded to withhold certain stories or to run certain stories, but the publication of the news is not the cut and dried thing that some militants think.

You see, the rich advertiser is not continually dictating to the publisher what to print and what not to print. He doesn't have to.

The publisher just isn't going to print a whole lot of what the rich advertiser doesn't like. The rich advertiser won't need to pick up the phone and tell the publisher he doesn't like the story. After some things get into print, the publisher will become aware that the rich advertiser doesn't like it. The point I'm trying to make is that the publisher and the advertiser think alike on most things, and it is their kind of thinking which consistently gets into the paper. So you don't need direct pressure from big advertisers or other well-to-do people, major politicans or influential civic or business leaders. These are the people with whom the average publisher and the average editor mingles socially anyway. He shares their ideas and their values.

Some young militants don't understand this. It is not the case that the advertiser is dictating to the publisher by saying Yes to some things and No to others. Sears Roebuck advertises in some of the black weekly papers and from time to time I know there are stories in them that Sears Roebuck doesn't like. But Sears still advertises because these papers reach the audience Sears wants to reach.

The same case can be made for a paper like the *Village Voice* in New York. It is doing well financially now, I think. The current wave of activism by both blacks and whites has given it a larger number of subscribers and, in turn, it has been able to get more advertising than it used to have. Advertisers will use the *Village Voice,* or any paper like it, if it can reach the audience the advertiser wants to reach. The clothing manufacturer may not like the liberal left-wing editorial line, but if it reaches people who will buy his clothes, he really doesn't care.

The only way to change this is in those few cases where a man, like Carlton Goodlet in San Francisco, has money but does not share the view of the upper class. The only hope is for a man with that kind of money owning a newspaper and turning his thinking to the lower income groups. You may know the story of Marshall Field III who, in the nineteen forties, was known for his liberal views, and at that time they must have been ultra liberal. He bought the Chicago *Times,* which later became the Chicago *Sun-Times.* He also started a paper in New York called *PM.* It eventually folded but it was a novel ideal in journalism, no advertising. The paper was extremely liberal, it had a lot of very left-wing people, some communists, on its staff. It reflected the concerns of the working class and those who were politically active and aware. But it folded because it couldn't support itself.

Does your work bring you into contact with the black gangs in Chicago?

Yes.

How would you describe them?

Numerically, I don't think any of the nationalists or Panther organizations are very strong. In Chicago, the largest youth gang is probably the Black P. Stone Nation which is actually a collection of black youth gangs on the South Side of Chicago, maybe thirty in all. The spokesmen for the Nation estimate membership at one hundred thousand.

I don't think they have anywhere near that many. My estimate is about ten thousand but they could possibly exceed that. Ten thousand is, I think, the peripheral membership, while the hard core membership is probably no more than three hundred or four hundred.

The other major gang in Chicago is called the Black Disciples. There is another independent gang that doesn't belong either to the Disciple Nation or to the Black P. Stone Nation. It calls itself the War Lords. Another large subgrouping of the Black P. Stone Nation calls itself the Cobra Stones.

On the West Side, there are the Conservative Vice Lords. It doesn't like to be called a gang, though the police call it one. It was once an out-and-out street gang, but it has made progress toward being a legitimate community organization. And there are the Egyptian Cobras and the Roman Saints, both of whom used to be very large, now they are small. Then there is a Puerto Rican group which calls itself the Latin Kings, and the Satan Lovers, another black gang.

The Panthers are not a youth gang. The GIU regards them as such, but it is entirely inaccurate to regard them as a gang. It is a political organization, a revolutionary political organization. The members are all young and they have a loose coalition with two other revolutionary activist groups. One is called the Young Lords. It is Puerto Rican and has a strong unit in New York City. The other is a group of young Appalachian whites in uptown Chicago which calls itself the Young Patriots. The GIU treats all three — Panthers, Young Lords, and Young Patriots as if they were criminal youth gangs, but in fact they are strictly political.

What are the attitudes of the youth gangs toward the criminal elements within the black community?

Well, first, there are criminal elements in these gangs. This is the principal difference between them and the Panthers, Young Lords and Young Patriots. Some of their members may be criminals, too. There may be some, but I don't remember offhand any member of the Panthers, Patriots or Young Lords who has been convicted of a criminal charge which I think is legitimate. They have been convicted of criminal charges, but most, if not all, were just frame-ups. The outstanding example would be the conviction of Fred Hampton who was convicted of armed robbery, maybe less than a year before his murder. It was alleged to be the robbing of an ice cream vendor of seventy-one dollars' worth of ice cream in Maywood, a western suburb of Illinois. It was such an obvious frame-up that nobody could really take it seriously. Nobody believed that Fred Hampton robbed an ice cream vendor. Panthers face criminal charges, but they are motivated by the fact that they are Black Panthers and it is a revolutionary group. Make no bones about it.

You have to make a distinction between the youth gangs and the Panthers and their revolutionary allies. The Panthers, the Young Lords and the Young Patriots are strictly and avowedly opposed to what you might call the criminal element. They are opposed to blacks oppressing other blacks through criminal acts, they are opposed to blacks selling dope and other harmful drugs to blacks. I don't think they have any programs which at the moment are designed to rid the community of these elements, but I am sure they are honest in their statements that they are opposed to it. They

259

think criminal activity is harmful to the best interests of the black community and against the efforts toward black liberation.

With youth gangs there are always varying degrees. There are criminals in some youth gangs, straight-out crooks. Some are specialists in extortion, others are specialists in intimidation. This is true, no doubt about it. There are some other youth members who stay in gangs, but who are opposed to individual acts of extortion or criminal activity. In my view, the most criminally inclined youth gang is the Black P. Stone Nation, but I think some efforts have been made recently at reform.

The Black P. Stone leadership in the last couple of years has tried to reduce the rivalry between Stones and the Black Disciples. Around 1965 to about 1968, there was intense rivalry between the Stones and the D's. Murders were very frequent, but the Stones actually came out better. There were more Disciples shot and killed than Stones. The shootings have not been eradicated, but they have been significantly reduced. The rivalry had to stop. That type of shooting simply couldn't go on. There are still shootings, but most of them are by young fellows, in the twelve to fifteen age group, who belong to neither Stones or D's.

An even more recent development has been the working relation between the Black Disciples and the Black Panther party. This was done largely through the efforts of Bobby Rush and especially Fred Hampton before he died. There is a greater awareness of black identity and pride in the community among the Black Disciples than among members of the Black P. Stone Nation. Some of the Stones merely give lip service to it. They don't really believe in it or work toward it.

How do the Chicago police, especially the black ones, respond to all this?

Badly. Some of the worst offenders in the department are black, though this is probably less true now due to the agitation of the black activists, new legislation and the work of the Afro-American Patrolman's League which is now fairly strong in Chicago.

The outspoken militancy of the Afro-American Patrolman's League in Chicago has given the impression that it was the first

260

major organization among black policemen. But the Chicago league is only the latest kind of black police group — one that has publicly split with its white counterparts. Black members of the Los Angeles Police Department had formed a unit a year ago in honor of a young officer slain in the line of duty.

The most notorious colored — I won't call him black — policeman we have in Chicago is a cop named James who uses the twin nickname Gloves or Duke Davis. His real name is James Davis. Gloves Davis has been on the Chicago Police Force for about twenty-two years and all these twenty-two years he has spent working in the black community harassing black people, trying to develop a reputation for toughness. He's succeeded. The number of black people he has brutalized is endless. He has shot people, and I believe he has killed others. He is the most notorious and brutal cop on the force, but there are others. I don't know them all, but I hear of them from time to time. Enough people tell me the stories so I know they are telling me the truth.

But as I say the number of brutal black policemen is probably smaller now than it used to be. There was once a time when almost any cop who wore a uniform, and who was black, was an asskicker. Some new blood has been infused into the force now, so percentage-wise the number of black tough cops is probably lower than five or six years ago.

To understand this fully, you have to understand the historic role of black policemen. They were never hired on any police force to enforce the law throughout the whole community. They were hired as colonial overseers to keep other black folks in line. This is consistently true. In no big city do black police in any significant numbers work in white communities. In Chicago it has just become fact that a token number of black policemen work in all twenty-one police districts. Up until about six months ago, there were six or seven districts with only white policemen. Now in these same districts there are only token black policemen. And even this token doesn't amount to much because the blacks don't really exercise that much authority — not nearly what white cops do in a white community or what blacks do in a black community.

The fact of the matter is that historically, black policemen have been used as subjects of the ruling political and social class to help enforce the law, and keep the peace in the black community. To that extent, blacks have been colonial subjects. So far as the black gangs are concerned, the police are constantly trying to get gang members to become informants. They make no secret of it. They have even been successful at it. They will favor certain individuals and use them to testify against other gang members at criminal trials. They make deals. And it is increasing.

I think it is an alarming tendency, especially on the part of the county prosecutor who will use one gang member to testify at the trial of another. They make certain promises of immunity to the one who testifies. This is standard criminal practice. And this practice didn't originate with the prosecution of gang members. It has been around a long time in Chicago.

What happens is that the prosecutor's office in any county will ask a lower-echelon syndicate hoodlum if he will testify against a higher-echelon syndicate hoodlum. If he does, protection and immunity from prosecution will be promised. Now there may be something to be said in defense of this practice, but I think more could be said in opposition to it — especially the way it is used against gang members in Chicago. The result is that the ones who win immunity from the prosecutor's office are not better, and perhaps more criminally inclined, than the ones the state's attorney prosecutes and sends to jail.

Another side of the problem is the black parent, especially black mothers and their sons. One said to me recently, "You got the cops on one side, the gangs on the other. And we can't find no way to deal with neither one of them." Thousands of other blacks in the big city feel like they are caught in the middle of a spiraling conflict between the militant youth and the hard-line surge of the law-and-order advocates. At the moment law and order is on top and youthful militancy on the bottom. I don't know who will win.

This dilemma is particularly difficult in Chicago. You see, the blacks see themselves victimized by the rising tide of crime but hesitate to call the police because they feel victimized by police misuse of power. And the relations between young blacks and the police have degenerated to the point where their struggle is engulfing all black people, regardless of how they feel about crime, the police or youth gangs.

What in hell are they going to do? Their kids are beaten up or intimidated by gang members at school and it is tough to go out at night for fear of being robbed. If they call the cops, sometimes they come, sometimes not. Blacks in Chicago don't feel right calling the cops because cops don't give a damn about black people, never have. The black mother is really bewildered and troubled on how to cope with the gang menace in her community other than by calling the police.

The police side of the story is that they are not indifferent to the plight of black people, and they, the cops, are fair game for attack themselves. Police in the Eighteenth District on Chicago's near-North Side estimate they were fired on at least thirty times in 1969 by snipers from one building in the Cabrini-Green project.* Several months ago two policemen, answering a call, were riding to an upper floor in one building when youths stalled the elevator between floors, then climbed on top of it and threw containers of flammable materials inside. They burst into flame but the policemen were able to put out the fire, then move the elevator to the next floor and get out. They were lucky.

I've checked four other police districts, the Second, Fifth, Eleventh and Twenty-first — and the number of attempts on policemen's lives is increasing at a rate approaching all-out warfare between police and community. In three of these districts there are public housing projects from which snipers fire on police, then vanish without being detected. In the Second District they estimate that firing at policemen occurs once a week, and half of the targets are black cops. Most of the sniping in the district comes from the high-rise, densely populated Robert Taylor Homes which, ironically, soars high above the sparkling new Second District police headquarters. Any reasonably good sniper could hit the station

---

* Since this interview, on July 17, 1970, two white Chicago policemen were killed instantly by sniper fire as they walked across a ball field in daylight opposite the same building in Cabrini-Green referred to by police in the Eighteenth District.

from any one of at least three Taylor project buildings. They are only one hundred yards away.

The overwhelming police response to the snipers is that either a hard-core criminal element is responsible or that militants like the Black Panthers or Black Nationalists are behind all of it. Very few see the incidents as reaction of the public to police practices.

On the other side, it is argued that the innumerable shootings and beatings blacks suffer from the police are the root cause of the antipolice hostility. Well, you can see that the two sides in this debate over practice are now further apart than ever. And the alarming aftermath of all this is that the black parents, law-abiding and hard-working, who would really prefer to get out of the projects, are the double victims of gang violence and police indifference and police hostility.

In the middle are the majority of black adults, themselves angry at both sides in the conflict, but not willing to completely join forces with either one. It is probably this reluctance that keeps this simmering warfare from becoming an all-out explosion.

What kind of police reforms would help?

A strong civilian trial board has to be established in every major city with a large proportion of blacks, Spanish-speaking peoples and poor whites. Trial boards which have representation from the local communities would be effective. I don't mean just a review board that makes recommendations. I mean trial boards with power to discipline policemen for acts of brutality against residents. It should be independent of the mayor, or any other office, and have the power to discipline the policemen directly.

A second step is to genuinely depoliticize the big city police forces. It is no secret that the police departments in Boston, Philadelphia, Cleveland, New York, Chicago and Detroit are too political. Promotions go to men who know politicians and who have done favors for them, rather than on the basis of merit. There are still too many policemen who get promotions because of whom they know. This happens even with civil service police exams. In Chicago it is notorious. There are ways of making sure the right policeman makes the right grades on the examinations.

264

A third thing is to hire more sensitive people to work on the city police force. A liberated black community which has a substantial measure, if not a full measure, of self-determination will demand policemen who are sensitive to the needs of the community. They will demand men whose primary responsibility and sympathy are toward the community's people and not toward the foreign power structure, the colonial power structure downtown. They will demand policemen who are agents of the community they serve, not agents of the white power structure, the white business community, or even of the white police chief. And just hiring more black people is not the answer, though some white liberals think it is.

The attitude of prosecutors has to change from tolerance of *any* kind of police behavior to recognizing that policemen have to be prosecuted for their crimes just like citizens do. The practice has been in all big cities that no matter how flagrant a policeman's abuse or insult to a citizen, especially a black one, he simply won't be prosecuted. This is backed up with the thinking that says, "If we do prosecute policemen, morale will go down and crime will go up." This is a preposterous and totally fallacious argument, but it has some slight basis in truth. White prosecutors think this way and some Negroes think this way: you can't tinker with police morale because crime will go up.

As a result there is a kind of gentlemen's agreement between the police and the white communities, and supported by some Negroes, that they will let the policemen monkey, mess over, and brutalize blacks and Puerto Ricans and Latins as often as they want, so long as they don't brutalize whites. They will tolerate brutalization of blacks and will not prosecute it. In exchange for white police competence in white communities, which keeps the crime rate down, the whites will say in effect, "We don't give a damn how much brutality there is. We want your morale to stay up, Johnny Cop, so you go out and mess over them niggers all you want so long as you perform in our community."

Deep down in his heart, the white liberal who lives in the suburbs feels that if he doesn't go along with all this, somehow the crime problem will spread to his community. So he says to himself, "Well, we really can't monkey with the police." This is the simplistic answer which the white liberal makes. He tells himself, "I'll kind of leave the policeman alone and let him go about his job and I won't bother him about brutality, particularly since the brutality isn't against us." Now of course if there is brutality against whites, then you may be sure white people will move on any policeman guilty of it.

These are the arguments which turn over in the minds of the white liberals as well as the white conservatives.

THE PREACHER
AND THE POLICEMAN

SINNER

I got high
last night
alone
I had an urge
to express
myself
so I started
talking to
the Bible
and it kept
telling me
to die.

— Norman Jordan
(Cleveland)

THIS PLACE CALLED HEAVEN

I've heard of a place called heaven
I don't know if I'm welcome there,
You see God painted black all over my face
And put a terrible kink in my hair,
My evening sun is sinking
I hope it goes down fast,
I've had such a hard time and miserable life
Without shoes, and a naked ass.
They keep talking about a man named Jesus
They say he died to set men free,
They must be calling me by the wrong name
Cause he's never heard of me.

— Jonathan (Beaver) Lowe
(Philadelphia)

BLACK THEOLOGY

What happens to you after you die? Do you know?

Yeah, I know. After they put you in the ground, your body turns into
— ah — bones, an' shit. Your spirit — soon as you die, your spirit
leaves you.

Where does the spirit go?

Well, it all depends. You know, like some people say if you're good
an' shit, your spirit goin' t'heaven . . . 'm' if you bad, your spirit goin'
to hell. Well, bullshit! Your spirit goin' to hell anyway, good or bad.

Why?

Why? I'll tell you why. 'Cause, you see, doesn' nobody really know that
it's a God, y'know, 'cause, I mean I have seen black gods, pink gods,
white gods, all color gods, and don't nobody know it's really a God.
An' when they be sayin' if you good, you goin' t'heaven, tha's bullshit,
'cause you ain't goin' to no heaven, 'cause it ain't no heaven for you to
go to.

Well, if there's no heaven, how could there be a hell?

I mean — ye-eah. Well, let me tell you, it ain't no hell, 'cause this is
hell right here, y'know! Yeah, this is hell right here!

What color is God? Black or White?

Well, if it is a God . . . I wouldn't know what color, I couldn' say, —
couldn' nobody say what color he is or really would be. But jus' sayin'
jus' supposn' there is a God, He'd be white, man.

Why?

Why? I'll tell you why . . . 'Cause the average whitey out there got
everything, you dig? And the nigger ain't got shit, y'know?
Y'unnerstan'? So — um — for — in order for that to happen, you
know it ain't no black God that's doin' that bullshit.

– Larry H.
(New York)

BLACK NIGHTS

Black nights
    And what did I see?
I saw an angel
    Black like me.

               – Ralph Williams
                 (Cleveland)

THE ELEVENTH COMMANDMENT
(WITH AMENDMENTS TO THE 6TH AND 10TH)

GOD:　　Thou may kill now, for business
or principle, and thou may covet
thy neighbor's ass.

But —

Thou shalt never print, publish or otherwise make known
those more graphic words per-
taining to the human genitals —

male or female,

or concerning the congress
thereof

or any other words which
might be construed by some as
being suggestive . . .

And thou shalt likewise

never describe, outline, or
portray those parts of the human
physiography directly or in-
directly (or not at all) connected with sexual intercourse

. . . (unless properly registered
as a "man's magazine")

MOSES:　　O.K. (pause). Can I say
"Fook?"

GOD:　　What?

MOSES:　　Fook. Can I say that?

GOD:　　Certainly Not!

MOSES:　　But it's not in the list.

GOD:　　I said No!

MOSES:　　But it's not —

GOD:　　Hey look, Moses. You want
to wake up tomorrow? Why
don't you go out and kill some
Canaanites or something?
Leave the morality stuff to me.

— Anonymous
(Philadelphia)

274

HATRED

"What is hatred?"
"What does it mean to hate?"
"Hatred is evil."
"Hatred is white on black."
"Hatred is Protestant against Jewish."
"Hatred is Protestant and Catholic against Jewish."
"Hatred is black against white."
"Hatred is violence."
"Hatred is the Nixon administration."
"Hatred is Soul versus Honkey."
"Hatred is 'black' versus 'toms.' "
"Hatred is old against young."
"Hatred is young not digging old."

— Anonymous
(Philadelphia)

NATIONAL BLACK INSTITUTE GREATER TRIBAL SYSTEM OF PHILADELPHIA

Behold!
The law does not concern itself
  with justice;
And men do not concern them-
  selves with virtue;
And society does not concern it-
  self with the welfare
Of its people

Wherefore, we are compelled to
  ask:
For what purpose?
Is all this business?

Even though it might be our
  swan's song

Nevertheless it is our will
To raise up the spirit of our people

To resurrect every man:
  giving strength to his character
  determination to his mind
  and courage to his heart.

Wherefore, we ask: bear witness.

The princes of this town are slow
  to action.
And the temper of the people is
  worn thin.

Corruption is the sweetmeat of
  judges
And sorrow is the product of their
  laws.

Reason and cunning, law and
  logic,
These have become the weapons
  by which to wreck the will
Of just men

Wherefore, we are overwhelmed
  by disbelief
  undermined by treachery.

Confusion and disorder creep upon
  us
And fear and doubt and tears invade our hearts.

Even friend and brother seek to
  leave us
And argue with us saying, they
  are wise.

These times are treacherous and
  governments are bad.

Wherefore, we ask:
  to whom shall we turn?
  Is there someone there?

— Anonymous
(Philadelphia)

Rabbi David Hill

Formerly Bishop of the House of Israel, David Hill is now a self-styled rabbi. His radio broadcasts each Sunday are powerful sermons against the white Christian churches. He is an orator of considerable eloquence and his wit and rhetoric make him a popular preacher. His usual theme is the Black Jesus.

Short and rotund, there is a quiet mirth and strength in him. He is a secure man deeply rooted in his religion and the need for black separatism now. He has been ridiculed and vilified by both blacks and whites, declared incompetent, a fool, and a tool. Few who have denounced him have ever met him.

Recently he was an important leader in a successful boycott of several MacDonald hamburger shops within Cleveland's Blacktown. These businesses were effectively suspended for weeks and months, and ownership is now passing into black hands. At the present time, Rabbi David Hill is in Cook County Jail awaiting charges there, after which he will return to Cleveland to face several grand jury indictments, including extortion.

I'm an orphan who lived on a plantation, in Nashville, Arkansas. We sharecropped. My father was dead before I was born and my mother was pregnant with me when she died. She died giving childbirth to me. I'm the eighth and the last. The plantation was owned by white folks named Walter Chandler and his family. They kept me till I was about nine then I lived with other blacks folks in the little community there. The blacks I stayed with would keep me in the summer and kick me out in the winter, you know, because they couldn't feed and clothe me and there wasn't any work except in the summer. I could sort of stand on my own by picking cotton and helping them make a little money, but during the winter they would find some reason to suggest that I move on.

There isn't really much difference between the plantations before and after the Civil War, or between the ones South and the ones North. I was owned. My mother, father, and the rest of us were owned by Mr. Chandler. If you left, you could be apprehended for leaving, arrested and sent back. There were about fifteen families and they had their own church and preacher and commissary there. We were paid in coupons, not money. But I was adapted to that way of life and wasn't rebellious. Nobody was. I was a typical colored boy or nigger or Negro — and from time to time they called you all of them.

There was mistreatment. The master, Mr. Chandler, and his son-in-law, they chastised you and whipped you whenever they liked, right in the field if you were picking cotton, or in the woods if you

"There is only one other place that white folks can send me, the grave. But my thing is winning. I want my people to win. I don't want to be a dead hero."

were chopping wood. They'd whip anybody, the husband, the wife, the children, you know.

The northern plantations are no different. Right here in Cleveland the slavemaster drives through his lands, not on a horse, but in black and white Fords with an inscription on the back which says "Our Men Serve All Men." That's a laugh! They beat whoever they like, the husband, wife, or children and kill them if they desire — same as on the southern plantation. There is rarely an instance where the slavemaster is actually charged with killing one of his slaves. Very seldom does he go to court. Today it is the same. There is no charge brought against a policeman for shooting a black kid down on the streets. It's justifiable.

The black people in Nashville had no one but themselves and their churches. But the religion of the plantation is the same as the religion of today, which is hoxie and phoney. What kept them there and what kept them subject to the conditions of the plantation was fear. This had been planted in black folks for years and years. This is why today many of them fear darkness, fear the cemetery, fear being out late at night, fear snakes. They were taught all this. This fear was what kept you on the plantation.

I was fifteen years old when I ran away. I went to Tyler, Texas, to find a better way of life. I felt there had to be one better than Nashville, one where you wouldn't have to pick cotton or corn or peas seven days a week and saw wood the rest of the time. There was a barber college, there, and though I didn't know what age you had to be, I thought I could learn to become a barber. I had just substituted one plantation for another. When I was sixteen — this was in 1944 during the war — I was apprehended by the police for vagrancy. They gave me a choice: go to reform school or volunteer in the U.S. Navy. So with the judge's permission, I put my age up one year; he signed as my guardian, and I was off to join the navy at Great Lakes, Illinois. When I finished my basic training they shipped me out to Hasting, Nebraska, for eight months, then to Camp Shoemaker in California and from there, overseas. The navy had agreed with me that they would not send me overseas until I was at least eighteen years old, but just as they lie about everything else, they lied about that, too. They made me a steward, working in the kitchen, until I got to Pearl Harbor where I became a gunner's mate, second class. Then I was injured in an explosion of an ammunition depot and was given a medical discharge, a hundred percent totally disabled veteran. I still carry in my back the mark, the bullet, that will go with me to my grave. They gave me the Purple Heart.

Just this year during our work with the Operation Black Unity,* they took away my disability pay. Somehow they decided I was no longer entitled to their benefits and they were cancelled. Just like that. They called me to the Veterans' Hospital one morning and the doctor said, "I'm to determine whether you'll receive money in the future, if any. I don't think there is anything wrong with you, a man who can close down a big operation like MacDonald's. There is nothing wrong with you." So a few days later, I received a letter saying that I was no longer entitled to any benefits.

After the medical discharge, I returned to Nashville to get my school girl friend, and we were married. Her father was a religious man and they were a religious family. They belonged to the Church of Christ. I was attached to that body, later becoming a minister in that denomination. The Church of Christ is one of the most racist denominations among the Protestants. It's predominantly white and they have few black churches. They send the black minister wherever they want to assign him.

Of course all churches in America are really two, one for blacks and one for the whites. It is so plain to see that they cannot be something of God. No person can take them seriously or listen to them because if it was really a church there would only be one where men and woman would assemble and give thanks to the God of the universe. There is not one church in America that is for all people.

I went through the formal seminary training, or brainwashing as

* Operation Black Unity is the general name given to the 1969 boycott effort of a dozen black organizations, from moderate to militant, in Cleveland which succeeded in closing down several, lucrative short-order shops owned by the MacDonald restaurant chain. The issue was black ownership of black consumer businesses. Rabbi Hill was one of the key leaders in the successful boycott effort which resulted in MacDonald's selling the franchise for two of the shops to qualified black entrepreneurs.

I now call it, at the Nashville Christian Institute. They call it a seminary, but I call it a cemetery because that's where they bury the truth. I was brainwashed in good fashion there until I left and was assigned my first church in Little Rock, Arkansas. It was there, in 1959, while I was pastoring, that Daisy Bates tried to integrate Central High School.

Of course I've been religious all my life. As a boy I was very religious. In fact when I was twelve or thirteen I was teaching Sunday school. At fifteen I was teaching adult classes. There is one thing that blacks have in the South and that's a lot of religion. They have plenty religion. None of it is any good, but they have plenty of it.

Nineteen fifty-nine was the turning point in my life. I guess it was just the Will of God. I was walking down Ninth Street in Little Rock, and here is a woman with a bunch of kids, two or three fellows, and a couple of signs. I passed by and spoke and she said, "Did you come to join us?" I said, "Join you? What's going on?" They were all black folks and this woman was Daisy Bates, though I did not know her at the time. She said, "Well, we're going to get into the cafeteria at Central High School. They won't let these black students in and we're going to get them in. They are supposed to eat in the cafeteria. They're hungry. Do you want to join?" So I said, "I don't care," and went along.

We went to this all-white cafeteria at the school and banged on the door and screamed and hollered and went on for a long time getting no place. The door was at street level and there was a school bus sitting there. The keys were in the bus, so I got in, backed it up and just drove through the doors right into this cafeteria. I was arrested and given one year on the chain gang. Daisy Bates and the children were given the Spingarn award of NAACP. It was in jail where I really began to think and look at society, at the conditions facing black folks, the schools, the churches. I looked at the whole system for the first time.

This time was so valuable and helpful to me because there I began to realize that calling myself a "Reverend" and a Christian minister and preaching the things that I had been taught to my folks was really supporting, condoning and strengthening slavery. I was saying to white America: I accept the position that you have put me in to help you make fools and slaves out of my people. I began to order books so I could read about Blackness. I got very angry at religion because this is what my people are all wrapped up in, and I said to myself, "They must be freed." I began to try to find a way to a more meaningful religion, one that would help free my folks rather than promise them heaven, milk and honey and a mansion as soon as they were dead and in the grave.

And I reread the Scriptures. When I was in that cemetery it had never dawned on me that Jesus himself could be black, and even the thought led me to feel somewhat guilty of sin. Such a belief was to degrade or belittle Jesus, for no one as good as Jesus could be black. My search led me to a book entitled *Sex and Race* by J. A. Rogers. It was this book which provided proof — beyond a shadow of a doubt — that not only did Jesus have black people with him, but he, himself, was black. Undebatable proof can be found in Revelations, chapter one, verses fourteen and fifteen:

His Head and His Hair were white like wool, as white as snow; and His eyes were as a flame of fire; and his feet like unto fine brass, as if they burned in a furnace; and his voice as the sound of many waters.

This description could not possibly speak of a Caucasian.

Then I read Jeremiah, chapter eight, verse twenty-one:

For the hurt of the daughter of my people am I hurt; I am Black; astonishment hath taken hold on me.

Here is Jeremiah, one of the oldest prophets, giving testimony to the fact that he is black. And of course there is the beautiful line in the Song of Songs of Solomon: "I am black and beautiful, O daughter of Zion."

When King Herod, the white Roman, sought to kill Jesus, Mary and Joseph, they were instructed to take the child and flee to Egypt, which was completely black populated land. If Jesus were white and his mother and father were white, no one would have advised them to flee into a completely black land inhabited by black people. A white family would have been spotted as easily as a sore finger.

The black historian, J. A. Rogers, went further to point out that the wildest imagination of any black person today would not permit him to think a white man with a pregnant white wife would have appeared at a hotel in Bethlehem seeking a hotel room to have a baby and being denied that privilege. Joseph was black. Mary was black. They heard the words that night which black people have heard ever since at hotels and motels: "There is no room in the inn."

Jesus was made white by the first white Christian church, led by the pope of Rome. This church sought to dominate the world and establish white Christianity over the majority of the people of the world, which was, and still is, black. It was under Pope Leo III in the last years of the eighth century where we find the first hint of — not only changing Jesus' color — but also the color of the original Jews who were black people. During the Council of Nice, the pope stated that to be a follower of Christ, one had to be white within just as Christ was white without.

From then on, slow but sure, white pictures were painted of a white Jesus and placed in Bibles, homes, schools and churches. Black people began to worship and accept this version as the Savior. The true black was once again crucified and nailed to a cross of prejudice.

It took me some time to find the real blackness in the Bible. At first I was trying to find it to fit into the church today. I did not see the black man coming away from the church and becoming a part of some other religion. It was my hope that he could find a way to fit into this church and find his own identity by so doing. It was a couple or three years later when I discovered that it would be humanly impossible for a black man to really be a man and be identified with what is commonly called Christianity in this country. I finally began to see that so-called Negroes in America were the children of Israel, the chosen race of God, the real Jews. So many Scriptures revealed this to me that I decided that when the door would swing open and I would walk out of that chain-gang pea farm I would have a different mission in life, that I would try to

awaken my people to what I consider the true religion for them —
the House of Israel. And through this religion they would discover
their identity.

How successful have you been in converting your own folks?

Well, when we organized the House of Israel in 1966 there were
four people involved, my wife and myself, her brother and his wife.
From four people we have in attendance at each Sunday service
about four hundred fifty to five hundred people and I would say
eight or ten times that many sympathizers and well-wishers
throughout the black community. We have moved out of our first
headquarters. We have large congregations now in five states.

Each time we assemble, a dozen "church-going Negroes" become identified with the House of Israel and leave various denominations. We are even taking pastors away from their Christian
flocks. My radio broadcasting especially is directed to this church-
going Negro, this colored man who goes to church and supports his
own enslavement each and every week. I'm trying my best to reach
him. To do it, I must destroy what he believes in the most, and
that is the slavemaster's religion, with the white Jesus and white
Mary and white Joseph. There is no freedom for the black man as
long as he's a part of the white man's religion. I often make the
statement that the first step is to remove the white man's cross from
around your neck.

Needless to say, my fellow ministers hate my very soul, in fact
many of them claim I don't have a soul. When it comes to Rabbi
David Hill, they can become un-Christian. They don't like it and
the fact that they are losing their members makes them fight even
harder. They tell all sorts of lies, for example, that I have my own
Bible. That is the reason I can come up with all this black stuff, you
know. Or they say I'm not an official rabbi and haven't been ordained in any rabbinical school.

Our service at the House of Israel is very simple. We have songs,
black songs that relate to life and to the struggle. Then someone
deals with black history for the period we call worship service and
then I bring a message. At the end of the service, you stand and
state the pledge to the nationalist flag, the black, the red and the

n — which symbolizes first, blackness, then red for the blood that must be shed, and the green for life itself. We ask everyone to stand and raise their right hand in the symbol of black power, a clenched fist, and state the pledge:

All power to the people, black power to black people, ebony power to the vanguard, one nation, one flag, uniting all brothers and sisters or perish. Salaam!

A greater number of blacks you can just forget, I'm sorry to say. They are so white in their minds that it's just like they sing in their churches, "Though you slay me, yet I'll serve you." In other words there is nothing that can be done to awaken them or bring them around. They are beyond help. But the young today, the young blacks, are entirely different. That is why the House of Israel is made up of a large number of young folks because they are the ones thinking different. Jesus said, "It is hard to put new wine in old bottles," meaning that it is really difficult to change old folks, so it is the youth we try to reach through our community programs. Their minds are ready.

When we do reach the older or middle-aged person he has to have had some experience with society. He works on a job and knows that he is the first to be fired because he's black or that the boss treats him badly because he's black. Or he has been involved with the police, with the law, or the city if he owns property. Surprisingly, a great number of folks that own property become members because they can easily understand what I am saying. They catch hell. They'll go and buy the old building that the man who lives in the lily-white suburb is going to sell. The building is run down and still he gets three times what it's worth. The minute he buys it, the city inspectors come out and condemn it. When this happens, they usually go out trying to find help. Then they come to the House of Israel. They've got to be convinced and this is what I'm trying to show them: that the system is against them. But as long as he feels that he is part of the system and that he's an American citizen and that this is the best of all possible worlds, you're just not going to reach him.

This is what made our MacDonald's boycott such a beautiful thing. It was really beautiful to see how a total black community responded to our pleas to stay away from MacDonald's shops. And they did. They really stayed away, in spite of the fact that the organized black leaders were telling them to open the shops and for people to patronize them. That successful boycott brought us many, many members. People with property began to see how it could be done. You don't have to burn it down. You don't have to shoot and kill. All you got to do is to stop his cash register from ringing. So they said, let's get with a group that is going to work along this line.

Black folks want to be free but they have such fear, you know. The slavemaster has put this fear in him, that he is going to jail if he does this or that. One thing black folks fear is jail, but many of them are waking up. They're stepping out of fear. We have had people on the picket line who have never been on a picket line before, not even with Dr. King.

This is the thing we try to give people that come to the House of Israel, true freedom. It's better to be a man just one day — even if it lasts only one day — than to be a boy all your life.

You see, the House of Israel advocates freedom, not violence. When we were preparing to move out against MacDonald's, the news media and papers said, "Blood is going to flow like water. The Black Nationalists are going to picket MacDonald's." They told lies. Later *Time* magazine said that not even the late Dr. King had ever carried out a boycott as peaceful as this one. Oh, he has the right to violence. Because of the violence inflicted upon him, he has the right. But he can't win through violence.

There is a better way. I believe the better way is by joining together, uniting together and using the sort of tactics that we did during the Operation Black Unity. There is no winning through violence. That is why in our instruction classes at the House of Israel we place great emphasis on the "coward with the gun." We put out a little bulletin showing a fellow with a gun in his hand and the caption reads: "I'm looking for someone to kill, white if possible, but anybody." We brand him as a coward because so many youth are in the street with a gun. It's not only whites they are destroying, they are also killing blacks. We now have a law that any person caught with a weapon that carries a citizenship card in the House of Israel is suspended for sixty days for the first offense. On the second offense, they are put completely out, excommunicated. It would destroy the whole movement if some John Doe who belongs to the House of Israel goes out in the street and shoots somebody with a gun.

We have a stronger weapon than a gun. We've got the truth. We believe that we should deal with the truth and convert the black people, the "Negroes," to this truth. There would be no power on earth that could stop us. My thing is winning. We're definitely opposed to violence, but you see it popping up. We look for it again this summer. I'm convinced that more white folks, especially those representing the law, are agitating and working toward this open warfare. They would like nothing better than to carry out their plans of genocide on a whole race of black people. In fact, during the early seventies I see a move toward genocide by the white racist police departments across the country. And when they speak of Black Panthers, they mean Black Baptists, Black Methodists and Black House of Israelites, and any other black persons that seek justice in this unjust society. We must hang together or we will hang one by one. I want my people to win and my theory is that we cannot win in the streets. I don't want to be a dead hero. I want to win by closing down businesses. I want to win by being able to control the schools. So through tracts, pamphlets, literature, and radio, from the pulpit and from house to house, we try to educate the black community to Black Christian Nationalism. And once this sleeping tiger wakes up, there will be no power on earth that can stop it.

What is Black Christian Nationalism?

It is what we preach in the House of Israel. It is a new church and a new theology. It means first that Jesus is a black man, in fact a Black Nationalist, a man very concerned about the nation, Israel. Being a black Jew his whole teaching was to pull out from under the yoke of the white Roman government those lost sheep of the House of Israel and restore their nation to them.

288

There is no time now to prepare man to die and go to heaven. We are trying to teach him how to live now, here on this earth: to control the black community, to control the dollars spent here, the school where his children must receive an education, the police department that sets out here on the plantation, the hospitals where he goes when he is sick. Everything that exists on the plantation, the black should control. This earth right here can become heaven. This is the heaven we are concerned about and the one I teach about, rather than the one you're going to fly to with some wings and with flowing robes on.

Black Christian Nationalism is the religious movement that is going to bring back the House of Israel, the dry bones that have fallen asleep.

We believe that we have already passed from death to life through that resurrection whereby one is changed from being a colored boy or Negro to a black man. When one has been born again, he is resurrected. So as long as he's scratching his head and saying "Yes, sir" and the things white folks want to hear him say he's a dead man. Once he accepts black theology and the doctrine of God's Will being done on earth, once he begins to relate to a movement that is working for control of the black community and a new identity for the black man, he has been resurrected and he will have eternal life. There is no "beyond the grave" anymore. Once he has been resurrected there is no death. He may go through other forms of change, but he now has eternal life.

I teach also that we're going to reign with a God a thousand years right here on this planet even after the changes we'll all go through, that we will reign with him right here on this present earth during the millennium.

This is a bigger and richer notion than Black Nationalism. I do not see a black political party coming into existence and becoming the vanguard of the movement. It will be a religious movement. I'm convinced of this; all history tells me this; the Bible tells me this. The black man will be awakened and resurrected through a religious movement. This awakening is really beautiful and it is coming on in Africa and around the world. Black people are beginning to resurrect and come together. That's why I know they will not

289

inflict upon the oppressor what he has inflicted upon them. I don't see blacks being capable of committing such sins and crimes as Gentiles have done. They are really soul people. They are God's folks.

You see, Israel, the black people of God, never had a separate government. There was the church, the temple and the rabbi; he was the spiritual leader, the judge and all. He was it. They dealt directly with him. This is what we teach: that there will be a theocratic government whereby the church, its laws and orders, will be handed down directly from the temple.

When you are able to give a person a religion he can identify with, he doesn't have to go around constantly trying to change his name, saying that he is Afro-American this or Afro-American that. Once he accepts the House of Israel, his history is laid before him and he can work in that framework. In time the House of Israel will become the religion for black folks across the country.

You spoke of Jesus being black. Is God also colored?

No. Neither is Jesus colored. God is black. If Jesus was colored, I wouldn't want to follow him. God is black and Jesus is black. If they are not black, there will be no black folks in heaven. You see, I cannot separate God from being in a body, incarnated. To me God manifested himself in Jesus. This is God in the flesh, manifested in the flesh. I do not see a trinity of Gods, three men sitting up somewhere in the sky looking down here on earth, you know, God the Father, God the Son, God the Holy Ghost. But I do believe that God created everybody. Yes, he did. This is contrary to some, but I believe God created even white folks.

In the House of Israel, we define the soul as being three parts. First there is the soul as the individual, the outward part you see here. The second part is what God breathed into man, the living soul. You cannot see the living soul. You are not looking at David Hill but only the house that he is in. David Hill is inside. The third part of the soul is that soul of God that's of man, also inside the individual person. I teach folks to begin to see God in us, in one another, and get their minds out of the sky.

290

Can God be in white folks?

Well, God can be any place he likes but inasmuch as he said he wouldn't dwell in an unclean temple, I don't think he'd be in no white folks; no, I wouldn't think so. They lost their last chance of salvation when they beheaded Paul. He was the apostle to the Gentiles and this was the last apostle God sent to the Gentiles.

Here I disagree with Reverend Cleage* who says that Paul was an Uncle Tom. I think Paul was a very clever man because when they caught him uptight and were about to kill him, he simply said, "I'm a Roman citizen." He was trying to save his neck and I think he was a wise man. Many times he had to condescend and wait till his right time came. He makes it very clear he was a Jew, that he was of the tribe of Benjamin. He was a great man, a black Jew and the last apostle to the Gentiles.

There will be no more apostles that God sends to the white man. Paul was the last. Every prophet from that time forward has been sent to the lost sheep of the House of Israel. You will read in the Bible that Jesus was very much a separatist, very much a militant. He forbade his preachers to preach to anyone except to the lost sheep of the House of Israel. The white man once had all the privileges that the black man has now, until he forfeited them. He had the privileges, the opportunity to be grafted, as Paul puts it, "to the wild olive tree." He had the opportunity but he lost it.

There are some fine and sincere whites and I must say that a great deal of my support comes from whites. I must admit this. I would say that half of the three or four hundred letters I get each week come from whites who are asking more about my teaching and who send donations regularly to keep me on the air. There are whites just as concerned about black control of the black community as I am, who are trying to see the real message and the whole truth without walking in the footsteps of the total race. Yet the pressures that will be brought upon them from the system and from society will almost prevent them from being able to come out and really support us in a true sense or take a stand that will be helpful.

* Reverend Albert Cleage of the Shrine of the Black Madonna in Detroit has expressed his views in *The Black Messiah* (Sheed and Ward, 1968).

And you know there is only one thing a white racist hates more than a black man, a white person who helps the black man.

I do not see the white race as a whole, as the white Gentile people, being accepted or being offered a plan of salvation now. Not that there is not one, but they won't change their ways and accept it. The one thing the white man won't change in his ways. At this state there can be no such thing as integration, but only separation.

Our black theology is saying that God must find a spot in your life to connect with that vacancy in your soul to make man complete. This is our argument in "Let us make Man." Today we are assisting God in making man. In Genesis 1:26 it says, "Let us make Man in our image and likeness and let him have dominion . . ." Today in black theology, God is calling upon the black man to assist him. God is saying, "Let *us* make Man. Let *us* make him in our image, after our likeness." God, being black, is calling on the black man to assist him in making man.

And this is what was meant in Exodus, "Out of Thee shall all nations be blessed," meaning *all* peoples. I firmly believe that what I'm advocating now — in spite of those five indictments* — is not just for black folks. As the late Dr. King often pointed out: his works and demonstrations in seeking better jobs for blacks would ultimately help the whites as well. This then is our teaching, "Let us make Man," and this reaches out. As the black man begins to elevate himself with the God within he will become more like God and so help man in general. Right now the black man must be separate so man can be made. Once the resurrection comes upon the black man there may be an occasion for the white man to join the human race. But at this point, there is no such thing as integration and no need to fight for this thing. Now we need to "make Man." Let man be elevated and resurrected. Let the grave open up, and let man be brought to where God ordains him to be. When these things happen, when man is no longer in the grave, no longer wrapped in grave clothes, when the stone has been removed, then we can say: let man work together for the betterment of all people

* Rabbi Hill has been indicted by the grand jury in Cleveland on several charges, including extortion, for his role in Operation Black Unity.

and let there be a heaven on this earth. But if there were only a black political party, none of this would be brought about.

It is through this black theology, taught by the House of Israel, that we must reach the young blacks today. We must show them how to have fine, clean, healthy bodies by purifying themselves of drugs and wine so they can be strong, both in body and mind. Then they'll be able to realize there is a Supreme Being. I've found so many young blacks as I've traveled around the country who have such great zeal and want to be black. They really want to belong, till they go out and then make fools of themselves. Usually the first thing they declare is that there is no God, to hell with God. Well, the House of Israel is trying to show them that you do not want to damn God because of the fact that you've been taught he is a white man. We're trying to reach the young with the idea of the black Jesus. If we don't reach them there is going to be trouble, riots, turmoil and killing in the streets. And that is not going to help either the white man's country or the nation we are trying to build. It won't help either one.

Who do you regard as the modern prophets of this new religious movement?

Well, it might have been Malcolm X had he lived. Some folks think Malcolm was a little confused when he came back from his visit to Mecca and talked about white and black people together. But it wasn't Malcolm who was confused, but the people who wrote about him. You will never convince me that he came back and decided that black and white people were going to join hands together and work for integration, that Malcolm was going to join the NAACP.

The two largest groups of blacks ever brought together in this country were brought by Marcus Garvey and the Honorable Elijah Mohammed. They brought many more than either Malcolm or Dr. King. Garvey was a pioneer in laying down Black Nationalism in this country and his value will not be clearly known for many years to come. And the Honorable Elijah Mohammed, especially when Malcolm was a part of it, was really moving. That is not true today.

I've been to many meetings where they say, "We won't have any leaders, just everybody do their own thing." I'm not of that school because I know where there's no leader, things are going to fall apart. A man will come forth.

I have even had a number of people who wish to make me a God. This was true with Jesus. Constantly they wanted to make him a king, or make him the Ultimate God, the Last Word. He was the promised Messiah, of course, and we accept him as the one to lead the children of Israel out of their white captivity. It is very, very dangerous to bring about a theology to deal with this problem. It is dangerous because we have many who sit in the temple who want to do away altogether with the idea of a Supreme Being or a Divine Being.

Not long ago I spoke to a group in St. Louis and I could see they were disappointed in me. It was written all over their faces. I was sorry because they were looking to find someone to endorse what they were doing. They didn't find it in me. What I fear is a black political or a black military party coming up, getting all the youth with their zeal and energy, yet lacking the genuine knowledge to build. This is why there must be something more than a black political party. If America is really going to be saved — and I mean both black and white America — it will be black theology that will save it. It is righteousness which will exult the nation.

The powers we are wrestling with are not the powers of the Jews versus everybody, or the Irish against the Italians, or the blacks against the whites. Sin is a reproach to any people, whether they be red, pink, blue or yellow. If you can let God come into your life, you begin to move against evil, not against the person. Paul said, "We are wrestling not against flesh and blood, but against principalities and power." We are moving against spiritual wickedness in high places. We're moving against that evilness and we purge it wherever we find it. It will make heaven right here for all men, for all people. Even the enemy will come to love you. The lion and lamb will come together.

So we need to become one, but not at present. Sometimes it is even important for a husband and wife to separate for a while so they might be able to come together later and find the real love they have for one another.

294

How dangerous is your work, Rabbi?

Well, there is only one other place that white folks can send me, the grave. I've cast my anchor here in Cleveland and here I'll stay. It's not the length of the ministry but the quality of it that counts. Violence is always present but again I say, my thing is winning. I want to win. I want my people to win. I don't want folks to read good books about me and say, "The Rabbi died beautifully . . ." I don't want to be a dead hero.

Gilbert Branch

Gilbert Branch is a member of two American minority groups, the black people and the police force. As deputy chief of detectives in the district attorney's office, he has earned an excellent reputation as a specialist in homicide. He grew up in North Philadelphia, spent two years at Virginia State College and served with the air force in Korea. He was a uniformed policeman and a detective in the homicide division of the Philadelphia Police Department for eight years, rising to sergeant and lieutenant before transferring to the district attorney's office.

296

Gilbert Branch has a brother named Stanley, a so-called black militant. Stanley also works for the black people, but he usually faces Gilbert on the other side of the line. It has been said that the white man turns black brother against black brother so they will destroy themselves, but this is not the case with Gilbert and Stanley. They need one another very much these days and so, one suspects, does the City of Philadelphia need both of them working together.

My mother and father were born in Virginia and my father's father in Haiti. My mother's parents were born in Virginia and my mother's mother was Indian and white, she married a black man. Most of my family are fairly militant. I find that the militant members of the family are lighter-skinned people. Complexion-wise, I'm about the darkest one in the family. My brother Stanley is almost as light as you are, with reddish-black hair.

There are six children in my family, three brothers and two sisters, at least three of them have been very active, especially Stanley who has been in the NAACP, CORE and many other groups.

I guess you are always aware of being a black person, especially when you are a very little boy, but then it is the shamefulness of being born black. When you get older it sometimes changes. I think now about an incident that happened several years ago when there was a riot in Newark in 1966 (??).

I was sitting in a hotel lobby just after the riot and there was a black power conference going on. People with all kinds of garb and strange dress were waiting around. I was then a sergeant in the police department and I was waiting to bring Floyd McKissick, my brother, my brother-in-law, and Rap Brown back to Pennsylvania. I was in a bar, in plain clothes, with all the news people. There was also another black guy who was pretty well drunk and also a couple of news people who were pretty well drunk.

You must realize I used to be ashamed of some of the things that black people did and I used to think that this was wrong in a white cultural system. But this day in that hotel when the bartender kept talking to me about this one colored guy who had been drinking

297

and was getting louder, I began to wonder. He said, "He's a disgrace to the race," and then told me I ought to take him out of there. I was just sitting there thinking that the two white news guys were making a lot more noise than the colored man but nobody considered them a disgrace to their race, nobody said they should be put out because they were white. And I thought then that everybody in the black society seems to be in one bag.

I started reflecting more on how I used to react when I saw a black person who wasn't properly dressed in a group, or didn't have a tie on in a restaurant. I thought about all the different garbs, no shoes and things like that. It meant nothing to me, it was just what he or she wanted to wear, like it was their business. Then I thought about all the other places I had been where the whites come and wear whatever they want to wear and it is accepted. No one says anything. Then I realized that there was nothing wrong with being black but you had been made to believe something was wrong — and you had to uphold positions for everybody else, especially white people.

Did this affect your police work?

I don't really think so. I have always felt that being a policeman is more than just a hard chore. I always felt like you were being used. For example, one time they called me in when there was a big to-do about a service building under construction; about no blacks working on the contract, no black electricians or plumbers. There was picketing and people lying in the streets and things like that.

My brother Stanley was in the movement to halt the construction and so they said to me, "Because of your brother and your relation with the militants, would you just go over there and work with them and let us know when they are going to picket?" They talked like it was a big benefit to society itself — and a lot less hazardous for them as well. I refused. I said that basically I don't think they would tell me because everyone knows I am a policeman. I also told them that, although I have been a black policeman all my life, I have got to be black when I am not a policeman. They said I had the wrong attitude, but from that time on, it was rare that I was involved in demonstrations.

What do you mean?

I mean that I am not going to go against my race. And I mean also that there is not a black policeman, or very few anyhow, that weren't raised in the black ghetto. And if he still doesn't live there now, he is so close to it that if he slips, he is going right back there. And when you think you can't understand the ghetto, you can't live in it, then you can't understand your people. You have forgotten your own culture.

I have worked with a lot of white officers on Saturday nights. We have walked down the streets of Philadelphia, on Columbia Ave. and on South Street. And they will say, "What's going to happen?" They can just feel tension, and yet it is just a normal Saturday night. It is no more different to me than it would be for someone in his white neighborhood to come over Saturday night and play pinochle or canasta.

When you have a black policeman forgetting that Saturday night on Columbia Avenue is just part of the black culture, he has been brainwashed. Sometimes he forgets and will think that something is going on when it isn't. The Lord forbid that he ever has to go back to that community again. They will recognize him for what he is.

Some of your black brothers would like to see you dead, right?

I'm sure of it. I appear to be part of a white power structure which has kept black people in ghettos. And I agree. I believe strongly that I have been part of the establishment and have kept them in ghettos. That is why I really can't get upset when they start hollering and having confrontations. We should have expected it to happen. We perpetuated it years ago.

Take my brother Stanley and me. We are very close and I suppose it is strange that we get along so well. I disagree sometimes about the way he goes about things but we never disagree about getting it done. The most important thing is whether it works or not.

I have wanted to quit and have even turned in my badge a couple of times. They didn't accept it, which may be good or bad. It is a terrible job but I feel like somebody has to do it. Somebody has got to represent the black community within the police department. Somebody has to stand up and say what he thinks is right. And if it is not me, then it will be another guy. I would rather it be me than another guy. I might as well stay and fight it out.

The only sure way is to make certain that now we are doing something. Maybe it won't do very much, but five years from now it will mean that somebody can get educated and have a better job.

Do you think Stanley wants you to quit the force?

I think Stan respects me more than anyone else. He is fighting policemen and getting caught by police so often, I guess he sees the problems better than most. Of course there is a steady stream of people coming in to see me with problems, and Stanley sends them. I am sure Stanley would be very hurt if I were to leave the police department.

Do we have equal law enforcement in the black and white communities?

No, surely not. There is no equal application of the law whether in the white or in the black communities. Some poor whites are worse off than the blacks. Of course I know the black ones better. I have done some service in white communities but I wasn't received too favorably. The white people would talk only to the white policeman even if I outranked him, and even when I was doing homicide work. They would direct their answers to the white detective rather than to me who was asking the question. But that is no different in the black community. My own people would rather talk to the white policeman than to me.

There is harassment of black people in general and there are selective investigations, whether intentionally or not. You must know that in a black neighborhood the kids will be chased off the corner and in the white neighborhoods the policemen will stand and talk to them or leave them alone. I try to do the same thing. I try to leave the black kids on the corner and just tell them to keep the noise down.

But it is more serious with groups like the Black Panthers. There has always been a "conspiracy" against anyone who says anything that is antiwhite, and the Panthers fit into that today. But it was always this way. Whoever is the big guy is the one to go out and get. Today it is the Panthers.

If you are picked up on whatever the charge and they look and see Panther literature, you will get twenty times the screening that you would have before. Having a rifle or shotgun in your house is no criminal offense unless a militant or Panther has one. Then it is like the end of the world. Recently four young black kids rented a house and they had five or six rifles there and they were held on fifty thousand dollars bond apiece. I expect they didn't intend to do much good with them but just on the surface. Not one of them had a record and the rifles were legitimately theirs. The reason for the heavy bail was they found some literature, not Black Panther literature, but involving some black movement which, according to our Civil Disobedience Squad, was closely aligned to the Black Panthers.

Now if this happened to the sons of white liberals, you would hear plenty and there would be articles and editorials. I am sure that when white people say that the punks should be smacked down, they mean someone else's kids, not their own.

These black kids will sit three or four months in the city prison and it won't make them any better. It's been said that jails are the best vice-producing institutions we have. There is a lot of truth in that because the young will associate with the older convicts who have been around longer. Today for example you may arrest a fellow for something and sit down and talk with him and find out he is basically a nice guy but got into trouble for various reasons. You feel a little compassion for him and you go into court. I never get mad about what they say about me. They will say I coerced a confession or whatever. I know I didn't; so it doesn't bother me.

There was a guy recently, about twenty-one years of age, who I talked to and he cried on my shoulder like a baby. We got to be good friends and then he had to wait in jail for about eight months before coming up for trial. I had occasion to be in the cell block to see someone else and I saw him. I went over to him for a few minutes. My job, after all, is to catch someone who has done wrong. I testified the truth in court. You do what you have to do, you win or you lose, but that is the end of the game. But not for this fellow. He was so arrogant he called me everything he could call a person. He was really bitter toward me. He wasn't the nice guy he was before. He was against the whole of society, angry about everything. You would have wished he hadn't gone to jail. He would have been a better guy if he had been freed. When he comes out he will be a real problem.

He may join up with young black ex-GI's, from twenty-one to twenty-five years of age. When they get started, they are the most militant of the militants. We don't have any gang structure like Chicago but we have probably more gangs. We have more than seventy-five different gangs, but nothing on the scale of the Black P. Stone Rangers or the Vice Lords. We have small gangs that take in maybe a block and a half. Some of these gangs have businesses of their own and one had a newspaper.* They have laundromats and car washes. I'm not totally against the gang structure particularly if you don't have a strong parental life. You got to have some control from somewhere and the gang is really the only thing that controls these kids. If it can be kept in proper perspective, it can give these kids pride and leadership.

When the black gangs move into the white neighborhoods there are bad problems. We have this particularly in West Philadelphia

---

* *Dig This Now!*, a South Philadelphia newspaper written and edited by young black gang members age eleven to twenty-one. Some of the poetry in this volume is taken from *Dig This Now!* with the permission of the editor, Otho Boykin, Jr.

and Southwest Philadelphia. White kids have their gangs already formed there and every once in a while a black gang will go over and run through and beat up everybody they see. And this brings up another problem. We had one white gang member kill a black boy, and he was released on nominal bail. In a day or two he got probation. There is no such thing as a black boy being released on nominal bail. This really creates problems, yet this is what the judge felt like in this particular case.

We do try to coordinate these gangs through the recreation department so they use the same field or center. We try to integrate some of them but most places just don't want these problems. If they keep gang members out and only allow the boys who are not going to do any fighting, it causes problems. If anyone even suspects a kid of being a member of a gang, or prone to any kind of violence, they keep him out of the recreation centers, off the yards. This doesn't help at all. But you always have a lot of people around that want to help the goodies, the ones that aren't going to fight in the first place.

In spite of these problems, Philadelphia doesn't have the gang problem, or the urban guerrilla warfare problem, that Chicago has. Philadelphia always seems somehow to be a few years behind. I think this may be good because we have more time to look at the situation and try to do something about it before it is really on us.

Is there a black policeman's association here?

We have what is called the Guardian Civic League. It is different than the Afro-American Police League which is probably a little more militant. What is happening is that there is an effort being made to set up a national conference of police societies which is a black national police organization. It will stand for more black policemen and better promotional procedures for black policemen. We want to make any black police problem a national one, just like the white policemen do. They have their organization called the Fraternal Order of Police (FOP).

303

Are you a member of the FOP?

Yes, but it would be better if all black policemen were in one strong black national police organization. The FOP gets into a lot of politics both national and at the state level. There can be a real conflict for the black policemen if you get mixed up in what's good for the policeman and what's good for the community. They sometimes get on opposite ends of the scale and whether it is stated that way or not the other end is usually the black community. The poor community is the black community. The crime-ridden community is the black community. And when you get a national or state leader of the FOP who comes out for George Wallace for President, and you should shoot all looters, you know he is not speaking for black policemen. And the black community knows that he is our spokesman and sometimes they think you are going along with this sort of thing. You get mixed emotions as a black policeman.

What does it mean to be a black policeman? How many roles do you have to play?

Well, any policeman is a member of a minority group. You have to be sympathetic to the policeman, black or white, because he is in a group all by himself. Many times he is isolated, an island. There is first the black at the bottom or the Puerto Rican, then the poor white and then comes the policeman just above them. If the policeman slips, he goes right back to where he came from, the bottom.

The black policeman plays lots of roles. He knows the black community where most of the crime is. He knows that the black criminal has always been a sort of society guy for young blacks. We didn't have any doctors or lawyers that came out of the ghetto. The only guy we read about when we grew up were the gambler and the big-time spender. So the black policeman is closer to this guy than he is to the doctor or the lawyer.

And today when we are producing a few doctors and lawyers, the situation is not getting any better. I once thought I could persuade some professional people to come to some of our ghetto meetings and get involved with the kids. But it turns out everybody has got other things to do. We couldn't get very many black middle-class people out at all. And the ones that came didn't know how to relate to them. It is amazing how quickly you can forget the language of the ghetto, and you don't even know what the kid is saying. You have escaped the ghetto and you don't want to come back.

While policemen are like these black professionals; they have very little dealings with black communities. They hear a lot of things but they just don't know how to react. They don't know how to handle a lot of young black kids. When you get a group around, if you don't have command of the situation, you are going to have a hard time. They are going to embarrass you and call your names. Take the word "pig." That doesn't particularly bother me so long as we have some kind of dialogue. If it is "Pig!" with a brick following behind it from the roof, well, that is a different story. But if we are having some conversation and we are talking, I don't care much what they call me so long as they listen and I listen, and we have some understanding. If the policeman gets turned off about being called a "pig," he will never know what the problem is because they always start the conversations with "Here comes the pigs."

The white policeman often feels differently about it. It turns them off. But that doesn't solve the problem. The problem means more than your little vanity.

Black kids do other things too that a black policeman knows about. A black policeman can walk quickly up to a troublemaker, say something, take his knife away and keep walking without ever looking around. And the community people will disperse in a couple of seconds. And sometimes the guy will continue to say something to you and you don't do anything positive in return. But if you do something positive, like pulling your gun, you have acted too fast. In two seconds time, that gun has lost all value. The gun is worth one hundred times more in your holster than it is in your hand, because now he is looking at it.

You see the biggest thing to any policeman is to be accepted in the community. He has got to be accepted. And to me this is not just by the white community or the black community but by the entire community. I would rather work in a black neighborhood. I feel I am doing more good in a black neighborhood. But I get as much pleasure, maybe more, being spoken to in a white neighborhood; because then people know I am there to help them as much as my own brothers. But hardly anybody says anything to me in the better white middle-class neighborhoods.

I'm not complaining. But I don't feel, as I once did, that there is more community support in the black community than in the white community. Truly I think all black policemen feel very uncomfortable in both communities.

Finally it may be something more than just being a policeman, black or white. It is about conning. I tell it like it is, though the black community sometimes wants me to call it more than what it is since they have been oppressed so long. They think a little lie won't hurt if you push it. I don't say it was right if it was wrong.

I believe that people are sophisticated enough that you just can't bullshit them any longer. You have to tell the truth. I just don't believe in lying to people about what could happen and what will happen. And there are so many things that have to be done. Certainly the communities need more black policemen. You need a real concentrated effort to get some decent homes for the community. You get tired of licenses and inspections when you still have to live and pay rent and you don't have any place to turn. There are so many things.

But the black community will have to stop conning everybody. You know that there are some liberal whites that have money for certain projects. So the blacks say, "This is just a big con job and I am going to get what I can get." Some of those liberals can really aggravate you too. At the meetings some black guys will come in and the white liberals will ask what they are doing, and the black militant will say something unintelligent. He should know better. And I will look at him and say, "Why the hell did you say that?" And he will say, "What's the difference? They liked it. They liked for me to be ignorant." But it is we who know more about the situation than the "do-gooders." It is such a big con game out here. The "do-gooders" don't know how often they are being conned. I know because I was part of the con myself and that is the worst part. You do whatever you got to do to survive, but nothing ever benefits. Somebody always get something out of these programs but there is never progress.

I think that the black community must stop feeling it has to bull-shit the world to get by.

THE TRIAD

AIN'T NO WAY TO FIX A DREAM

Ain't no way to "fix" a dream, brother!
Long phrases, and pretty words only confuse me.
Wide open hurt, exposed astonished.
Gone are the moments, tender in themselves.
As gone are they, so goes my mind — my residence.
Thinking during peace — leisure, love, and leaving.
Call to swift meadowlarks, quickly gone.
Demand response of walls — or images at church.
But no longer desire an answer of the past.
It has fled, a dream broken . . . wake up, brother!
Ain't no way to subdue me, brother.
No, just ain't no way.
Disappointed, worried, YOU are the failure.
Lost are your attempts to walk above me.
As lost are they, so lose your words *with* me.
Laughing at your depth, your authority — your trifling.
Reach out to stop me, but it's too late! !
Keep me from jobs, and positions you pride.
But do not deceive yourself that I am beaten.
For I plan, *unsubdued* . . . watch out, brother!

– Tamera Brown
(Cleveland)

ATTENTION: ALL NIGGERS

Niggers of the world,
The hour of decision has come.
Procrastination has been interred
With the bones of Malcolm, with
The dreams of Martin, in
The ashes of Detroit and Watts.

Sons of slavery and oppression,
Awake and live.
Awake or die.
Live, Die.
But, for God's sake, do something.

— T. P. Mathis
(Philadelphia)

ADAPTATION ON THE BURNING OF TROY

Walk lightly down the dark hallways of Priam's palace
upstairs a sniper is waiting
outside the walls of Detroit are burning
Cassandra screams as the National Guard beats her and takes her away
Pyrrhus rushes up and into the blackened room
a quick burst and it is all over for the Viet veteran come home
an old man tied up in the corner curses silently as he watches.
meanwhile — Aeneas and the palace guards are throwing bricks and
    pop bottles from the roofs and windows
the police and Guard arrive in new force —
Aeneas and his followers hit the well known alleys and back streets and
    disappear to strike again
as Pyrrhus and his men curse them.

— Melvin Johnson
(Cleveland)

MOTHER TO SON

Well, son, I'll tell you:
Life for me ain't been no crystal stair.
It's had tacks in it,
And splinters,
And boards torn up,
And places with no carpets on the floor —
Bare.
But all the time
I'se been a-climbin' on,
And reachin' landin's,
And turnin' corners,
And sometimes goin' in the dark
Where there ain't been no light.
So, boy, don't you turn back.
Don't you set down on the steps
'Cause you finds it kinder hard.
Don't you fall now —
For I'se still goin', honey,
I'se still climbin',
And life for me ain't been no crystal stair.

— Langston Hughes

ABOVE KARMA

In the last
days
All — things
become what they were
Desert people become desert
people
Sons return to their father
All mix-breeds become pure
The seed returns to fire
peace becomes peace.

          — Norman Jordan
           (Cleveland)

Ahmed El Ibn Said (Fred Evans)

Ahmed El Ibn Said, born Fred Evans, is a thirty-eight-year-old black man who was convicted by an all-white jury in May 1969 of seven first-degree murder indictments connected with the shoot-out between Black Nationalists and city police in the Glenville district of Cleveland, on July 23, 1968.

He is an astrologist and served in the U.S. Army overseas during the Korean War. He is tall, six feet four, well-built, a heavyweight boxing champion at his army base. He has detractors and sup-

317

AHMED EVANS
VICTIM OF
RACIST COPS
UNITED FRONT FOR POL. DEF

"I have come to learn that fear is worship. Whatever you fear is what you worship. I am no longer a Negro. I am a Black Nationalist, a black man, a man. I am not afraid of anything. I don't fear anything anymore."

*porters, black and white, but there is no doubt he has been influ-
ential among some young, black, alienated youth in Cleveland's
inner city.*

*The following statements have been edited largely from the
courtroom transcripts of the Nondu El (Lathan Donald) trial held
in July-August 1969. Ahmed did not testify in his own trial but
took the witness stand for the defense in the trial of his young
lieutenant.*

What is your name and where do you reside?

Ahmed El Ibn Said. You know that as **Fred Evans.** I reside at
the Ohio State Penitentiary, Death Row, third floor, cell sixteen.

Where were you born and how were your early years spent?

I was born in Greenville, South Carolina, on May 23, 1931, one
of fourteen children. My father's name was John Henry. In the late
nineteen thirties John Henry and Ora, my mother, brought the family to Cleveland and we settled on the East Side.

I went to Rawlings Junior High and left in the ninth grade, or
rather the fifth grade for that is the interpretation of whatever the
education amounted to. I was transferred from one grade to another because I was always too big for the class I attended. The
fact is I couldn't even sit in the desks. I was the tallest kid in my
class and the others called me Big Dumb even though I was the
smartest. So I got out.

I have lived in this city for some thirty years or more. I have
always lived in the same environment that is known as the ghetto.
And I know what the ghetto means. At an early age I wanted to
know why things never changed. I knew I had a good mother. I
knew I had a good father. I knew I belonged to a good family but
conditions never changed. All I ever heard was promises and promises and more promises.

After I quit school in order to help support the family, I began to
wonder more so because I saw within my own position the things
that never changed. Either I didn't have enough education or
wasn't trained for the job. Here I was, a man who had imagination,

who had loves and desires and needs and no way to express myself, no way to let it out of me, and it began to grow and grow inside.

What sort of jobs did you have?

I've only had two jobs, being a laborer and being in the army. I joined the army in 1948 when I was seventeen, lying about my age. I received the basic training of a soldier and some leadership training at Fort Hood. I was camp boxing champ, heavyweight. They probably still got a picture of me hanging on the gym wall.

After completing the course, I became a member of the Eighty-second Airborne Division and went overseas to the island of Guam. Then I received further training, for combat, at Camp Ord, California, and went to Korea. I was a member of the Seventy-third Combat Engineers Battalion. We were back-up troops for the Third Marine Division. We supplied them with bridges and roads, laid mine fields, what-have-you.

It was in Korea that I saw the useless waste of lives. I saw people stacked like cordwood. I viewed all these things and saw how cheap life can be. After a year in Korea, I returned to the United States, was discharged and came home to Cleveland. I drove a bus for the Cleveland Transit System for a while and then decided to re-enlist in the army. But I had symptoms of battle fatigue and was subject to blackouts. During one of these, I struck my commanding officer and received a general court martial. I was convicted and sentenced to two years of hard labor at Fort Crowder, Missouri. But I didn't serve the two years. After seven months, I received a letter from Washington stating that my sentence had been remitted and that I would receive an undesirable discharge.

By that time I had earned the expert rifleman's badge and was authorized to wear the National Defense Service Medal; Korean Service Medal with one silver and one bronze service star; United Nations Service Medal; Army of Occupation Medal with Japan Clasp; Presidential Unit-Emblem with Citation Star; Republic of Korea Presidential Unit Citation Badge. That was in 1956. I then came home to Cleveland and secured a job with the Pennsylvania Railroad. I worked for them for ten years until I quit three years ago.

What led you to this decision?

A number of things. You may remember the Mack Charles Parker incident in 1959. He was a twenty-three-year-old Negro who was awaiting trial for the alleged rape of a white woman. A masked mob threw Parker in an auto, killed him with a rifle and dumped his body in the Pearl River in Poplarville, Mississippi. It was the Mack Charles Parker thing that first got me interested in the cause. After that, I became what you probably would call an agitator. At this point in my life, I had given up to the system. That is to say I had come to realize that my pursuit of happiness was irrevocably blocked because I was a Negro. I had given up. But when the Parker thing happened, something was born in me. I made up my mind that it isn't right to give up.

Then in 1962 I saw a UFO [Unidentified Flying Object] at Seventy-ninth and Kinsman. It hovered for a while and disappeared. That started me thinking about the stars and God and I thought that here I was thirty-three and Jesus had died at thirty-three and I hadn't even got started yet. So I moved off by myself to study the science of astrology and philosophy. I wanted to put things in perspective, to know the whereabouts of things, the history of the matter. The position that I occupied in life was definitely not suitable to me and I wanted to know why. In astrology I found a never-failing relationship of cause and effect which teaches one lesson: that which ye sow ye also reap.

I heard of a group of people who were in the process of forming a sort of unity among members of the community. At this point it wasn't known as Black Nationalism. It was just a group of young people. We met wherever the situation occurred. It might occur in the park. It might occur at my house. Or it might occur at someone else's house. We had no permanent place.

These are ghetto people I am talking about. Don't ever forget that these are the only type of people I associate myself with because that is where I am and where I will be. I found that there was no age limit at all, that anyone interested in uniting to alleviate the conditions that we are living in was perfectly able to participate.

I found it was honest, not a bunch of people stuffing their pockets with other people's money, having no interest in the people at heart but living high lives, driving beautiful automobiles, wearing fancy clothes, eating elaborate meals, and giving elaborate speeches to a bunch of people who couldn't understand what they were talking about. So I joined these people.

Then I got interested in the JFK* House when it opened. The kids who hung out there began asking me for advice. I began making astrological predictions and to have faith in myself. In 1964 I visited the headquarters of the Black Nationalists in Harlem and became a member. On my return to Cleveland, I became a full-time member of an organization known as the Black Nationalists of New Libya. I was a slave until 1964 when I became a Black Nationalist.

By this time I had become Ahmed. I wasn't Fred Evans anymore.

What have been your activities since this time?

They have been devoted to helping the Negro. I had this desire to show him who he was, what he was, what was wrong in what he had been doing. I felt I had the ability to do this and I began to give lectures on African culture and African history. And there were times I would lecture on the economic situation and anything else that would deal with our becoming a self-determining people.

Then after the Hough riots of 1966, I began to speak out even more. I pointed out that I was a soldier, that I have a role to play and the Negro leaders had theirs. I said I was willing to follow if they were willing to lead. But they disappointed me, and it seemed that we were all heading for the streets.

Then about this time, early in 1966, I predicted there would be trouble in Cleveland. I said it would happen in the months of June or July, and the Hough riots occurred in July. I could do this through the studies I had undertaken in astrology. I knew that this location, these longitudes and latitudes, were influenced by the stars. About a year later, a reporter for the *Wall Street Journal* said

* The Jomo Freedom Kenyatta, or John Fitzgerald Kennedy, House. See Harllel X interview.

I predicted another disorder for May 9, 1967, but I didn't make that prediction.

In March of 1967 we started an Afro Culture Shop at 11105 Superior Ave. We had sets of carving tools, art materials, paints, hammers. We decorated it and had hangings on the wall, with the signs of the zodiac and information relating to astrology, numerology and philosophy. And we had a Black Nationalist flag there, black, red, and green. It had the crescent and the star on it.

And we had what was known as a wall of truth. On the wall we had data from newspapers and magazines concerning the plight of the Negro. There was one of a policeman with a dog on a leash attacking a black man. We had a picture of Malcolm X, the original leader of the Black Nationalists in the United States of America. We had pictures of Jomo Kenyatta, Frederick Douglass, Marcus Garvey, and Patrice Lumumba.

I have been asked by a lawyer why we didn't have pictures of Booker T. Washington, George Washington Carver, Senator Brooke of Massachusetts on our wall of truth. I told him that these men were Uncle Toms and Senator Brooke is a traitor. I have also been charged with marking for death the persons of Mayor Carl Stokes, William O. Walker, Leo Jackson, Officer Payne and Councilman George Forbes.* But Black Nationalists never kill black people even when they serve the oppressors. Both the brothers Stokes, perhaps subconsciously, are furthering the cause of oppression. They are perfect examples of the extreme that Negroes have come to in this society.

We stayed in our shop on Superior for a year until the police drove us out. They used an order from the sanitation department and condemned the building. We moved to 6605 Hough Avenue and started to clean it up. It was in terrible shape, rubbish two feet

* Carl B. Stokes is the mayor of Cleveland and his brother Louis, U.S. Congressman from the Twenty-first District (Ohio). William O. Walker is the editor and publisher of Cleveland's black newspaper, *The Call and Post* (see Annie Lee Walker interview above). Leo Jackson is the city councilman for the Twenty-fourth Ward, Officer Payne is a Negro member of the Cleveland Police Force, and George Forbes is the city councilman for the Twenty-seventh Ward (see his interview below).

324

high on the floor. We cleaned it out, scrubbed the premises and disinfected it. We painted it inside and out.

It was my intention to make this place a cultural center. We had all types of skills there. We had seamstresses. We had artists, brothers who dealt in oil paints and all the arts. We had carvers and sculptors. We had musicians and dancers. We had just about anything you can think of. You name it, we had it.

By making these skills available to the people, to the young people of the community, we could stop them from killing each other and become assimilated to what we were. We heard groups standing on the street corner singing better than some records we had heard. It was my hope to become an outlet for these musical groups. We wanted to make a teen-age club where they could perform. They were suppressed because there was no outlet.

The skill was there. All sorts of things were possible. We could have been a very beautiful success. In fact, I had seen success in this, and I will add this has been a lifetime dream of mine, ever since I can remember. I had always wanted to work along these lines. Here was the opportunity.

You spoke about the police. What contacts did you have with them?

It started the moment I began to work with groups of youngsters. I was more or less an adviser for them. They would come and ask me for advice on different things. They wanted a change in life. One of the young men was Brother Nondu El [Lathan Donald]. He was a very intelligent young man, very eager, easy to catch on, and very adaptable. We had a beautiful relationship and were constantly in each other's company.

It was then the police began to raid my apartment. They came to ask questions at first, then they came with a sledge hammer and broke the windows of the shop and wrecked the joint. There was constant harassment by the police. They came in numbers, sometimes forty or fifty. They had various weapons, submachine guns and sometimes hand grenades. I heard that once they brought a bazooka, but I didn't see it. We were always under surveillance.

Sometimes we were accosted here and there on the street. There were incidents in which young ladies were harassed and abused. I was clubbed in the head any number of times. Once I was taken to the Fifth Precinct while walking my girl home. I was never charged with anything but they clubbed me on the way to the station. When I got there, they tried to make me say my occupation was "murder teacher." I have been clubbed, stomped, spat on, kicked. I have had my wife paraded around in the nude in front of policemen.

There were particular incidents with different policemen. Once, after being beaten unmercifully at the station house a lieutenant came by my cell and asked my name, then spat on my chest and said, "That's you, Ahmed." Another time Officer Payne came to the shop with a sledge hammer and broke the window and then attacked me. I disarmed him and we had a little altercation. He made an effort to draw a gun and I pinned his arms to his side. After that I was arrested. When released, I told Brother Payne that I was very sorry he found it necessary to be a liar, and a worm, and to accuse me. I definitely don't like to be falsely accused, but when we parted he said he was sorry and I forgave him.

And I knew Sergeant Ungvary* well. We had, well almost, a friendship. He also is born under the sign of Gemini. I once said to him, "If we were in a revolution and I was fighting for the black cause and you were fighting for the white cause and I saw you, I would shoot you." And he said, "I would shoot you, too." This is the type of understanding we had.

What is the black cause? What is a Black Nationalist?

A Black Nationalist is a man who has grown out of the bonds of being a Negro. He is a black man, the same as a Negro, but he doesn't think the same as a Negro. A Black Nationalist is a black man without the title of Negro. He thinks for himself. He does for himself. He doesn't need anyone to guide him by the hand. This man has aspirations and he has ambition and he has love and desires. He has pride.

The principles of Black Nationalism are to believe in God, to know and understand God. We have the words of Jesus and Jesus was saying that we cannot obey, we cannot serve God and Mam-

* Sergeant John Ungvary is head of the Subversive Unit (sometimes called the Red Squad) of the Cleveland Police Force.

mon. Mammon means the state. It means we must serve God in all circumstances. If it means your life, it means your life.

A Black Nationalist will fight back in self-defense, which I have done myself. There is such a thing as a breaking point. In Negroes, this is nonexistent. There is a point where you take as much pressure as you can take. This is where you stand up like a man and you dish out what is necessary to dish out.

A Black Nationalist has knowledge of the human race. He has a comfortable knowledge of procedures of things and society. A Black Nationalist is a man who has learned who he is, as a black man. To understand what a Black Nationalist is, you must first understand what a Negro is.

A Negro is a person who has crossed the boundaries of choice. He has obligations to everyone. You see, being a Negro means you sometimes sleep in a car, sometimes you have to beg for a meal, sometimes you have to steal one. It is doing whatever is necessary to survive.

I don't mean that to be a Negro is a despicable thing. There is a reason why black people are Negroes. Black people were not always Negroes. There were black people before the pyramids were built, before the ancient cities were built. There were black people before white people or of any other race. It was necessary that black people became Negroes, not in the way you may think because they are stupid or inferior in any way. They became Negroes because of the exclusive will of God and that is why they are Negroes now. They will remain Negroes as long as God wants them to be Negroes.

Once I was a Negro. I was afraid of everything. I was afraid of my mother, my father, my sister, my brother, my neighbor, and especially the white race. I was just a body of fear. I was afraid of being hungry, of losing my wife and child, of being ridiculed, afraid of society, afraid of life. I was afraid of the grave. That is what it means to be a Negro. You have to know what it means to be afraid of everything. You just have to be a coward in every respect. You have to be able to endure.

Negroes are wonderful people. They have exhibited the most superior ability to endure I have ever witnessed. I have never known, read or heard of a race of people who endured such extreme circumstances as the Negroes of America. They have endured this with faith and they have been a wonderful people. I love them. I have dedicated my life to the betterment of these people.

I realize that the Negro people themselves do not understand Negroes and white people do not understand why Negroes are Negroes. But they are a wonderful people and are under the influence of the real God. They will remain this way until the time for initiation is over and they will come out of it.

As I know the world, the world has violent people. Everyone has violence, and I would say if you think Negroes are nonviolent, you don't know Negroes. They may be nonviolent when it comes to white people, but they commit wholesale genocide on their own race every Friday and Saturday. The Negro has never been nonviolent. They kill each other like flies.

Martin Luther King was a great friend of mine, but a nonviolent man in a violent world is a fool. I felt he was leading the people astray. He was adding to their demise by giving them a false illusion. I can't conceive of the police department or the Ku Klux Klan — or any organization known to be violent — ever adopting a nonviolent policy. After he was dead, it really didn't hurt me at all, because I knew this would happen to him. He dedicated his life to nonviolence, and I could not see this. I still don't. I mean if a person is violent to me, I will be violent to him. If he is nonviolent to me, I will be nonviolent to him.

My philosophy is fight fire with fire. It's simple. If I am attacked by anybody, and I do mean anybody or anything, I will defend myself at all costs. But I would not attack someone who is not attacking me. I never had the liberty to enjoy such an emotion.

As I look upon the situation today, there is a great deal of fear around. Even in the courtroom I saw fear on the faces of many people. I have come to learn that fear is worship. Whatever you fear is what you worship. If you fear a state, or a particular person, that is the controlling element.

As I said, I have been a coward. I have been afraid of anything you can imagine. But at this moment I have no fear whatever of losing anything. This is due to my knowledge of the situation, my studies in astrology and numerology and philosophy. I have knowledge of reincarnation and know that death is just another side of living.

I realized I could have died in Korea. I had prepared myself for death there and it didn't happen. It's like looking death in the face and seeing it walk away. The twenty-third of July was another opportunity I had to see apparent death real close by. I wonder why I am not dead today. I believe that everything that happens is destined to happen and, under the circumstances, I have no choice but to accept what happens.

I am no longer a Negro. I am a Black Nationalist, a black man, a man. I am not afraid of anything. I don't fear anything anymore.

Following the trial and conviction of Ahmed El Ibn Said (Fred Evans), the Common Pleas Judge, George J. McMonagle, permitted him to express his views. Afterwards, the judge himself made an extended comment, relating the actions of Ahmed to the younger black generation, especially the students at Cornell University who, in the spring of 1969, had armed themselves during the take-over of a university building.

AHMED EL IBN SAID

I don't think there is any doubt that the people of my race have every right in the world and have every reason in the world to resist and to reach out and become what they were created, me — not symbols, I mean — not half anything, but whole, as I am now whole.

I fully understand the ways of life as they are now, and the truth of the matter is I have no regret. That is to say, I have no malice towards anyone, white people or anyone else. Just the reality of the matter that counts.

As you know, I am an astrologist and this gives me insight into the future so I see anyway, you understand, but this will not end by the means that have been used today against the black men who are willing, who are able, who are strong enough to stand up.

The electric chair or fear of anything won't stop the black man of

today. Like, I fully understood what I might encounter when I became a Black Nationalist; but I didn't become a Black Nationalist to sell out my people or to use them for malpractice. I became a Black Nationalist because I wanted to help. I felt that I had something to give them, to aid them, and I did.

I feel justified in that I did the best I could. And, of course, concerning these charges, I am not a murderer. I don't think that any record that I may have made proves me to be a murderer.

However, I want it to be fully understood that all the men that I have known and all the people whom I have associated with, that they are on the right path because when you are on the right path to righteousness, in a world such as we now live in, you are bound to run into opposition, the likes of this.

This is to be expected. I mean, you just can't say that you are going to turn away from a world of inequity and walk along a red carpet. It is not that way, I mean, when you turn around from evil and wrong-doing, you are bound to run into all these types of oppositions; and I fully accepted them and I do now. Thank you.

COMMON PLEAS JUDGE GEORGE J. McMONAGLE

Mr. Evans, I want to make another public statement as to the adequacy of your defense and the zeal and the endeavor that these men put forth in your behalf.

Now, if it can be said there was any defense you presented or interposed as far as this case is concerned, it was that you did not agree with our laws, and apparently you were not bound by them and it seems to be that this carried over in this statement you made to the court today.

I think it is perfectly obvious that we cannot have a system where every man is his own law. There is some mention of your being a student of the Bible; and if you go back to the Book of Judges in the Old Testament . . . the Scripture says:

"In those days there was no king in Israel — every man did what was right in his own eyes," and it was recorded, however, that anarchy reigned.

In our society no man can live in human society and make his own law.

Now it is an adjudicated fact that you, personally, caused the perpetration of crimes as horrible, actually, as any that have been perpetrated or committed in any civilized community. These were horrible, not only because of the manner and extent of their perpetration, but because of the misery and trouble that they caused to many men and their families, including young boys and their families who were misled by you.

You know, actually, before we had this Glenville incident, that has been adjudicated as caused really by you, there was never any open display anywhere of firearms by youngsters.

Now boys of the same age as your followers and who are, however, college students, they now feel that apparently it is the proper thing to do and the legal thing to do, to have a show of rifles, shotguns, bandoliers. Basically these children are really emulating the example that you set as a part of this incident which is now coming to a conclusion.

You have caused the infliction of a horrible wound on the minds and souls of people in this community. Let us hope that the punishment will be a deterrent to others.

Nondu El (Lathan Donald)

Nondu El is the fourth child, and fourth son, of Alice Johnson (see below). He is also the brother of eighteen-year-old Bernard Donald, also called Little Nondu, who was killed in the shoot-out of July 23, 1968. Now twenty years old, Nondu El is serving the first year of a twenty-year prison sentence for his part in the alter-cation. He was charged and convicted of seven counts of second-degree murder, with a plea for clemency because of his age.

Three years ago, as Lathan Donald, he was a student at Glenville

High School in Cleveland, Ohio. He met Ahmed El Ibn Said (Fred Evans) in his junior year. School records show him in the top 10 percent of his class in ability, yet his grades were mediocre to failing. The scholastic exception was the English class where, under a white teacher, Judith Williams, he did outstanding work.

The profile of Nondu El is unlike others in this volume. It is drawn from several sources, including letters to his mother, Judith Williams, and the courtroom transcript of his trial.* Questions I constructed were put to him, through his mother during visiting hours. He memorized the questions and responded later by letter to his mother. Nondu El's form of response is rarely direct. Unlike older persons, the question does not call forth a web of reminiscences. The form of response is pensées, *brief philosophical rejoinders in the manner of epigrammatic writing. He quickly seizes the truth or falsity of the question or issue and deals tersely with it. His letters are passionate affirmations and denials.*

For this reason, the profile of Nondu El consists of passages following a rough chronological order. The statements are divided by topics.

Like many men before him, both black and white, Nondu El will have time to reflect upon his life and develop his thought, behind bars. Unlike them, he has not been isolated in the middle years or late in life, but at the beginning of his young manhood. Nondu El could be released from prison in his thirties, but not as a free man. In the Ohio State Penitentiary in Columbus, Ohio, he is a free man today.

TO JUDITH WILLIAMS

Salaam Judith. Dig the familiarity. Three years since I've seen my old school marm! During that time I have had mixed emotions concerning our past relationship. After much consideration and due reflection, I have learned that it was quite fruitful and a rewarding experience. "All praise is due to him who neither sleeps nor forgets."

---

* Prison officials refuse to allow anyone, except his attorney and members of his immediate family, to visit him.

First, why do you say that the letter was strange? Unexpected, yes, surprising, yes. But strange, no. This is typical of your benevolent nature. Many times in the past eight months I have picked up a pencil with the intent of writing to you but something always stops me. For one thing I didn't know how you would react toward a letter from such a dubious character as people have been led to believe I am.

Nay, I have done no writing since I left school. Indeed, my mind has been a turmoil of thoughts and ideas burning to be released, but I could find no reason for putting them on paper except for personal reference. I felt that I had ceased to exist in your mind, or maybe that too was a product of my imagination.

You are right in saying that anybody can latch onto a doctrine or ideal. But in my sphere of existence there exists only truth and falsehood and by using my ability to reason rationally I have latched onto the doctrine of truth.

I am a complex individual, with moods, thoughts and ideas as numerous as the sands of the sea. Aren't we all? And yet a wise man is one who is able to interpret the things that unfold before his very eyes. So be it.

So far as how things look to my mind's eye, they are the same. What was, is now, and will be. Life was, is, and will be, an eternal fight to retain sanity in a society of lies, deceit, filth, transgress and blasphemy. It is a maelstrom of hate, a holocaust of confusion. Negative, irrational reasoning, phantom ideas, grotesque schemes; bloodlust, cunning and blasphemy combine to create an imaginary heaven and a concrete hell.

I have reason to believe that my position is quite clear and concrete and no power on the face of the entire inhabited earth will shake the foundation of my convictions. The element of fear has been removed from my being and I will pursue my chosen course of life as long as I exist.

I have mixed emotions concerning my being married, even though it has been approximately two years and my lady shares the same philosophy as myself. And even though it may be me on Death Row, physically, mentally and spiritually she will be present.

I am a man and death is the culmination of my ideal. But emotionalism reigns supreme in the female. Need I say more? Much to my sadness, I have no sons, or daughters for that matter. But so be it.

335

As to your thoughts of me, thanks and no thanks. The fondness part is hip, but anguish is negative. All the things that I have done and all the bridges I have crossed were with eyes open, flesh and spirit eager and willing.

How long ago it seems, the time when I was confused, utterly, totally and completely confused. But that was yesterday and yesterday was the beginning. Time soon exhausted this form of emotionalism and the seemingly senseless life cycle evolved into organized symmetrical meaning.

INFLUENCES

My early life was uneventful as far as race relations are concerned. I was aware of the difference in tones of color and an unexplainable hatred on their part. This developed into a hate that hate produced. It was later replaced by my understanding of their ignorance. I saw the unlicensed prejudices on the part of those who were supposedly upholders of the "law." And therefore I developed a total disregard, dislike and, in short, total indifference toward authority in all aspects. This carried over to this very day, only now I apply intelligence with dissent!

A black life in a black ghetto explains itself.

As for people that influenced my life, before I met Ahmed, I must give due credit to Mrs. Williams. I hold this woman in very high esteem and will continue to do so until she changes my opinion, if ever. She planted a seed that is bearing fruit to this very day. She nurtured, cultivated, encouraged and praised what little ability I had. At last I found a vehicle in which I could express my thoughts, ideals and emotions and I indulged feverishly in creative writing. That was a major episode in my life that I thank God for letting me experience. That eventually led me to discover what I had sought for seventeen years, a reason, a purpose for living — my people. I learned very little in school other than how to read and write. Her constant coaxing to expand my literary efforts enabled me to obtain a vast amount of knowledge. I devoured books as fast as I could get my hands on them, on all subjects especially Negro literature. You cannot begin to imagine how exceedingly this broadened and, if I must say so myself, enlightened me as to what was going on outside the small world of my experience.

Glenville High merely gave me the chance to become acquainted with a woman whose unselfish concern paved the way for me to express the world of feeling that was crying for release. This turned out to be the spark that started the bonfire to burn. And then I met the man who gave me the key to unlock the doors!

Writing was not the end, but merely a means to an end. I met the master Astrologer, one who was able to relate intangibles to tangibles, physical effect to spiritual cause, one who was endowed with incredible — I repeat, incredible — insight, foresight, intelligence and understanding. I totally respect intelligence. Ignorance appalls me no end. There is no excuse for it. Desire coupled with willpower overcomes all obstacles, all oppositions. I vowed to myself, to my people and to my God, that as long as I had breath in my being I would channel all my body, mind and spirit towards a cause that was worthy of my blood, sweat, and tears. So I embarked on a course that I knew would eventually lead me to these walls or to eternity.

THE WORDS OF AHMED

In the words of Ahmed . . .

Seek ye a thief?
Then look to him who is rich and when he says, "I have saved," say to him, "Lay up no earthly treasures." When he says, "I was wise," say to him, "You are subtle and greedy. With nothing you came, so shall you return."

Seek ye one who was robbed?
Then look to him who was hired, and when he says, "I have a good job," ask him if he works for the Creator, and if he says, "No," then tell him he has been robbed . . .

Seek ye a prophet?
Then go into the multitudes. Look for him who has one pair of sandals, one garment and carries neither purse nor script. If you do not find him there, seek out the dungeon of the persecuted. When you find a bearded one of ebony countenance, ask him why he is there, and if

337

he should say, "It is the Will of the Father," say to him, "You are the true prophet."

Seek ye the devil?
Then look to those who are judging the earth, for he is the Beast of the earth. And if they say, "I judge in the name of God," then say to them, "And they will be Twelve, you are the children of Jacob."

Seek ye the Father?
Then look to yourself, for never was there a time when man was not, nor will there be a time when man is not. If then you find that you have been whipped with many a stripe, remember what the prophet said, "It is the Will of the Father," then say to yourself, "Thy will be done Forever."

ON JUSTICE AND JAILS

Past, current and future events — named, the incarceration and preparation for execution of Brother Ahmed, and I might add myself — deem it necessary for me to deal strictly with reality, and at present the major portion of my mind is preoccupied with this circus I am about to attend.

Let it be understood that nothing I could put down on paper concerning the Black man and American justice (?!) could more vividly describe the living example of it that is about to be perpetrated in this den of inequity.

That courtroom scene was weird, my soul was vexed no end. I realize it was purely retribution, and no one escapes its effect.

The old form of justice, blind as hell, still stands. Justice! Oh, of all the ridiculous, insane happenings of today, the justice of this paranoid, psychopathic society is in a class of its own. None but my Creator is fit to judge me. He alone can reward me for the fruits of my action, whatever they may be!

The vibrations emitted from this dungeon of the persecuted are strictly negative.

I can't stand to see anyone suffer, regardless of who they are.

338

ON IGNORANCE AND FEAR

Universal knowledge is the key that unlocks the doors of obscurity. The Revelation of Alpha and Omega. The eyes devour the words, the ears receive the verbal prophecies and decrees, the mind defines and analyzes, the lips utter the testimony of truth as ordained by the law of justice.

Knowledge is entrusted neither to the timid nor the haughty.

Once man gets off his knees in submission to the ignorant and to fear, he becomes what he was created. He becomes aware of the fact that he is a product of the Universal Infinite Spirit. This changing over that we call death is merely a process that must be carried out in order that we may re-unify with the source from which we come — call this source God, or Allah, or Jehovah or whatever.

Once an individual loses his fear and couples this peace of mind with intelligence and understanding then he is free to pursue the path of duty and right action unhindered by the thought of what the consequences might bring. The consequences are secondary when you consider what has been achieved and, more important, what can be achieved in future activities of similar nature.

Those who seek to destroy the continuance of the brothers in this place fail to realize that the element of fear is nonexistent in our beings. "Fear of death is but a delusion, hovering in the breast of sages. For one who has lived a single springtime is as one who has lived for ages." Yea, my brother evolved with this thought instilled in his mind. For El Jihad was proclaimed and Allah's will was done. "El Jihad — the Holy War. Death means paradise, victory means peace, and defeat means the chance to try again."

The full appreciation of wisdom is so only when the soul places the attaining of it above all materialism. When dreams are accepted at their useless face value, when the veil of fantasy is lifted from the face of reality, when the cycle of life is exposed as a minor phase of existence, then the soul lives. Then man's spirit is resurrected from its stagnant state of decay. Then you can truly say, "I am free."

The most awesome foe one must overcome before he can even begin to activate a method of reformation is ignorance, and out of ignorance is born fear. Let me emphatically state that we regard fear as a grave evil. It is negative, inhibiting and incompatible with progress.

It has its uses: physical, for self-preservation; mental, to stimulate foresight. Yet even here it is a force then that can be replaced with a better. The wise are not concerned with the interests of the self save as they are beneficial to the whole. All living things are bound together by the same common cord.

Inasmuch as fear is often used as a weapon, a form of intimidation, it should be sought out and destroyed. The crippling effect of fear on all activity needs no further emphasis. It is a profound force that is inhibiting on the physical, emotional and mental plane — as we can see every day as applied by the oppressors against the oppressed.

Fantasy and ignorance is the order of the day.

ON WHITE SOCIETY

It has been a common occurence for these people to underestimate our intelligence, ingenuity and determination. These same people, in support of their egos, are anxious to believe that the spirit which brought us to this point has miraculously been broken. But when men get involved in activities they know are right, and are willing to sacrifice for it, there is no stopping short of victory.

All over the country the vigorous reaction of our struggle has put fear into the hearts of the ruling clique. Like cornered animals they strike out wildly. The persecution increases as they are driven to commit even greater crimes, violating the pseudo-democratic constitution which they have sworn to respect. Any attempt they make to remain in power will be in vain. Their end as a ruling clique is in sight.

It is inconceivable for me to even imagine that merely because a handful of men has been displaced, that the ideal also has been hidden or destroyed, or even seriously hindered.

Having grown up in the ghetto, I had very little contact with the Caucasian race, or white people, but my opinion of the white race was that they were misled to the point that they had considered the black man subhuman.

As far as people saying that we were warmongers, or racists or that we talked hate, that is wrong. Speaking for myself, there is only one thing I hate, ignorance. We were trying to achieve understanding and communication between us and the white people, all those we came into contact with. We were trying to show them that even though history shows a number of heinous crimes burdened on the black man by the white people, we bore no malice toward them. We felt pity that they could not see and understand what they were doing, violating the universal laws of justice.

ON BLACK NATIONALISM

I have been for five years, am now, and will always be, a nationalist. In essence, a nationalist is a social reformer one who utilizes every weapon he has at his disposal — whether military or otherwise — in protest *for* the people against *their* oppressors.

The nationalist fights to change the social system that subjects un-armed peoples to injustice and poverty. He acts against the negative conditions of the social order in whatever manner the circumstances permit.

When I became a Black Nationalist I was aware of the attitudes that all of this society harbored toward anything they do not under-stand. I know they fear the unknown.

It was our desire to clarify our concept of what this organization stood for, using our astrological knowledge in our approach and in our methods. The brothers and sisters drove home the realization of how vast and potent a source of culture, endurance and willpower we possess as a people. The brotherhood made us all realize that racial arrogance and discrimination is promoted by a few demi-gods that stand to profit by dissension and unrest among the masses of people both black and white. And therefore our greetings and parting words on encountering anyone was the Arabic word, Salaam . . . Peace! They showed the beauty, strength and contentment you feel with unity of thought, purpose and goal.

Salaam comes from the Hebrew word "shalom," and it means peace. And the clenched fist, the gesture, is one of unity and strength. You can interpret that two ways. With unity you are physically stronger. And also with unity you can pool your resources and mentally become stronger.

341

I can tell my people many things, but I can show them much more.

We sought to build an organization of intelligent men, fearless men and yet cautious, discreetful men who could not be bought, deceived or frightened out of doing what is right, what is just and what is necessary.

When an individual was initiated, so to speak, into our organization, he was taught how to think for himself, then go on from there. My own philosophy differed from Ahmed's because he was older than I and had naturally seen more. We had what we called a competitive opposition. Some things he held I didn't agree with, quite a number of things. I considered this healthy because it would keep everybody on their toes.

Brother King said, "When men are dedicated to a cause they know is right, and are willing to sacrifice for it, there is no stopping point short of victory." And Brother Castro said, "When men become involved in certain activities neither prison walls nor the sod of cemeteries can separate them. A single ideal, a single belief, a single memory, a single cause, a single spirit, will sustain them all."

What we sought to do was lift as many people as possible from out of the stagnant pool of iniquity and transgression that they had allowed themselves to fall into because of that indomitable, repulsive foe called ignorance. It was not our objective to sell out the people or use them in hopes of material gain or to achieve personal satisfaction. Indeed, we felt we had something to give them.

However, there were those who felt that this action was a threat to their already uncertain security and so came July 23. Action brought reaction, and so the hate that hate produced came forth. Blood was shed, lives were lost, freedom was curtailed and irreparable damage was done to attitudes that took so long to establish.

If and when I return to the streets, whenever that may be, I will continue to uphold, defend and advocate the very same cause that brought about our present demise. As long as I exist, in whatever environment I may be in, I will defend my ideal under all circumstances!

ON RELIGION

I am religiously inclined inasmuch as I try to be a Muslim. I will be religious so long as whatever religion teaches does not contradict the laws of nature, that is, the universal law of justice.

The entire universe and all other life travels in a cycle so that what you sow you must also reap — so says the Christian, the Islamics, the Jews, the Buddhists and the rest.

Religion should be a spiritual ladder instead of a mental crutch as so many unknowing people make it.

Religions are man-made forms of apparatus for the worship of some God. These may be rafts, to be used to cross the stream life, and to be left beyond on reaching the other shore. Or they may be shields from the truth which the seeking mind is unable to face when found.

In the same way, God may be a substitute for the effort to stand alone. To use a crutch knowing it to be a crutch is one thing: to use it while claiming to walk unaided is a lie to oneself, the most detrimental of all.

I cannot conceive of a God that would be content with me existing in any capacity other than what he created me, a man. A man is one who does not allow himself to become merely a symbol of what is contrary to his true being.

Man can understand no eternal truth until he has freed himself from pretension. The mind, subjected to centuries of slime, is saturated with the repulsive stench of illusion.

Struggles of the battlefield pale into insignificance when man first contends with inward enemies. These are not mortal foes to be overcome with an ominous array of might. These foes are omnipresent, unresting, subtly equipped with hypnotic weapons.

Thoughtless is the man who buries his ideals, surrendering to the common fate.

The vast majority of religions stress moral and ethical concepts. All codes of morals consist of a series of precepts designed to prevent the evils done by one man to another, stressing respect for his body, his good and his reputation. This true relationship involves the maximum

343

of self-control, that is, control of the desires of one's self where they conflict with those of others. With the dawning consciousness of a greater "Self," the need for rigid rules, whether imposed from without or within, give way to the true essence of life.

Ethics therefore is the school wherein the individual learns to subdue the desires of the part to the greater needs of the whole. As such, it is of immense importance. However, the greater majority of religious schools of thought fail to produce results on this elementary plane.

Religious schools of thought fail because a point is reached where ethics is transcended and a greater force is felt, a greater clarity of insight is needed. This force joins the will to the deed, fantasy to fact, the ideal to the real. It is through this force that all lives must sometime pass in one of its incarnations. And beyond this force lies the realm where mind — not matter, not the body — is ruler.

The body will use the utmost of its energies, acquired in many lives of self-indulgence, to hold the spiritual traveler back. This explains why so few of our splendid plans for spiritual growth materialize. They all involve the subjugation of self, and the lower desires resent being subdued.

The force or energy that pervades the universe is what I call Allah (for lack of a better word). Sufi Islam is the closest religious concept I have so far come across. I have found others, such as Zen, that hit fairly close to the meaning of existence.

This Allah, this force we call God sustains all life. Every atom of every element is totally a universe. And the universe we conceive is merely an atom in the body of a greater universe.

The mind is the womb of all material manifestations. Our meager intelligence of space does not allow us to see that there is no end to the infinity of worlds. Hell then is merely an extreme state of mind, wherever you find it.

When you reach a point in spiritual evolution you become aware of the fact that death is a minor transition from one state of existence to another. So finding something to die for is a trivial matter in itself. You need only see that the means by which you evolve run parallel with the cause you embrace.

However finding something worth living for is a task, within a task. And even the fulfillment of my cause cannot express fully the total me.

ON THE FUTURE

My future life — whether spent in here or out of here — is primarily dependent upon the length of time it takes a substantial number of people to realize that whether confined by walls of concrete or confined by walls of ignorance, fear and oppression, we are all, nevertheless, "confined."

The future lives of all of us depend upon the dictates, whims, prejudices and benevolences of those who are presently in control of the apparatus that has been fairly effective thus far in keeping us in situations like those which exist "in here" and "out there." There is no difference in the condition.

Alice Johnson

Alice Johnson is a housekeeper's housekeeper, efficient, swift and pleasant. She is much in demand and it is easy to understand why. More than a housekeeper, she is a wonderful companion. She handles any conversation, any domestic situation, with humor and wit. She seems at home in any home.

Now forty-eight, she has had twelve children by three husbands. Seventeen years ago she married her present husband and ten years later they bought a house in the Glenville area of Cleveland, Ohio.

346

*Two of the children, Lathan and Bernard, were involved in the
July 23 shoot-out. The older, Lathan, is now serving a prison sentence and the younger, Bernard, was killed.*

*Alice Johnson calls herself a "black, Negro woman." The de-
scription is apt if you take "Negro" to mean she can move easily
in white society and "black" as the capacity to deal with her own
people. She is a good example of the bicultural character of many
black people today. With an eighth grade education, she moves
easily in educated or uneducated circles whether black or white,
young or old.*

*She is now living for her other children, but in another sense,
she is living for herself and always has been.*

It is true as Lathan said that he did not know many white people. When he grew up there were only Negroes living here. But that
is not the way I grew up or the way it was when he was small.

Tell it from the beginning, will you?

All right, I will. I was born right here in the city of Cleveland,
born and raised here. I was raised up with the mother and father of
my four sisters. My mother died when I was eleven years old and
then I really knew what hardship was. My father took to the bottle
and my older sister played both the mother and father role until she
married and moved away. How we survived those years, I'll never
know.

I went to school until about age fourteen when I became pregnant without knowing anything about the facts of life. I left school
in the last quarter of the eighth grade. In the meantime, my sister
had separated from her husband and she sent me to the Mary B.
Talbert Home for Unwed Mothers. I stayed there for about six
months till my baby was born, then I went to live with my sister. A
social worker helped me get on welfare and moved us to a bigger
home where my other sisters joined us and we lived together. I
worked at various jobs, usually as a domestic, and then seven years
later I got married.

Eugene was my first child, then when I married I had five more

347

children, all but one were boys. There was Richard, William, Lathan, Bernard and Alice. When Alice was six months old, I terminated that marriage because I didn't want my children growing up in another drunken environment. I knew all about that. So, when my husband started drinking, I left him and took the children.

Several years later, I met my present husband and we got married. We have six children which brings the grand total to twelve, six boys and six girls.

I had plenty of jobs in the course of those years. You name it and I did it. There was work in a packing house, with great big slabs of bacon and ham to carry around, and then in a bakery. For a while I worked in a restaurant, in the kitchen part, then as a domestic in different homes. For thirteen years I worked in a hand laundry my stepmother had. I did so well she turned the business over to me and I raised my children in that laundry. That's why I hate to iron right now.

We knew a lot of white people in those days, especially Jewish people who lived in the neighborhood. There was never any talk of prejudice, of black or white. We played, slept, ate together. By sleeping with them, I mean we stayed the night over at white people's houses and they stayed over at our house. We would cook something like tripe and they would send down a platter of food. We would visit with the people upstairs, you know. Or we would go down in the gully and steal coal, or catch frogs together. There was never any race talk.

There was a Mrs. Katsenstein who was one of the nicest persons I have ever known. She changed her name to Kent because her little boy couldn't spell Katsenstein. She loved antiques and would go to the shops and come back with small trinkets which Mr. Katsenstein would call junk. I worked for her mother and her brother too. Sometimes Mrs. Katsenstein and her mother would stay up all night baking cookies. Nobody asked them to do this. They would get the kids together and take these cookies out to the State Hospital and give them to the patients, then provide a little concert for them. After her husband died she stayed on in an apartment nearby and continued collecting antiques.

I have warmer relationships with white people than I have with my own. That is the truth. William doesn't have any colored friends. His roommates were always white. Eugene, my oldest, is the same way. It is nothing I have said to them; I guess they found out they can get along better with white people. I know I can. Right now I have only one colored friend, but we don't usually visit. There is nothing we wouldn't do for each other, but seldom visitors make close friends. Everybody likes me and I am what you would call a "telephone friend." I do a lot of talking on the telephone. I love people but I was never much of a visitor. I don't hate the blacks, it's just that I get along better with the white people. William and I laugh sometimes when we make the statement, "One thing I cannot stand is a nigra." That's what the southern white man used to say, "nigra."

Tell me about William and the other children.

Well Eugene is the oldest, he is thirty-one. Richard is twenty-four, William twenty-two and Lathan twenty. Bernard is deceased. Alice is eighteen, Kathy is sixteen, Michael is fourteen, Jeannette is thirteen, Sibyl is twelve and Lois is nine. Who did I forget? Oh yes, Patricia, she is eleven.

My first six children except for Alice who is talkative like her mother, were very quiet. Eugene is quiet and so were Lathan and Bernard, and Richard will sit behind his shades laughing and say nothing. None of the boys talk much, probably because all of their lives I have been screaming at them.

Eugene graduated from a community college in New York and went on to be a male nurse, then a supervisor at a hospital. Later he wanted to go into the banking business and he is now a foreign correspondent investigator for the First National Bank in New York.

Richard was always good with automotive mechanics and when he graduated from high school, he was determined to be a paratrooper. He is now a Green Beret, a specialist in a demolition unit. Next year he plans to reenlist and make the army his career. He married a girl from Okinawa and plans to buy a home there. We don't talk much about the war but he says he has seen some terrible things.

William just graduated from Oberlin College where he studied business administration and became very interested in modern dance. He has now moved to New York and found a job with Trans World Airlines. He is trying to make the necessary connections so he can go into theater work.

He and I had a great time at the Oberlin commencement last June. I was waltzing around the campus looking it over, and thinking how maybe my husband and I might move over to that county when the kids are grown. William came running up and said that the president's wife gave him a note for me. I put it in my pocket and said I would read it when I got home. He said I had to read it right now. It was an invitation to lunch, so I said I would go.

I really enjoyed myself and put on a pretty good show too, hobnobbing with the filthy rich. It was plush and comfortable up there on the second floor of the dining room. William and I were the only black ones there, but nobody was looking or staring. I sat next to the president's wife at the table, and I didn't have a quarter. I wasn't very hungry because I had just eaten a big ice cream. They were talking about politics and I know nothing about politics. I didn't know what I was talking about but it was accepted, probably because no one there knew what they were talking about either. Maybe I was just a little giddy but they were all a little drunk too. One of the men said he thought I was the only one at the table making any sense. I never felt so happy.

Lathan was a very bright boy, very quiet and not a leader to my knowledge. At least he wasn't until he met Ahmed Evans, then he became a teacher. Once he wanted to be a carpenter because he was a jack of all trades. Lathan was greedy for books. Greedy. When he was nine years old he could quote passages from the Bible. I would check later to see if they were right, and they always were. In summertime when you have got to have fresh air and sunshine, I would just force him off the back steps where he would be with gobs of books. I would tell him to read, learn something and understand what he read. And he did.

A friend of mine was talking on the phone about Lathan just this morning and she said she remembered how her boys were always talking about Lathan having his head stuck in a book. She would call and ask where the boys were and I would say, "Lathan is up on the third floor reading and the other kids are all up and down in the street." Later he would tell them about different things that he had read.

He played the drums too and loved football. When the games came on TV, you could hear him screaming for twenty miles. For a while he worked up at the University Hospital and he got passes to go to the games. You know, I never had one minute of trouble out of Lathan.

Bernard was my problem child. He was the type of child that needed more attention, a slow learner. It was always easier for Bernard if somebody said, "Let's go steal a bicycle," than if somebody said, "Let's go and read a good book." He wasn't aggressive but one who would follow the leader, and usually it was Lathan he would follow. He got into a lot of trouble with various boys who stole automobiles and things like that. You couldn't really call them gangs, they were just a bunch of boys like himself, slow learners that didn't go to school.

Alice just graduated from Glenville High and she is now a keypunch operator at General Electric. She has an apartment of her own. The rest of the children are fine, a little too early to tell how they will turn out but they are doing fine work so far. Lois, the one who is nine and in the fifth grade, is doing very well with an I.Q. of about a hundred and thirty. She may be another Lathan, or another William.

There weren't too many sorrows. We were a close knit bunch of people and we not only worked together but played together, something like brothers and sisters. Eugene played the trombone, William played it too, then Lathan played the drum and Alice sang in the choir. Now Sibyl plays the flute, Michael the drums and Patricia and Lois are in the school choir.

I don't have any grandchildren yet. Eugene hasn't married and I guess he never will. William says he is not going to get married until he is forty. I think that is best, if you haven't got all the play out of your system. Then you don't mess up some other woman's life. Some men never do, and I won't mention any names. Take my husband. He still thinks he is a young man. We were laughing about him this morning. He never takes his shades off in the house and I asked him what he is doing with them. They are for teenagers, I say. Then I ask him why he gets his trousers so tight the stomach hangs over the belt, and he says it is the size he wears. I tell him it was the size maybe he used to have. If he knew how much we talked about him, he would drop! He is a quiet person and doesn't have the sense of humor we have. If he says something funny, he doesn't know it and I will laugh.

We had a lot of fun at Christmas. You should have been here. Everybody but Richard and Lathan were here. I'm a kind of comic. I have a comical way of talking, and we had a tape recorder. We snapped pictures with the camera I got for Christmas. William played back the tape and you couldn't hear nothing. There was so much screaming and laughing and acting, I guess people said, "Those folks are just crazy."

Of course I'm not always laughing. I wasn't laughing two years ago when Lathan and Bernard got into this trouble. I even stopped going to church and reading the Bible. I said, why did this ever happen to me? I got to the point where I said there isn't even a God in heaven, because I don't remember ever willfully mistreating anybody and if I did I apologized or asked God to forgive me. I didn't think there was any point in me praying or anything else. But this year I got over that. I said, you're not better than anybody else. There are other women who have gone through the same thing, or maybe worse. My husband tried to explain to me that it wasn't anything I did.

I was just going through a suitcase that has all of Lathan's and Bernard's report cards, old Mother's Day cards and things like that. I was saying to myself: why did something like this happen? I like peace, quiet and tranquillity and that just blowed everything up. It was spread all over the world by the newspapers. This address was probably known in Africa.

At Bernard's funeral, which was packed, they were looking for a great big crying and screaming scene. But I do all my crying in private and very little of that. I cry when I am happy. When I see a beautiful sunset or beautiful patch of flowers, I will cry. Sometimes when I am all alone, and nothing is wrong, I will have a weeping fit.

After the funeral, people said that they didn't see how I could have stood up under it without screaming or crying. But my conscience is clear, that is one of the reasons I wasn't fainting and falling out.

Bernard and I used to go to the Methodist Church. He and I were the church fiends, the only ones who really attended church almost up to the very end. He didn't want to go to the Black Nationalist meetings. He told me this. But nobody made him go, he was just following Lathan.

They both got interested in nationalism through that bastard, Ahmed, that immigrant from hell. He tore down everything I tried to build up. I call him the Pied Piper of Cleveland. I never could understand why he never did use that soft, persuasive, hypnotic voice and teach those kids, talk to them about finishing high school. He could have done a wonderful job if he had kept talking to those kids. He could have done a better job than we parents, and gotten them to finish their high school education.

Did you ever meet Ahmed?

No, I didn't, but I know some of the other nationalists. Lathan wanted me to meet him, but I told him that I didn't want him here at all. Now I wish I had. I don't know, maybe things would have been different. Maybe, but then again, maybe not. Lathan was just starting high school, in the tenth grade, when he met Ahmed. I didn't want to move into the Glenville area. They were just writing in the papers about the conditions there and how things were deteriorating. But I wanted some room for the kids to stretch out. We got a three story house and for the price and the space it was just perfect. If we had just stayed where we were . . . but I don't know. I think it was their destiny, things were just fated that it was going to happen anyhow.

You see, Ahmed was talking about some of the things Lathan wanted to hear. And then maybe there were a lot of things Lathan was teaching Ahmed after they got into it. In the beginning, one of

Lathan's friends, Leslie Jackson, introduced him to Ahmed. They were both about fifteen or sixteen at the time. They talked a lot about Ahmed, sort of worshipped him. They would come back here after seeing him, and study and study. In Bernard's case, he was just following behind Lathan. I don't think Bernard really knew what was going on.

Bernard would say he got tired of going to those meetings, and we would slip away and go to church. Bernard would come to me sometimes and try to talk astrology. He wasn't really making any sense, because I read those books myself. I don't know too much, but what Bernard was talking about nobody could understand. It was pathetic, I would sit down and listen to him as long as I possibly could.

One day Lathan was begging me for five dollars and had told Bernard he would get it because it was in the horoscope book they had just bought me from the drugstore. I'm Scorpio, you know. So I went along and tossed him the money to make him feel good, making him think the book had something to do with it. I heard him tell Bernard, "What did I tell you?" But the book didn't have a damn thing to do with my pocketbook. I let him figure the stars are right.

I see Lathan regularly and he looks fine. I get a letter from him every week. He is more mature than he was before, a serious young man. No monkey business. He is in the best of spirits, thank God, no moping. And he has gained weight all in the right places. He is razor slim and his shoulders broad. Last year his face looked puffy, and his cheeks discolored, but now he stands tall and looks good. Actually his spirits are better than mine. He cheers me up, and to see him in that kind of mood makes me feel better. Lately he has been studying law. All he could talk last time was the law but I couldn't understand any of it.

How do you and the nationalists get along now?

Oh, very well. I am popular with them because I am the only one who can communicate with Lathan. The real joke was when one of the nationalists came over after the incident in 1968 and said he would have come over sooner except that he was afraid of me. He remembered the times when they were all up on the third floor, smoking after school. I tried to be nice, and a lady, by asking them to leave. I would ask Bernard to step down for a moment. Then I would tell him to get his friends off the third floor. But by the second or third time I would put my foot on the step and use a few, tart, choice words. You should have seen them move then!

When they come by now, they are all courteous and nice. They want to know how Lathan is doing. They provide him with reading matter and send him books from the publishers.

Not long ago some of them came in their nationalist garb. My daughter said, "There are three nationalists at the door, Mom, and they want to see you." I don't know what made me scared, but when I went to the door they were all standing together right there in the vestibule. I saw this towel or white cloth wrapped around something and they said, "It's a Valentine present for you." I thought they were going to blow me up with whatever was inside this towel. So, I thought about the kids and said to myself: if it is a bomb, we will all go to hell together. I closed the door to the vestibule and we were all squeezed in there. I never moved till they threw the towel back and I saw it was a copy of the Koran. It had been sent all the way from Arabia to Lathan.

Nationalism means mainly violence to me, but some of the young ones have come over here and talked about it, explaining it to me. They say they are not going to take what their parents did. They won't go through that: putting up with things, sitting back and swallowing it. This is a whole new generation and I told them I see their point. If I were young, I would be right in there with them, raising hell, and getting our rights. There was a time when nobody would listen to an Ahmed, but no more. If you sit back and never speak up, then you will always be sort of a slave, to white people and everybody. So it is a good thing, if it doesn't get out of hand. That is the thing about it, that they don't let it get out of hand.

But when it does, you can't give anybody advice. Suppose one of my other children should get involved with one of these groups out there preaching violence. I wouldn't know a bit more what to do about it now than I did then. If you were to find out your child was taking dope, you would probably do the same as thousands of

355

others and say it is a phase they are going through. It will pass. You really don't know what to do. You might say you would do this or do that, but when it actually happens . . .

What does the future hold for you?

Well, I have never been further than Detroit, Oberlin, and Columbus, Ohio. So I just got an airplane ticket — fly now, pay later. I told my husband and he almost fainted. I am afraid to fly but in two months I am going to New York. After that, I bet I never stay on the ground.

I would really like to go to Paris, maybe with Eugene or William who are interested in the same things I am. I would like the side streets of Paris where the books and antique stores are. I love artwork like Mrs. Katsenstein. I may not understand it but I love it. The kids broke my ceramic that cost twenty-five dollars and I could have killed them. I would love to go to Paris because of the art museums. And I just may do it. I'll fly now and let my husband pay later.

BLACK PROFESSIONALS

SUPER STAR

Super niggers
Ultra feminine Julia,
Super masculine Sidney,
Immaculate in speech,
What happen to mother fucker
Listening to Bach and the Beatles,
What of Trane and Sun-Ra
of Pharaoh and Monk.
Super niggers,

White society's super androids
Black society's Frankensteins
Super niggers,
White society's mythological
    beings.
That Super masculine Blacks
    will never let exist.

> – Wm. Johnson
> (Philadelphia)

To HELL!
With the Spider,
Stick your hands
In the cobweb of Life.
                    – Norman Jordan
                    (Cleveland)

360

RESOLUTION

Cool it, man . . .
You've got to know, an' understand
That every black man, everywhere
Has known frustration an' despair;
Has yearned to break the barriers
That hold him in a lowly station.

But, cool it, man . . .
Blind rage won't win you anything.
Nobody but a simple cat
Will play the game of tit-for-tat,
An' 'cause he's mad at some low louse
Whose skin just happens to be white
Goes out an' burn his own damn house!

So, keep your cool . . .
An' use the brains you say you have.
To put the squeeze on politicians
To make them change long-held positions,
To water seed already sown
In carving our black unity
To bring up leaders of our own!

So, cool it, brother.
An' figure out a way to bread:
For bread can build a firm foundation
To new respect throughout the nation,
So, as you leave old sixty-eight
Be cool and take advantage of
The breaks we've made in freedom's gate!

And cool it, baby.
In a world that's in confusion over peace and war
'Cause we must learn to get ourselves together.

— Alfred Williams
(Cleveland)

361

THE BLACK MESSAGE

Yeah! your skin is black
And that's a natural known fact
But that's bout all there is
To being truly black.

Your skin is just a symbol
Your Afro's just a style
If you don't know the meaning
of being black and proud

You may wear African Garb
And talk about liberation
But if you can't explain your rap
You're in a tight situation

So get yourself together
And do your thing up right
So we can holler loudly.
We will not stop our fight.

Then no one can ever stop
Though they will try it now
No one can ever stop us.
No way. No matter how.

— Dorothy Collins
(Philadelphia)

Ernie Green

Until his retirement in 1969, Ernie Green was one of the most destructive blockers and consistent runners in the National Football League. He spent seven years as an active player with the Cleveland Browns and now serves as a scout. Though his lifetime rushing average is 4.9 yards per carry, he served the Browns best by running interference for Jim Brown, and later, Leroy Kelly.

Ernie Green is highly respected wherever he goes. Cocaptain in his final playing year, he served several years as the player–

"I have three boys, ages thirteen, six and four. I tell them I don't want them to be the success in athletics that I was. I'd rather they have an obsession for something else, maybe law or teaching."

representative for the Browns in meetings with other professional teams. Upon retirement from professional football he accepted the position of assistant vice-provost for student services at Case-Western Reserve University.

An elegant dresser, intelligent and courteous, a good listener, Green at thirty-two years of age has successfully begun a new career in university administration. One gets the feeling he may have several more.

I learned my football first at Spencer High School in Columbus, Georgia, where I was born. My coach, and my history teacher, was a graduate of Spencer who went on to Alabama State College. He realized the importance of a good education, and the fact that a lot of athletes were coming through school and not getting educated. He told us that someday we might wake up with nothing decent to fall back on.

He taught us to play football, too, to play every aspect of the game. If you are going to play, you got to block, you have to tackle, you have to kick the ball, catch the ball and run the ball. He taught us to do all these things. By the time I got to college I could do these things, but I found that not everybody else could.

My father and one of his friends also had a good deal of influence on me. This fellow liked to antagonize my father's children. I remember an early conversation with him when I was in high school. I told him I wanted to be a professional athlete, like Jackie Robinson maybe. When I said that, he laughed and looked down at my feet and said, "Your feet are too big to be an athlete. You can't run, you're too clumsy." Well, this angered me and I never forgot it. Always in the back of my mind, I felt I had to prove to him that I could run. By the time I made the pros, he was still alive and I went back to see him. By then he knew all about me because they were getting our games on TV. It was a big thing for a guy from Columbus, Georgia, to make it in the pros.

My father did the same thing. He would challenge you. We could never satisfy him, though deep down we knew he was proud. He used to go with us to baseball games or wait up for us when we got back. If we won, he would say the other team wasn't so good. If we got two or three hits, he would say that the pitcher was weak. So we were always trying to get him to say that we had done a great job. He did it occasionally, but not very often.

We lived in a pretty rough neighborhood, an area with little bars and honky-tonk cafés. There were four in our neighborhood, so we heard everything we wanted and saw everything we wanted, right there from the front porch at home. There were always a lot of people visiting in our house. My mother worked and when she did, we had to do something for the other people in the neighborhood. If we did something wrong, they would tell her. Usually she would lecture us and a spanking would accompany it. She would say, "I don't have time to work all day as hard as I do and raise impudent children, so if you are going to act this way, I am going to kill you." We knew she wouldn't, but at the time it was something to think about.

There was one black high school in Columbus and three white high schools, very strictly segregated. There was no crosstown rivalry because we never played each other. And there were two conferences in Georgia, a white and a black conference. In my junior year, we won the championship in the black league. I was fullback on that team and pretty big, as big as some linemen. When I entered high school I weighed a hundred and sixty-three pounds and I graduated at a hundred and ninety-three pounds.

We used to watch the white teams play and then read about them in the newspapers. But we could never find anything there about us. So we developed a kind of complex that they didn't really care about us. But because we had played some of the best black teams in the state we figured we could beat any other team. We had size going for us, and we had experienced guys who played together for many seasons.

One thing I noticed was that no matter how prejudiced or bitter white people were they were just as happy and proud as the next black person when Willie Mays or Jackie Robinson came up to bat. And these people were also pulling for Joe Louis and Sugar Ray Robinson to win a fight. Regardless of how they felt about black people, these guys were heroes. I think that those of us who were aware of their feelings felt that if we did the same things, they would change their feelings. The idea in back of my mind, and I'm sure in the back of other black athletes' minds, was that if he can accept you on one level, there is a possibility he might accept you on another.

For instance, professional athletes become very close during the season, but who knows what's going to happen when the season is over? You might go back to your home in Mississippi and because we were able to get together as athletes, you invite me out to your house, expose me to some of your friends. Maybe by that association I realize that you are not such a bad person. Maybe we could exchange some ideas and attitudes. Sometimes it works this way and sometimes not.

Of course it takes time for a person to accept you as a man, or a human being, in athletics. The first thing they will respect is the ability to block, tackle and run the football. The other part doesn't enter in right away. Later they might conclude that Green is a pretty good man, but the only thing they are concerned with right away is, can he run with the football? After that other things might get started.

When did you leave Columbus, Georgia?

In 1958, the same year I graduated from high school. I had been thinking about it for some time. You see, when I grew up there was a feeling that if you wanted to succeed you had to do it outside of Georgia, maybe up North where, we heard, things were better. For years I had seen guys graduate from high school and just stay there on the street corners and become bums. I was convinced that if I looked at the two groups — those that stayed and those that left — those who had done something worthwhile were the ones that left.

Even though my mother still lives there, and two of my brothers, I don't like it at all. It was the attitude more than anything else. Unless it was absolutely mandatory, you didn't come into contact with white people. As I got older it bothered me to have to wait an extra ten minutes to get waited on. White people always got served first. This happened even fairly recently when I went back home to pick up my wife, during my first year with the Browns.

369

I went back home because my wife had just had our baby in a Columbus hospital. I went to pay the bill and get her out. I'm there with my checkbook waiting while three or four white people, who came in after me, get service. The cashier would reach over my shoulder to get their money and leave me standing there. Anywhere else, I would have walked out and bought the item in some other place. You see, they didn't care, didn't give a damn who I was or how much money I had. I was black or, I suppose, Negro.

In Columbus the only white people I met were the ones I was supposed to hate: the ones I fought with as I passed through a neighborhood, or the ones who came in ours, or the bill collectors. To this day, I don't have a bill collector come to my house. In the South it is routine for them to come by and raise hell if you haven't got the money. I'll never forget them.

The way I got out of Columbus is interesting. I was pegged to go to Tuskegee or to Florida A & M. But there was a young man, named Andy Walker, who had gone to the University of Louisville, in Kentucky, and done very well. When he was set to graduate, the Louisville coach called Walker's high school coach and asked him if he had any other good ballplayers. The coach suggested he call the coach of Spencer High because we had just beaten his team badly.

I like to tell this part of the story to young high school ballplayers when I read that a California university sends a private plane to Cleveland to pick these fellows up. You see, this coach sent me a Greyhound bus ticket from Columbus, Georgia, to Louisville, Kentucky, a trip of about nineteen hours. When I got there, nobody met me and I sat around for two hours. Finally, some people at the bus station found the name and phone number of the coach and he called an assistant who was supposed to have met me.

So I stayed a couple of days and they showed me around. It was track season then and they wanted to check out my speed. Lenny Lyles, who played with Baltimore for eleven or twelve years, was in his senior year at the time. He was perhaps the fastest guy in college ball, until Hayes came along. So they asked me to run against

Lyles. For a while I didn't do too bad because I was always quick on the start, but of course he outran me. But they liked what they saw, and we talked about a scholarship and then they laid out a contract.

At Louisville I came to know white people and it was a different kind of experience for me. I had lived much of my life without any relationship or friendship with them. Because of my life in Columbus I was a little skeptical. They were going to have to prove themselves to me, prove that they needed and wanted me. As a result I developed some friendships I will cherish the rest of my life.

I remember in one of the first practice sessions there was an older player who kept calling me "Boy." I told him to cut it out, but he persisted. When he kept pushing me around I took it as long as I could and though he was smaller than me I punched him. I told him I would do it again if necessary. Well, he stopped and we became the best of buddies. Even now we call one another up if we are in the same area.

I didn't have the usual problems that black students have regarding dating because I was already married. Since my wife was living at home with her mother when I was in college, I had most of my relationships with fellows. There was no interracial dating in Louisville then. If somebody did, the dean would call and stop it, or else you just went home.

I was very sympathetic to Martin Luther King's movement. His home in Montgomery, Alabama, is only sixty-five miles from Columbus. I was very aware of what he was doing and very much in his corner. I knew first-hand what some of the problems were, and if changes were going to be brought about, count me in, I'm with you. Of course, there wasn't much activism on the campus. Out of five or six hundred students there were less than fifty blacks.

What is the difference playing college and professional ball?

Well, in my case there was some similarity. Because I had been taught well in high school, I could do some things other guys couldn't. So when I became a halfback I used to lead plays for the fullback. The fullback would do the running and I would get the

371

blocking. So when the fullback graduates, I am the biggest thing in the backfield and I become the fullback. But we now have a small halfback who can't block. So I lead the plays for him.

When I come to the pros, I run into the same thing. Jim Brown is here. He needs a blocker, so I am the one to lead him. I did it first for Jim and then when Leroy Kelly came, I did the same for him.

In pro football the only thing we are interested in is winning. We know it is not going to last forever and if we do well and win, we are going to be able to do those nice things for our families that take dough. So any person whom we can depend on in those third-down-and-one-yard situations is the guy to bring in to do the job. I don't give a damn what his attitude or belief is if he can help us win. What he does with his time and energies off the field, I could care less. Again, it is nice if he is a nice guy, but the only thing I am interested in is good results. If we get good results, that is all that matters. If you throw that block for me, and I score that touchdown, you are going to get the same benefits I am. That is what we work for.

Jim Brown had his greatest years as a pro in 1963 and 1964. He gained eighteen hundred yards in one season. People knew Jim Brown. He was a household word so far as football goes. And he is one helluva football player.

Sometimes teams with superstars don't win championships. As great as Brown was, the Browns didn't win a championship when he was breaking all the records. Another example is Sonny Jurgenson. For the past five years Jurgenson has been the greatest passer in the game, but the Washington Redskins don't win.

Of course you use what you've got, but I look at the number of backs that the Browns, for example, must have gotten from 1958 to 1964, backs who didn't make it. What I'm saying is that we will never know whether some of those guys might have helped make the Browns a winner. We will never know that. The Browns didn't have to carry five backs like other teams because Jim Brown was almost indestructible. They said: Jim Brown is always going to be there. And in those critical situations when the ball was given to

Jim, sometimes he was stopped. Perhaps if someone else had done it, while they were expecting Jim, the results would have been different.

What part do personal attitudes, particularly about race, have on the field?

Well, take Brown again for an example. Despite his greatness, there were people who couldn't stand Brown because he was black. You remember the remark of Tommy Smith, once the world record holder in the hundred-yard dash, "On the track I'm the world's fastest human, but off the track, I'm just another nigger."

And some guys can be the greatest people in the world, the greatest football players in the world, until certain things happen. We can be "buddy, buddy," drink from the same glass, spend the night at each other's house, but the moment you see me with a white girl, it is all gone. There is a possibility it could affect play on the field. There is always a chance that because somebody saw somebody with that girl, a block will be missed or a play won't get called. But in pro ball everybody suffers because of your feelings.

If you get into an argument with the quarterback, it is possible he won't call your plays. They tell a story about one leading quarterback who used to take some of the guys out on week nights and booze them up pretty good. He would try to get them as drunk as he could so the next morning with a big hangover, he could work the devil out of them. It was his style: if they go out and booze it up, they should be able to take it the next day. What I am really saying is that other guys in their own way do the same thing as this quarterback. When we have feelings and when we react, I may do something to hurt you. But half the time I am probably hurting us all.

It can sometimes work the other way. A perfect example is Lenny Lyles, the guy I raced at Louisville. When we played the Baltimore Colts, we would always chat before the game. Once when I was just standing around watching Jim Brown run a particular play, and not blocking, Lenny almost took my head off. He knocked me down, and said, "You'd better pay attention to what's going on around here." Then he helped me up. Later in the game, I looked for him and got him back, hit him pretty good. I think the guys play just a little bit harder against their friends than they do against guys they really hate.

Race plays a big part at the box office. Before Jim Brown, there was Motley of the Browns. He was the Joe Louis of football. Black people started to get interested in the Browns then because they had Lynn Ford, Marian Motley, Bill Louis. And Jim Brown came along right after. Last year I think the Browns had something like fifteen black football players. It used to be that way with the Cleveland Indians, with fellows like Larry Doby, Luke Easter and others. Here was the feeling of a black guy out there and doing a hell of a job. Now that the black stars are not with the Indians, black people have no one to identify with.

Is athletics the way for young black people to establish their identity?

Today they can find their identity in a number of ways. There is the study of Afro-American civilization which we never had. I think it is wonderful because when you start talking to other people one of the most embarrassing questions is, who are your folks? Where did you come from? Years ago people didn't come up with ideas about our black background and heritage. I would love to have that for my children.

Another way is to work within the system and to improve it. There are difficulties about this today, especially among college-age students. I think one of the best ways to change the system is to get involved in it. The students argue differently and we can learn a lot from them. I know I have. People are my bag, and whenever there is a group of people, especially young people, with some problems, that is what I like. Students today are more aware of world problems than we were. We were not as knowledgeable as these kids because most of them have grown up with the situations which are taking place right now.

We have been in Viet Nam for nine years, so if a kid is nineteen years of age, that is all he has heard about. This is a major concern

374

of today's young people, but when I was in college the kids only wanted to go to parties on the weekends and drink beer. Today's kids are more knowledgeable, they don't mind saying what they feel, whereas we couldn't or didn't. If we talked loud or raised too much hell the doorman would come and throw us out of school. Now kids do exactly as they want. They take over the dorm, take over the president's office. Sometimes they get spanked and sometimes they don't.

We have good discussions. I agree we should get out of Viet Nam but I question the ways they have for implementing their ideas. I don't think disrupting classes, burning buildings, taking over classes and interrupting the education of others is the right thing. I tell them not to force their own feelings on others.

Students are also critical about the system, about whether or not they should get into it. They say that once you get into it you don't want to change it. Some of the kids who leave college and get involved in the system you never hear of again. I wonder what happened to their philosophies, their ideas about changing the system. I would be interested in looking up a group of activists four or five years after graduation to find out what they are doing.

When I was coming up, the way to get accepted was the way of Willie Mays. I felt in the back of my mind that if they accept you because you are an athlete, later they may accept you in other ways. So first I was accepted as a football player and now, because I am doing something else, I will be accepted another way.

More and more black parents aren't encouraging their kids to get involved in athletics. I talk often to high-school students and attended a meeting not long ago. One of the parents suggested to me that I play down athletics. So I told them that athletics are great, but not the most important thing in the world. I tell the same things to my own children. I have three boys, ages thirteen, six and four. I don't want them to be the success in athletics that I was. I loved it, but with me it was an obsession. I'd rather they have an obsession for something else, maybe law or teaching.

There is no problem about blacks being accepted in athletics any longer. Everybody in the world knows that black guys can become

375

pretty good athletes. But now there are other areas, other professional fields. We can also become great doctors, great educators, lawyers and the rest. These are the areas that we are now going to conquer.

Robert Storey

The three-storied house is large and comfortable with a lawn sur-
rounding it on all sides. It is across the street from Saint Paul's
Episcopal Church and Robert Storey is at home. The children are
dressed for bed, watching television's "Bewitched." I shake hands
with the boys, and they return to the set.

Robert Storey is in his early thirties, a pipe-smoker, an attorney
and an elected director of the Associated Harvard Alumni. Almost
a native Clevelander, he nonetheless spent eleven years — from age

377

"The whites keep asking, 'Who is going to be the black Moses?' Well,
who in hell is going to be the white spokesman? Who in hell is
going to lead this country?"

REBMAN PHOTOGRAPHERS INC.

fourteen to twenty-five — on the East Coast, in Boston and later at Quantico, Virginia, with the Marine Corps.

Bob Storey identifies easily with his race and always has, and he is also a black professional man. He can walk both sides of the street. And while he has hopes for America's future, he senses the present lassitude in race relations and doesn't like it.

I suppose you might call it a kind of "sustenance" theory or something — people helping each other by knowing them before — but I really didn't have any problem with overt race prejudice either at Phillips Exeter Academy or at Harvard College. Let me put it in context. I came to Harvard from Exeter and I had a number of close friends, one of whom was black and we lived in the same dorm my freshman year at Harvard. I saw him along with other people I knew, people I met. It wasn't a matter of blacks seeking out blacks. You would probably have to say that my experiences at both schools was atypical, but let me tell you something about the other black students who were at Exeter at the time.

There was a fellow named Monty Dowling and we ran together on the track team, both hurdlers. We became friends because we were on the track team together. Today Monty is a doctor in New York. Another fellow, very quiet and sensitive, was Nathanial La-Mar who was a senior when I first arrived. Nate is from Atlanta where his mother is a school teacher. He was a writer and went on to Harvard. I think he once won a competition with the *Atlantic,* now he is an editor in a New York publishing house. Harold Scott was a class ahead of me at Exeter. He became interested in dramatics, and is still an actor. His father was a doctor in Orange, New Jersey. Scotty went into theater at Harvard, got together with two other actors and put on the American premiere of Jean Genet's *Death Watch.* One of the students bought the American rights to it and they put it on in Cambridge. Drama critics came from all over the eastern seaboard to see it. It ran to tremendous audiences and then went to New York. Later he became an original member of the Lincoln Company of the Performing Arts and appeared in the

379

play *Cool World*. Another classmate was Tony Miles, who was with me both at Exeter and later at Harvard. Tony is now in Washington, a lawyer with the Securities Exchange Commission and his wife is a child psychiatrist.

I say all this to show that there was just a handful of black people there but they all reached some level of distinction. Those of us who became friends did so because our paths crossed one or another area of common interest, not because there was a black solidarity movement. There wasn't.

Of course it would have been different if you didn't have the advantage of coming from the same prep school and having a group of friends there. For a black student, say from Cincinnati or somewhere, to come in cold to Harvard, he will probably feel somewhat overwhelmed. He would have the initial burden of being black, then coming from a distant place and falling into an entirely different environment, a high-powered rich society.

For example, I remember one of the questions that was asked on the Exeter application: what was your home address and what was your summer address. It seemed quite strange to me that one would have a summer address; you know, why weren't they at home in the summer? Exeter was a whole new experience for me. I had never known people from that eastern seaboard culture before, people with two sets of parents, who took summer vacations in Europe and winter vacations in the Bahamas and Florida. It was a whole new world. I never knew people like that.

I grew up on Cleveland's East Side though I was born in Tuskegee, Alabama. My father had seven brothers and six sisters and lived on my grandfather's farm there. When I was about two or three months old we moved first to Detroit, Michigan, then to Cleveland. I can still remember my grandfather because I returned to Tuskegee when I was fourteen or so. He was then in his later seventies still living there and trying to take care of the place, an independent man who — even with all his sons and daughters scattered about — refused to come live with any of them. I have an older brother and my father works for the city. We all — including my mother of course — lived in public housing. During the Second World War, those with sensitive jobs connected with the war effort were given preference, so new housing units became available for Negroes. It was a predominately black area but there were some white families, but not too many. Really it was a mixture of people. I never thought I was living in a ghetto or anything. None of the people were wealthy, but some had far less than others. They were all your friends, and while I had a brand new baseball glove more often than the others, nobody made much out of it. Parents didn't pick your friends because of what your friends' parents were or weren't. Today I think it is a bit different and the urban setting, especially the black urban setting, lacks alternatives. It is one of the tragedies of the kind of society we are creating today that there is a sameness about life in the ghetto, an economic and educational sameness.

In the elementary school, for example, my homeroom was in the library and we had all the newest books and equipment with people coming down from the board of education giving us everything from finger painting to Spanish and French. We had radio programs on elementary foreign languages, music and art.

Of course at that time I had never heard of Exeter, but some of the teachers had and they talked with my mother and father encouraging me to apply there.

So unlike some black people who moved from the South to the North, you really moved from West to East?

Yes, and at an early age. I was fourteen, and the only black student in an entering class of two hundred thirty-five freshmen. The whole school had at that time seven hundred fifty students and about six were black. There were difficulties. I never worked so hard in my life. There were kids there that had been in private schools from the beginning, places like Buckley and Trinity-Pauling and Fessenden. I would be in my room studying after dinner and these kids would be out in the halls playing or fooling around. I couldn't understand it. I thought I must be the dumbest guy in the world. I didn't know how to study. It was the kind of thing a lot of people from public schools in those days didn't learn. At places like Exeter and Harvard you really learn how to study, knowing what is important and how to select what is important — good training later on for law school.

What did you do outside the classroom?

I was tall for my age and had played a little baseball in Cleveland, but the track coach wanted to make a hurdler out of me. Somehow I figured out those strides between hurdles and by the spring I had made varsity track in my freshman year. Later I was vice-president of the senior class, cocaptain of the track team and on the student council. At commencement, I was the first class marshal, an elected position, the fellow who leads the class at graduation.

Discrimination? Well, as I said, no overt discrimination ever, but there were some experiences. You see the town Exeter, New Hampshire, had about five thousand people and there were no black families. There was perhaps a kind of innocence on the part of many people there, much like the reception that black people got when they first went to Europe. There were black people in Portsmouth, New Hampshire, and in New Bedford, Massachusetts, there has long been a black community. They were involved in the whaling industry, skilled craftsmen who were respected.

I recall once when I rode my bicycle through town, one of the faculty children rode by me on his bicycle, then stopped, pedaled back and asked me, "Are you from Japan?" He obviously had never seen a Negro before. Another time I remember a visit to a family in the town that I had gotten to know rather well. The mother was telling me that her son Michael, who was in the seventh grade, asked her what they meant in the civics class when they said they were studying the Negro problem. He wanted to know what a Negro was. So she told him, "Bob is a Negro, what did you think he was?" He said, "I thought he just had a good suntan."

My favorite story about Exeter though is about my first day there. I was a little hungry and decided to go out and get a hamburger. I bought two, brought them back to my room, ate one and didn't want the other. So I looked around for somebody who might want it. I saw this kid down the hall, a tall stringy guy and I went over and told him I had this extra hamburger which I didn't want and would he like to have it. He looked at me and said, "No, thanks." So I said, "Okay, if you change your mind, let me know. I have it down in my room if you want it." Later that evening I went down to dinner and a fellow came up and introduced himself to me and said he was from New York City. We stood talking there until this same tall fellow came down the steps. My acquaintance said, "Do you know who that is?" I said, "No." He said, "That's John D. Rockefeller's boy, John D. IV." Later John and I became good friends.

Was it automatic that you would go on to Harvard?

No. Actually I thought I would go to Oberlin College, near Cleveland. My class graduated two hundred seventeen people and about ninety of us were accepted at Harvard, about thirty-five to Yale, about twenty-five to Princeton and sixteen at Dartmouth. The class went overwhelmingly to Ivy League schools, but I had no orientation to any particular college. I felt I had had enough of New York, Boston and Philadelphia. I mean that I had seen enough of the eastern establishment, and wanted to go back to the "good, old, wholesome Middle West" and to a different kind of school, a coed school and all the rest. I had applied to Harvard, Yale and Oberlin. I was admitted to Oberlin right away, long before admissions from Harvard and Yale came back. So I wrote to Harvard and Yale and told them to withdraw my application. Then something happened over the summer to change my mind.

I went to England for the summer as a Winant Volunteer. Boys from Exeter had been involved in the Winant Volunteer Program since Ambassador John Winant, ambassador to the Court of Saint James and the former governor of New Hampshire, had suggested the idea of having young people from America come to work as camp counselors and lifeguards in London's West End in the cockney district.

There was a great shortage of young men to do this sort of work. My family paid part of my way and there was a partial scholarship so I could go over. The fellows I went with were all going to Harvard and I got a different perspective on things there.

I was assigned to a place called Bethnal Green, in the industrial

East End of London. I can remember Peter Duke, the head of Oxford House where we worked, saying then that it was interesting I got along so well with the people there because there were very few black Americans coming over at that time. Of course I was in the company of other teen-age Americans who were a bit older, and I suppose they made the assumption I had to be rich like all the other Americans.

The London experience was important to me because before then I had no awareness of political problems or matters of foreign policy. These things never interested me, even at Exeter. But while I was in London for that summer, I became an ardent reader of the *Times* and the *Manchester Guardian*. I began to look at world problems and politics because I found they played more of a role in the lives of English people than here at home. So, for the first time I developed a political awareness and sensitivity.

As I look back upon these experiences, and on my admission to Harvard, I think my initial feeling to get away from the East Coast may have been emotional, at least a little. It benefited me greatly to go away to London and have an opportunity to remain in a milieu which had really become part of me. It was something completely natural to me. And then later when I had a chance to be at a great center of learning, with people studying there from all over the world, well, I never regretted not going to Oberlin.

At Harvard the big names were often boring in class, while some of the lesser known ones were simply great. I recall Professor Philip Rhinelander, who is now at Stanford, a dean there. He lectured in Humanities Five on "The Ideas of Good and Evil." He was a very good lecturer, extremely popular, but got canned, I think, because he didn't publish. He was a very gifted man. There were others, too, especially in my field which was government. I had started out in history but switched because of my interest in the undeveloped areas of the world, Africa, Asia and the Middle East; at that time there were no courses in history in these areas, but only in the department of government.

Another professor I recall was Professor Merk, who taught American history. He was a student of Frederick Jackson Turner and a delightful old man. In the worst storm of the year he would put on his galoshes and his muff and come to class, even if there were only six people there. He would lecture to six or six hundred in the same way.

I responded to teachers who put something into the course. And when the lecture was dull, I just stopped going to class, feeling that I could spend my time more fruitfully than just sitting in a dull lecture.

I liked social life, too, but you must realize that none of us had any money. Going out was very expensive. A weekend of football, for instance, was very costly. If you had a date coming up, you had to have a place for her to stay, unless she came from the local area. The only way I cut it financially was to operate a newsstand. In the beginning of my sophomore year I started it in the Freshman Union, and I did it for three years. I made a little bit of money by selling *Playboy* and *Escapade,* the *New York Times,* cigarettes and candy. This provided me with pocket money to do what my roommates were doing with their fathers' money.

The social life at Harvard was a little easier for me because I had a backlog of friends and associates. It was a major difference between me and the other black students there. They had trouble relating both to their brothers and didn't really feel a part of Harvard either. I remember going out to a party in Roxbury during my freshman year with a fellow from Boston. He was always after me to come to parties and I kind of resented it because I really didn't know this guy. You see, I had already been brainwashed. I didn't really know him, so why should I want to go to a party with him on the weekend when I had parties of my own to go to?

At that time parties were outside the context of my life and not something I wanted. It was rather a continuation of the kind of social life and activity I didn't really have to go to Harvard or Exeter to find. I don't want to put a worse connotation on it than it was, but I found what was happening at Harvard much more interesting and stimulating.

F. Scott Fitzgerald said that black people have a great capacity for participating, yet withdrawing. I think it is true that the black professional has of necessity had to bridge two cultures, play both roles, to be at the same time the actor and the writer or observer.

385

For the black man to survive in American society he has had to be comfortable both in the worst ghetto and in the plushest white home.

For example, we went to a party in Glenville with another black couple last week. It was a very unpretentious party and we really enjoyed it. The people were all ages, dancing and laughing, very uninhibited. There was no pretense, no sham. You didn't have the sophisticated conversation you get at a white middle-class party, or the phoniness that goes with it either. It was a tremendous and relaxing evening.

After Harvard, what?

I was in a marine corps platoon leaders' program where I spent two summers, six weeks each, during my last two years at Harvard in prebasic training. At graduation I was commissioned and went to Quantico, Virginia. I was in the marine corps for three years. I took my basic training at Quantico, then went to Japan for fifteen months and concluded my tour of service in California.

It was here I saw overt racial discrimination, not only in the corps but in the South. In the course of a year, five classes would go through, maybe twenty-five hundred marine officers. At the most, I saw about ten that were black. The highest ranking officer in the corps at that time was a captain. I believe he is now a colonel.

I can recall that we would go downtown to restaurants where I couldn't be served. I would put on a suit and walk into the restaurant and sit down, pick up the menu and see the people freeze. I wouldn't put on my uniform but even if I had, they wouldn't have served me. Once I threatened to do it, but when I told one of my friends, he told me they would declare the whole place off limits. He talked me out of it, saying that it was all well and good, but what about the rest of us, where are we going to eat? So, I didn't do my "uniform sit-in."

One time I went into a place called the Dixie Pig, put on my three-piece tweeds, sat down and picked up the menu. People looked around but nobody said anything till the waitress came up. She said, "I'm sorry I can't serve you." I said, "Why not?" She said, "It's against the law and we'll lose our license if I serve you." The interesting thing was the real look of apology on her face. She really meant it in my case. I said, "Where can I eat?" She said, "Out in the kitchen." I left, telling her that I would not eat in the kitchen.

There was only one restaurant in Quantico where I could get served. I guess this guy felt that anybody who was a marine officer could eat in his restaurant. Yet there was a real danger that he would lose his license.

On the base, too, there was some discrimination. I ran into that separate-but-equal bit in Quantico. The marine corps was one of the last of the services to integrate. It struck me as being fifty percent Catholic and fifty percent southern. The corps attracts a lot of guys from small towns, towns in Ohio, and everywhere. There was some antiblack feeling. On the other hand, the marine corps has a motto about the good "gyrene," a real marine. I found that any guy who approximated that won respect. Of course, there was a lot of racial kidding. Any guy from the South was always a hillbilly, and a guy from Chicago was a gangster. This is always true in the service and will probably always be. But if you proved yourself, you won respect.

Following my tour of duty in Japan and Oceanside, California, I returned to Cleveland, married and now have a small son. I had wanted to go to Columbia University but it would have been expensive and difficult to find a place to live nearby.

You know that most black professional people today in Cleveland are not from the area. Most of them come from the South or from some other city. Very few lawyers, and even fewer doctors and dentists, were trained here. They came from other places because they had heard it was the promised land for blacks, flowing with milk and honey, you know. Even when I grew up here, it was looked upon as a sort of Mecca for black people. Cleveland had black judges before other northern urban communities. It has school teachers, assistant principals and principals. You have had black people working as clerks in the black community here when stores in other cities still had white clerks. And blacks were working for the dairies and in the steel industry. Cleveland had the first

387

black ballplayer in the American League. It was a swinging town for blacks. I can remember when *Ebony* ran an article praising Cleveland as a great city for black people.

The law, however, has not been a promising career for a black man in Cleveland or anywhere else. At Western Reserve University, I was the only black student in my class and there were only two others in the whole law school — neither of whom graduated. Partly it was money. Those who do try go to law school at night and work during the day, maybe the post office or selling real estate. And if he graduates, the black lawyer rarely gets a crack at the corporate client, sophisticated real estate problems or tax work. His work is usually restricted to the police court, to bread and butter matters such as divorces. It is tough to make a living as a black lawyer. For this reason, guys who have the means and who can afford higher education often go into careers that promise immediate rewards: medicine or dentistry, teaching or the ministry. In these areas, you know you can find work. It is changing, but slowly.

I'm working just now in a program called the Ohio Law Opportunity Fund to provide money for minority students — Spanish, Asian, black, Appalachian white — in the form of scholarships. There seems to be money available for medical and teaching scholarships, but not much for law students.

Where are we going in America today?

I think we are in a post–civil rights period, at least if you mean by the "civil rights period" a common front with heavy white leadership, the nonviolent approach, the Martin Luther King era, the March on Washington. Probably the march in 1963 was the apex of the civil rights movement and to the extent that the promises of that march have not been forthcoming, we are in a post–civil rights era.

I don't mean there is no place for a white man in the liberation of the black masses. To say that is stupid. Not only is there room for the white man, there has to be. Not one problem affecting the black man today can be solved by the black man alone. Do you want to talk about housing? Who are the major developers? Who

are the lenders? Who owns the land? If you talk about jobs, who
are the major manufacturers? Who has the power to hire and fire in
American society? Who are the investors and stockholders? Who is
on the board of directors? What I am saying is that there are no
problems in America that black people can solve alone or that the
white people can solve alone. Anybody that advocates total separation of the races is out of his mind.

Separatism has many connotations. Obviously physical separation doesn't make much sense, but that is in fact what we have in
America. It is part of the problem. I'm not for picking up black
people and moving into six states in the South saying, "Okay, fellows, you are now on your own." That's forty acres and a mule
again, and we went through that.

From now on no white man will be able to tell a black man what
to do, or to say that a black man is inferior because he's black.
There is a heightened black consciousness that is very healthy. It
will never happen again that a white man will define the black
man's place. Today's generation has a greater philosophical solidarity and black pride. I don't mean the Afro bit. It's a lot of hog-
wash. You don't see Africans walking around with dashikis.
They're going to Brooks Brothers to buy their clothes. There was a
time, you know, when an African coming to this country would
wear native garb so he would not be confused with an American
Negro, feeling he would get some kind of preferential treatment as
an African. But no more. He *knows* what kind of treatment African garb will get him today!

I remember Richard Wright went back to Ghana thinking he
would be returning home. When he got there he found nothing, no
magical awakening. One friend of mine in the Peace Corps was in
Ghana for a while and when I asked her what she thought of it, she
said, "Thank God for slavery."

I do believe though that black people have got to get together in
the sense that they meet each other with a sense of pride and rec-
ognition. This is a great problem in the black community. For too
long has a black man had to lose his identity as a black man in
order to succeed. There was always a sort of feeling that you had to
get away from your blackness as conceived, and preconceived, by

389

the white man. You see, I don't think it is a white world, but rather a society that has been largely conceived by whites and administered by whites.

Going to Exeter was a great help to me in this respect. It let me know at a very early age that there were a lot of things I could do better than they could. I learned that I put my pants on the same way those guys did. I discovered that if given an opportunity, there wasn't anything a black man couldn't do just as well as a white man. I found out that I could make my way in what has been defined, wrongly I think, as a white man's world. This is what more and more black people are going to have to do.

It is in the white world where the power is, not in the ghetto. If you're talking about real power, effective power, political power, economic power, it is in the mainstream. We have got to go out there and compete in the mainstream because that is where it is at. We have had over one hundred years in this country of separate-but-equal, but it didn't do a hell of a lot for the South and it isn't going to do much for the North either.

There is now a sense of liberation that is widespread in the black community. I trace it back to Malcolm X. Malcolm X was the central figure in the attack on nonviolence of action and spirit. He was a man of great talent and insight whose ideas converted the intellectual and biracial civil rights movement into a struggle for identity for the masses of black people. Whereas King sought to appeal to the minds and hearts of all Americans, Malcolm aimed for the jugular of what he termed the collective white man. The nonviolent civil rights movement was bound to fail, in Malcolm's view, because if appealed to instincts and qualities which were present in too few white Americans.

I think it was Malcolm X who drove the nail into the coffin of the civil rights era, the one that is over. Malcolm X got right down to the nitty gritty. He talked to the hard-core black man and used language that this man used. When Malcolm X talked, he expressed thoughts that this man had. He was the first great mass leader, probably because we are in a time of modern communication, television and the recorded word. We probably will never know whether Marcus Garvey was a mass leader because he lived before this time.

Martin Luther King spoke in the traditional vein of the cultured, educated man in America. He spoke the wisdom of the ages and placed everything in a historical context. I remember when he spoke at Saint Paul's right across the street. He quoted Thoreau, the American Constitution, the Declaration of Independence, the Bible — the collected wisdom of Judeo-Christian society. In that sense, he was a mainstreamer. Uneducated and simple black people would hear Martin Luther King and be right with him, but not really understand him. They admired him, yes they admired him, but they didn't know who Thoreau was.

Malcolm caused the first stirrings in the bosom of the little black guy. He turned this whole thing around. And there is nobody around to replace him. I don't think there will ever be another Malcolm X any more than there will be another Martin Luther King. They were unique men. Ralph Abernathy is not Martin Luther King, and Stokely Carmichael, Rap Brown or Eldridge Cleaver are no Malcolm X's. Nothing is more transitory than a militant leader.

When I was in New Hampshire recently, David Susskind was there. His son was being enrolled at Phillips Exeter. We got into a discussion with some black students there from the Afro-Exonian Society. It is the Afro Society of Exeter. The school now has about forty or fifty black students. I was rapping with some of them and Susskind was there listening. It was shortly after Martin Luther King's death. He asked me who was going to fill the void. I told him the man I thought most likely to emerge as a national leader, as a nationally recognized leader, is Carl Stokes. And I think my prediction was borne out of *Time* recently in a national poll when he was named the black man most respected by other black people in the U.S. This man's potential is virtually unlimited. He can easily become Vice-President of the United States.

The quality he exemplifies is that if you take the rules and play the game, you can win. Working within the system does not necessarily mean defeat. If you use the ballot box, use the elected offices, just like every other group in American society, the blacks can win. Since he has been elected mayor of Cleveland, there have been more black guys involved in more significant levels of political and economic life in this town than ever before. He has succeeded in the system. He has beaten the people who, to this day, cannot accept a black mayor.

My own feeling is that if you're going to bring about change, the only change that is valid and lasting in American society comes within the institutional framework. Mass leaders who emerge on the scene overnight disappear overnight. This is true even of Malcolm X. I think Malcolm himself had reached this point in his personal philosophy when he was killed. If you recall in the *Autobiography,* his trip to Mecca transformed him. For the first time in his life, he said he could see the white man as a brother. I think in a sense Malcolm X experienced in Mecca what I experienced at Exeter and Harvard. I could then see people as people. I didn't like every guy I met at Exeter, but I didn't dislike him just because he was white.

What I mean is that Mecca or Exeter could be anywhere, anywhere from this point of reference. When Malcolm had the experience, for the first time in his life, of seeing people as black, as white, or Asian, he saw them as people. They were there in the name of Islam, so there was this community of feeling between them.

When I saw that something similar happened at Exeter and Harvard, I mean that out of these experiences came lasting friendships between blacks and whites, enduring ones with real love and affection. I don't have any hangups about distrusting Whitey, or getting Whitey. There are a lot of fools and bastards in this world. Some are black and some are white.

Martin Luther King makes this point in another way. The genius of King is that he took what had been described as a Negro problem and made it into an American problem. He properly linked the struggle for Negro rights to the great cause of human rights. He lifted things up beyond Montgomery. It wasn't just some poor old darkie woman, an uppity type, who wouldn't sit down at the back of the bus. It was a great act of rebellion on the part of a human being, crying out for dignity. Martin Luther King took the Rosa Parks incident and made white America see for the first time what the black man was asking for. It was an idea whose time had come. He was a prophet. He was demanding nothing less than the constitution, nothing less than the Declaration of Independence.

There are some who will say that the reason for his death, the manner in which he was killed by a white man, the way he was beaten, also showed black people just how bad the white man is. But the white man also killed John Kennedy and Robert Kennedy. A white man shot Lincoln. The white man hung Jesus, we are told. That is nothing new. There are a number of people who can't be trusted and many of them are white.

We did not only lose Martin Luther King, we lost the Kennedy brothers and many other leaders. Perhaps in no other time have we lost so many great men in our country over such a short period of time. There is no one in the white community that is filling the void today either. What we are really facing is a lack of the kind of leadership that can bring us all together, yet I hate to use that word because it has been prostituted by President Nixon.

The momentum gained during the early sixties, the civil rights period, has been lost. The desire to commit our national resources, our national morality, to solving social and race problems has been dissipated. And I think it has been deliberately undercut by the present Administration. Nixon is trying to put the lid back on, trying to turn back the clock to the Eisenhower era when the Executive Office just didn't get involved in these matters. It didn't, of course, and we are now paying for it. We are going to have a helluva time in the seventies. The present Administration is catering to people who want to put the nigger back in his place, who want to put the students back in their place.

My generation was called the Silent Generation, because we didn't cause any problems for anybody. We were slotted into the system. Kids aren't that way today. We are now living in an age of participatory democracy, and the participants get younger and younger each year. There is today a greater interrelationship between students, both black and white. They aren't hung up personally about color, but only on strategy. Kids today know nothing about separate-but-equal. You've got to remember that 1954 is sixteen years ago. They don't know anything about a segregated army. You walk the streets today and you see many black and white couples. The kids don't have our particular hangups, and they are going to keep things boiling.

What we really need is the political leadership that can bring this whole new effort into the mainstream. The kids can't win. It will be Chicago all over again, misguided idealism ill spent. I think it was Sammy Davis, Jr. who said once, "There ain't yet been a razor made that can stop a tank." That's what I'm talking about.

In Chicago incidentally a lot of white people for the first time saw what the police can do to you. This didn't surprise black people. It did surprise white people though who saw their own kids getting leaned on. They never thought it could happen. But it did.

I suppose I'm coming back to that old pitch again about being able to recognize individual qualities and not get hung up on color. Carl Stokes became mayor of Cleveland not just because he was black. The same thing was true of John F. Kennedy, the first Catholic President of the United States. This didn't mean that any Catholic can become President. The fact that Carl Stokes can become Vice-President of the United States doesn't mean that any black man can do it. Look at Richard Hatcher of Gary, Indiana. I'm talking now about the qualities, personal and political, that individuals have. Look at all the white mayors there are in this country. Only a handful could be called distinguished or truly outstanding.

Because the white community knows that it has not been treating the black man very well, he is nervous. A guy can put on a dashiki and get on the street corner at noon and declare himself a black leader and the media will go around and lionize him. Ahmed Evans became a national figure because the *Wall Street Journal* quoted him as saying the world will come to an end, on May 9, I think. Nobody had even heard of Ahmed Evans before. So when the black man says no instead of being nice and quiet, white people think maybe he's going to kill them.

This is just another part of that make-believe world in which white people try to imprison black people. For the longest time, white people felt that because a Negro was serving their food and smiling he was very content, very happy and had no problems. And

394

now today because some guys are frowning and calling them names, they have just flipped over. They think that is the real side, the true feelings of black people. As usual, white people are looking for a single answer for black folks. They never demand a single answer for white people.

They keep asking, "Who is going to emerge as the black Moses?" "Who is going to be the black spokesman?" Well, who in hell is going to be the white spokesman? That is more of a problem. Who in hell is going to lead this country? There are a lot more whites, with a lot more training, with a lot more money, a lot more prestige than there are blacks. And at the moment the white community is not producing this kind of leader. So I think instead of running around trying to find out who's going to lead the blacks, white people better find out who is going to lead the whites, and therefore lead this country.

George Forbes

George Forbes is tall, maybe six-foot-six. He is thirty-eight, a college graduate, a lawyer, a councilman elected from the all-black Twenty-seventh (Glenville) District, reelected three times. He has grown in his perception of black pride just as his constituents in the Twenty-seventh District have. Forbes has often led the way. He understands and appreciates the demands for black self-determination but he also knows the real power is downtown. He said recently, "You know, just looking at a fox hunt you would think

"Black folks hate white folks and white folks hate black folks, but it has to be put in context . . . until you recognize hatred, you can't overcome it."

the fox is leading the chase because he is out in front. Actually, the hunter, carrying the gun, is the leader."

Forbes went to the "Mountain Top" two years ago, out into his own ward to talk to Fred Evans (see interview with Ahmed El Ibn Said) and his young nationalists who were under police surveillance. He was the last person to see Ahmed before the shooting started. Gunfire prevented his return.

When you move from the South to the North you don't see any apparent differences, except that you can ride in front in the streetcars and buses. But it is only apparent. Black folks live together. White folks live together. A segregation existence. Perhaps I appreciate the segregation in the South more than in the North. Down there, there are no ifs, ands or buts about it. You know that white folks are opposed to black folks. Up North you have entrepreneurs who say things out of one side of their mouths — like "let's get together" — then they hire you to go to their factory where it's all white and you sweep the floor.

We have a saying: "In the South, you only have a few white friends but they are good ones; in the North you don't have any at all."

My home was in Memphis, Tennessee, and I went to Manassas High School. We also had a Booker T. High. There's always a Booker T. Washington high school in southern cities. My folks were typical southern Negroes, sharecroppers. My dad worked in a factory and lost an arm about the time I was born. He wasn't guaranteed any lifetime job because there was no such thing as pensions and workingman's compensation so far as Negroes were concerned. So while he farmed a little, my mother cleaned white folks' kitchens for three dollars a week. There were nine children in the family. What white people we knew, we knew as lords and masters. We never had a chance to associate with them. I never had a white teacher till I came North to college.

We were told to rise up and get an education, then leave. I don't feel that way today, but at the time it made sense to urge young black folks to go North.

398

I was attracted to Cleveland because my brother lived here, and it was during 1948, the year of the Olympics when Harrison Dillard was running, that I visited here. I'm no track star but it created the feeling that Cleveland was a good place for blacks to go to school. I had done two years in the marine corps so I had the GI Bill. In 1953 I entered Baldwin Wallace College, a Methodist School. I'm a Methodist.

There were twenty black students there at the time and I wanted to be a minister; would you believe it? After one course in the New Testament, I said to hell with it. We blacks hung together in order to survive. You see, it was a typical midwestern small college and they allowed twenty blacks in, a sort of quota system but they wouldn't admit it. I was older of course, twenty-three or twenty-four and wasn't much interested in the panty raids and all that crap. I was there to get an education.

I never ran for a political office in college. What can you do with twenty votes?

My major was American history and political science. I wanted to know from the historical viewpoint what this country was all about. I guess I took about every damn course they offered in American history. I didn't go to school to become a politician. I went to study government, what made this country tick. Of course, I knew I had to survive, so I got a teaching degree in social studies. I wanted a complete background. I wanted to learn what this country was all about. My term papers were always about the Negro in politics or the Negro in the New Frontier, always centered around research for the Negro, though there was very little done unless you read John Hope Franklin, W. E. B. Du Bois and people like that.

I'm not one of these blacks who desire to go to Liberia or Ghana. It's here. This is where it's at. It is here in this particular time and in this country. No ifs, ands, or buts about it. This great country survived because of strength. Right is right at any particular time, but this country has not done everything that was right. There were plenty of incidents, like World War II when we removed the Japanese. But during that particular time it was the right thing to do. So you go through the process and you learn from history.

399

Somebody has got to chart the course. What you do is appreciate the good qualities and try to rectify the faults. That is the basic philosophy I have. I'm both trying to make the damn thing work, as a politician, and also trying to understand it. This is one of the greatest problems we have, lack of understanding.

After college, it was an old story. Since I had taken a few extra courses to be a teacher, I applied at the board of education. I was turned down by a Negro woman. I can't remember her name, but she played the role of good nigger and Uncle Tom. She's dead now but maybe she lived too long. She would turn down blacks just as fast as they would come. So I did what plenty of other guys did: went to work for the post office. It is a fairly common story if you want to survive. For a while, they let me substitute, then I spent half a year teaching, then I left to become a housing inspector and later went to law school at night.

For a while my working schedule went like this: during the day I was substituting in school, went to law school three nights a week, drove a post office truck two nights a week. And by using Saturday and Sunday I got another forty hours a week as a truck driver.

While I was a housing inspector, I moved into the Glenville area. It was rapidly changing from white to black. So when the election of 1962 came up, I said, "What the hell, I've got the qualifications. I'm going to try to be councilman." And I didn't even have the support of the black paper in town, *The Call and Post*.

Anybody encourage you?

Well, the year I was elected, 1962, I finished Cleveland Marshall Law School. But I had worked for a fellow named Bill Sweeney, the incumbent, a year or two before that. So when my family and I first moved here, he saw the problems were rapidly changing. There was a problem of white folks understanding and interpreting the needs of black folks. Bill told me he didn't understand them and would rather step down than to half represent the ward. He had been born and raised in the neighborhood, but he didn't understand problems like welfare.

You see blacks don't have the parish priest to talk to about this type of thing. So they would come to Sweeney and ask him to solve this or that problem. Black folks call on their councilman for every-thing. In a white area people are too sophisticated to call city hall on certain problems. Well, this was getting to Sweeney and he said, "To hell with it."

The area used to be Irish and Jewish. Sweeney was the Irish candidate and there was a fellow by the name of Jerry Goldman who ran and several others. There were seven in all and I came out on top in the primary and won the general election. I hadn't made any promises except to provide good government. I never went out and said that I'm going to do this or do that. The longer you are in this business, the easier it is for you to do things or see that they get done. I know this ward now backwards and forwards. So I didn't make promises. I responded to the people, to what their problems are and their needs. Some problems I can't solve, of course, because they don't come into my province.

Don't misunderstand me. There are plenty of things I can do, especially with a black mayor in city hall. The greatest thing that could possibly have happened for the people in my district is to have a black man become mayor of the city of Cleveland. We want for very little so far as city services go. We get a better deal than we have ever gotten before, and not to the detriment of the white wards either. They are still getting services. But we are getting more than we have ever gotten before. What goes around comes around.

This is a point that my white colleagues cannot always under-stand. They are used to serving under white mayors, but it is just a matter of giving up the throne. When Anthony Celebreeze was mayor, they would call him Tony, play golf together, go to Mass on Sunday together.* So, what the hell, they would pick up the phone and say, "Honey, put the mayor on. This is George." And they told him, "I would like to have this or that." Now I'm entitled to it, because when the mayor runs, out of my thirteen thousand registered voters he gets most of them. When you go to a West Side district with thirteen thousand registered voters, maybe he picks up one hundred votes.

* Anthony Celebreeze, later secretary of what is now the Office of Health, Education and Welfare, was mayor of Cleveland from 1956 to 1962.

How would you describe the Twenty-seventh District today?

The median salary is six thousand to seven thousand dollars a year, for people who work at Republic Steel, Fisher Body, Alcoa and that kind of plant. This is their first chance to buy a home, it is an honor for them and they want to keep it that way. They range in age from forty to fifty years and have been here about ten years. They are hard working, honest people when they are left alone. They are probably more conservative in their views than the average person. But when there is a confrontation, that upsets the balance. I mean the black and white thing.

Our kids range from fourteen to eighteen and they go to the local high schools. They recognize that there are problems between black folks and white folks. They are not militants, they are not fire-bomb throwers. They don't wear dashikis and tikis and this sort of stuff. But they know what is going on and they make the difference. The kids are the ones that are carrying the message to the families. They know that their folks can work at Republic Steel the rest of their lives, but they are not going to be able to buy it. This is how the influence is reaching the parents.

Now this is my role. On the one hand we try to fight to maintain the status quo and on the other hand recognize that things are not like they used to be. Certain changes must happen. We don't try to duck the issue. Sometimes I'm caught in the middle.

Have all city services been improved for black folks, especially the police?

Well, the police department is an entity in itself. That is a problem that no one understands. They are an independent, autonomous unit. And the police in this town are more aggravated because the mayor is black. But so far as the number of men assigned to black areas, there has been an increase.

The police are special. It is in the nature of the job and it is a historical concept that the guys live by. They have to recognize that there is a social change taking place in this country. If a guy wants mainly to have a gun on his side, then there is something wrong with him anyway. I realize that they have got to have one, but there

402

is a social upheaval taking place in this country. The sociologists realize this and a lot of politicians too. But some politicians won't accept it. They say, no, we are going to have the status quo, and the bastion of the old is the police department, the men in blue. They draw the line here.

Let me give an example of what I'm talking about. Last night in city council meeting we had something like three hundred or four hundred whites come down to complain about some housing project they were particularly interested in. They had about five policemen in the council chamber. Two weeks ago we had forty black high-school kids come to the chamber and they had about eighty policemen there, maybe two for every black. I commented on this to the law director, but he can't do a damn thing about it. The mayor recognizes this thing too. The police view themselves as the old gods that have to keep everything in order the way it used to be. But, you see, time marches on.

Young blacks say, no, it is not going to be this way. And then you've got some whites who are trying to overthrow the establishment. They don't know what the hell they want. The difference between the young blacks and the young whites is that the blacks want in and the young whites don't want anything. You see, everybody is raising hell and still we are trying to maintain the ideas of 1890 in 1970. Until the time comes when the police departments can accept the fact that things have changed, there will be trouble.

The police department itself must change and adapt itself to new times and trends. This is something the criminal element understand quite well. The average criminal out there recognizes that the police department is frustrated and he is really outfoxing them.

The policeman, for example, never goes back to school. I don't care if he stays on the force for forty years, he never goes back to school. There is no such thing as in-service training. He goes to the range and shoots his pistol, maybe once a month, and that is it. He doesn't stay abreast of Supreme Court decisions and amendments to the decisions, to sociological changes going on in his community. Every policeman should go back to school every year for a week or several days or whatever, so he can be brought up to date. When you enforce the law, you've got to know what it is all about.

403

And pay is no problem, at least here in Cleveland. We've got the highest paid police department in the state of Ohio. Our men make about ten thousand dollars a year.

There are some related problems too. There is a lot of silent approval outside my district, in the suburbs, for what is going on here. And not only outside it, but inside too. Let me give you an example. We have an omnibus crime bill now pending in council which says that when you see three or more people standing on the corner, and the policeman feels they are capable of committing a felony, they can be held for seventy-two hours as suspicious persons. I was just standing out there a short time ago with two other fellows. With this damn crime bill, I am subject to being arrested.

White people want it passed because once it is passed, you can keep the Negro under control. This is what it is all about. They are kidding themselves. Where do you have the highest rate of unemployment? It is right down here with black folks, so if a man can't get a job, should he have to stay in his house all day? He can't work. His check is late. So he can't stand on the corner. What you are doing is to leave it to the discretion of some guy who happens to be driving around in a police car to say that he is capable of committing a felony.

All of us are capable of committing a felony. The bill will not be equally enforced in white districts, but it will be enforced down here in mine.

Probably the worst job in America today is to be a black policeman. No question about it. The role of the policeman is to be the protector, the enforcer of the law, to enforce justly and impartially. But to the blacks the law has always been the white man's law. So when you bring in a black policeman who is enforcing the white man's law, he is immediately labeled an Uncle Tom. And this has a very devastating effect. In our town we recruit hard to get blacks on the police force, but they want no part of it, especially if they'll be assigned to my district. And, too, there is a trend toward private police forces which hurts recruitment for the city police. And the black policeman feels the injustice that has been put upon his people for years, for years and years, and he will be caught up in the middle of it.

404

Do you think that black folks hate white folks and white folks hate black folks?

Yes, I do, but it has to be put in context. You see, when we have some kind of confrontation between whites and blacks, it is usually over housing, or education, or jobs, increase in welfare, or something like that. But these things are spin-offs of the basic problem. The basic problem is that there is a vast dislike or prejudice that exists on both sides, black and white.

And the Constitution has caught up with the white folks. The difference between life today and two or three years ago in my District is that the black folks have read the constitution. They recognize that they have got the right to bear arms too. So they bear arms. Nobody can do anything about it. They have got arms, they have got them all over my district. When they didn't have them, it didn't make much difference. Now people don't move in on them the way they used to.

But this feeling of black folks against white ones is a very new phenomenon. It was not expressed so much in the past. And when it was it was not an open thing. Black people were afraid to come out and say that they hated white folks. There was a southern teaching which said, "The Lord would make a way." But how in the hell can he make a way for me, when white folks are making it for themselves? Negroes began to find this thing out. So, they don't depend so much on the Lord as they do upon themselves.

Let's talk about housing. Let's say that the white folks are going to be good and build houses for black people. We must face the issue that people must be housed in this country. So white folks come along and build them right back in the same ghetto where the old ones are. But we may want them to put them up in suburbia, wherever it is. We expect a black man to live like a decent human being and we will do all we can to build him a house in order to uplift him. The white man has got to respect the rights of the other party. Then we are facing the issue.

You see, hatred does exist and if we're going to work on the problem of hatred, you do it not on any one Brotherhood Sunday of the year, but every day. Then housing and other problems will fall into place.

Until you recognize hatred, you can't overcome it. When you recognize it, it is a simple thing to eliminate. You take a black who says, "I don't like honkies." Then you take a white who says, "I don't like niggers." Let's be realistic about it. During a school dispute here, there was a white guy they called Chief. He and I talked. He told us that he and his friends just didn't want niggers out there. Now I could have jumped him and knocked him down, but Chief was just being realistic. I said, "All right, you have got your job and I have got mine. We have got to keep our people under control" and he did. And I did. That is a first step.

When men recognize what the basic problems are, then you can proceed. You can call it separatism or integration or anything you want to. But you must recognize what the problem is. Unless we find a solution along these lines and work on it fast, I don't see anything but chaos in this country, a little Nigeria maybe.

White people get concerned about this separatist talk but the black man has a point. It derived solely from the fact that the philosophy of Martin Luther King was rejected by young blacks. Why was it rejected by blacks? Because it was first rejected by whites. Whites wouldn't go along with it. So now blacks are saying, "If you won't let me in, I'll do my own thing in my own way." And this is your black separatist thing in a nutshell.

How much longer do you intend to be a councilman?

Not very much longer. I have come to the conclusion that you do what you can. Like Dr. King said, "I've been to the Mountain Top." I went to see Ahmed at Aburndale and 123rd Street. I was the last guy to see him, along with Walter Beach. I talked to him and told him to cool it and I would be back. When I went back, I was shot at like I was a rabbit.

You know, you do your thing. I fought for the faith I thought was right. And you are castigated by whites too. They call me on the phone and say nigger this and nigger that. I have an obligation to my family.

Ahmed is a very intelligent man. He felt deeply about the injus-

406

tices that had been inflicted upon black folks. He was a leader in the movement, especially among the young people. He understood that this is where the next thing is coming from. He hoped for changes with the young people. And there are a lot out there who feel this way. He taught them not to be afraid.

The hope is with the next young black generation. He has strength and he has pride. I suppose I'm fortunate enough to be in a position where I appreciate the old, but I'm young enough to understand the new. The new ones coming along don't care a damn about the old order. His hair is long. His hair is nappy, but that's the way it is with him. That's the way he wants it to be. He isn't worrying about hot combs anymore. It is that black pride that is going to lead him through. And us with him.

REDCAP

GRAFFITI IN DIALOGUE

Black and White together now!
Why should they want to?
Because brothers and sisters should live together
Blacks smell
Come Together Right Now
Black is Beautiful
Black Power!
You nigger lover!
Power to the people!
Blacks bite Rats!
All Power to the People!
Bigot.

> — Taken from back of a
> student's chair in the
> classroom of a white
> middle-class high school
> (Cleveland)

TIME FOR A COMMERCIAL

Friends, are you having trouble trying to sleep nights?
Worrying about the war, rioting, police brutality
   and poverty
Is that your problem, Friends?
  Well, put an end to your sleepless nights;

use

New Improved Democracy with BLACK PEOPLE in it
New Improved Democracy with BLACK PEOPLE in it
is sure to deter riots, end poverty, stop police brutality,
and let you sleep so soundly, that you won't
want to make wars, or meddle in foreign affairs

New Improved Democracy with BLACK PEOPLE in it
is guaranteed to work, not just for today
or tomorrow but for life
So remember to ask for and use;
New Improved Democracy with BLACK PEOPLE in it.

— Mary Mason
(Cleveland)

TRUTH

If I ill fit
your picture
Cry not
at what you
see
Rather,
stab the blame
within the hearts
of those, who gave to me

— Mary Mason
(Cleveland)

James O. Cannady

At age sixty-three, Jim Cannady is a kind of senior executive. He has been on the job as redcap for thirty-nine years in the Back Bay Station of the Pennsylvania Railroad in Boston, Massachusetts.

He is well known among the urban travelers and visitors who pass through the station and has maintained friendships with regular commuters which span decades. Part of his notoriety is due to the fact that he has kept up a dialogue with the passengers while he carried their bags. He has been a friend, adviser and teacher to

"Since I moved outside, I don't belong. I sometimes wonder if the white man actually realizes what he has done to black people."

thousands of people over the years. A kind of black Socrates he has asked as many questions as he has answered. Lately the topics have been urban riots and black power.

As a result, he has been asked to talk before many white groups, over a hundred. Yet he remains discouraged at the results. As he says, "Educators misinform students. The churches don't live up to the standards they preach. And the government has simply not done its part."

Jim Cannady is the last profile in this book because he represents what many white people have recommended for black people. He is well-educated and industrious, intelligent and friendly, and he has attempted to live in an integrated society. All that the best in the white community have asked of black people, Jim Cannady has done — and more besides.

But Jim Cannady at sixty-three is a dissatisfied man, a little more bitter than he was ten years ago, and now ready for retirement.

I came out of the army in 1945 and bought a lot in Sharon, an all-white suburb of Boston. The colored lady I bought it from needed the money and sold it cheap, three hundred dollars. Soon after that I got married, but it wasn't till 1953 that I could build a house on the lot.

When I got the permit to build, the people of Sharon used a technique that is not known by many people. They wanted to know what kind of a house I was gonna build. This is a method they use in order not to convey the fact that they are prejudiced. I had to get a lawyer for the day of the hearing when twenty-one people showed up to deny me the privilege of living in Sharon. My lawyer gave them twenty-four hours to grant the permit or he would seek further legal procedures against them. Rather than have the whole town going into this legal matter, they granted the permit.

So I built a Cape Cod with a shed dormer, two rooms and a bath upstairs, two bedrooms downstairs, living room, dinette area and kitchen. But it wasn't the house they objected to. It was me.

There was a white neighbor next door who had bought his house from a colored man. When I moved in, he bought a big black dog and called him Blacky. So I bought a white cat and called her Whitey. And these two animals became very friendly. They would go out on the lawn and lay down side by side with no friction whatsoever. The neighbor got a bit disgusted with this and one day he threw a can of his garbage over on my lawn where the dog and cat were sunning themselves together. So I just went over and picked up the garbage and put it back on his lawn.

On the other side there was a good neighbor, an Italian, who incidentally worked on the railroad with me. He offered to loan me any of his tools, and when I moved in, he asked whether there was anything he could do for me. Nice man.

Perhaps my daughter found it more difficult living in Sharon than my wife and me. She is graduating tonight from high school and she won't even go and pick up her yearbook. The kids in Sharon have been awfully cruel to her. She has had very few playmates. Some of the families would allow her to come into their homes but not allow their children to come into mine. It has left a scar on her. This is the tragedy of moving into suburban Sharon.

She had a party the second year we moved in, and we invited forty-two children to our house one Sunday afternoon. We had about seven black kids from Boston and the rest were white. Not one white kid of those thirty-five we invited ever asked her to their homes.

My daughter is a very good pianist, and organist in our church. She was asked by her teacher last year to get a little musical going, with some singing, for the last day of school. The teacher gave her a list of ten or twelve girls in the class she could call upon to work with. Well, Nadine, my daughter, became very engrossed in this and when they needed an organ or piano, she said, "You can practice down at my house." Six of these girls went home to ask whether they could go to my house for the rehearsal. Not one of the parents would allow them.

Now I admit I'm no angel, but I try to keep a respectable home. My home is very presentable. In fact, I was out there some months ago cutting the lawn when a man came up and asked me what time the owner of the property would be in. I said, "If you come back about six or seven P.M. you will find him then."

I have tried my best to go into the details with my daughter of what it has meant to be black and to have survived in the America we have today. I told her she had to have a unique education, that she had to be, if not better, at least as good, to get a position in most places in America. Therefore, she had to study harder and see that her marks were better than most kids. She also had many black history books which I bought for her. We have just about the complete set of works by Dr. W. E. B. Du Bois, Carter G. Woodson and many others.

What is most interesting about the treatment my daughter gets is that most of these are church-going people. I have been a member of the First Baptist Church of Sharon for the past fifteen years. I've held about every position in the church, including filling in as the minister on Layman Sunday. I've been chairman of the deacon board; I've been a deacon, an adviser, been a teacher in Sunday school. And I find that basically speaking the thinking of the majority of the people of the First Baptist Church hasn't changed. They still look at black people funny. They have this peculiar perspective simply because this is the way they have received their religion.

When I gave the sermon on Layman Sunday, I told them that unfortunately most of the hypocrites I know in Sharon are sitting in front of me this morning. I said that if I had no more respect for the teachings of Jesus Christ than you have, I would never come here to say that I worship him. Of course they didn't like it. I have now finally given up on them, not because they have hurt my faith, but I gave up because I just don't see how there is gonna be change with them.

You see it is always good to look at a thing objectively and also subjectively. You have to look at yourself. I'm no theologian but I can read the Bible and interpret it for most people. My interpretation is that God wouldn't love me until I first loved myself. I don't believe I have the capacity to love God unless I love myself. This is strange to a lot of people. They think there is something selfish about it. But before I can convince you of something I have got to convince myself of it.

I have gotten a tremendous insight into human beings by working with the Salvation Army. They have what is known as the Un-wedded Mothers Home. Each Sunday morning they have a religious service but it wasn't possible for them to get a minister. So, for years I went up to the home and spoke at least twice a month to these young, pregnant eighteen- and twenty-year-old girls, both black and white.

It amazed me to see how many of their parents disowned them because they had done the most evil thing in the world: have sexual relations with another human being. They just cut them off. Ironically, especially for the white parents, I went to some of their homes and told the mothers and fathers I would be ashamed of myself to have as fine a daughter as they had and to treat her that way. In a good many cases, their friendship was rejuvenated.

I remember one man that I wasn't able to reach. He was a minister of one of the large churches in Boston and his daughter became pregnant and he put her out. I went down to talk to him in his office at the church. I said, "Regardless of what your daughter did, she is still a human being and your flesh and blood. And I would dare to say to you that most of the things that happened to her were not her fault, but yours, because you didn't show the proper respect and love for her. It was for this reason that she had to seek other avenues to get it." And when I said, "But if that is your religious faith . . ." he just showed me right out the door.

Have you always been outspoken?

Almost from the beginning. I graduated from Johnson C. Smith University in Charlotte, North Carolina, and then got my master's degree in education — just thirty-nine years ago.

When I came out of school I started teaching in a high school. In my first year I made a statement to the class which you can believe if you find it necessary. I said that we were all by-products of our mothers' and fathers' enjoyment, that they had no idea about us but were only satisfying themselves. I told them this was an instinctive desire of man, because I was comparing the reaction of sex in mankind to that of the lower forms of animals. So I was asked to get up and apologize to the student body for this statement. They said they couldn't afford to have me in the school as a teacher if I didn't do that.

Well I refused, so I was kicked out.

Couldn't you have gotten a teaching job elsewhere?

No, because every school that you go to would ask for my previous record. This was a tradition among black educators: once you have a guy who speaks out of line you have to make sure he doesn't get back into the school. I did look for work elsewhere, and that is how I came to Boston.

I was interested in psychoanalysis, and had a very good training in education and psychology at Johnson C. Smith. One professor who had taught me, a fellow named Bill Knox said, "Jim, if you're going to Boston, and if you want to further your education, I have a friend named Edward Titchener." Bill Knox had gotten his degree at Harvard.

So he wrote to Titchener and I went over and met the famous English psychologist. He permitted me to work with him and we were doing fine until he had a heart attack and died shortly after I got there. He was a very fine professor and I would probably have gotten a degree in psychology if he had lived.

Well, I needed work and there was a job as a redcap there at the Back Bay Station. That was in 1931 and I have been here ever since, except for the three years I was in the army. By this time I am the senior man, but when I started here there were thirty-five redcaps in this station, now there are three. We are what is known as privileged trespassers. I have never been able to find out where this legal word came from, but we are the privileged trespassers at Back Bay Station.

I've met a lot of people in that time. And some of them I have made very upset. They won't come back to this station, they get off somewhere else rather than to face me. But there are others. In a morning, there may be four, five or six hundred girls coming in here and I wave at them all as they go to work. They have gotten to know me and if I am away, they want to know whether I was sick. These are girls who have never had any contact whatsoever with black people.

I've met famous people too. I was a good friend of James B. Conant, the former president of Harvard and a good friend, too, of Senator Henry Cabot Lodge. There were a number of people, including Michael Curley. I could tell an awful story about him, but I won't. Robert Frost was another. He was a very good friend of mine and wrote two poems which I have, still unpublished. One was for my daughter and the other for Jack Kennedy's Caroline.

My daughter knew, loved, and worshipped Robert Frost. She wrote an essay on him in school. The teacher read it and said it was very good, but the thing she didn't like was that it was written as if my daughter had talked to the man, actually met him. My daughter said, "Well, I have." The teacher told her that she must be kidding. So, that night when Nadine came home, she said, "Daddy, can I take this poem of Mr. Frost to my teacher and let her see it?" So she took the poem and a snapshot of her and Mr. Frost taken at my house. The teacher said she was sorry, that she had been mistaken. My daughter said, "Okay, but don't let it happen again."

When Frost died, another amusing thing happened. The reporters went to his office for a story and the secretary told them to come over to the Back Bay Station and ask for Mr. Cannady. She told them that he, perhaps better than anybody, knew the story on Mr. Frost. So they sent three people from the Boston *Globe* over here. They walked in and asked me where they could find Mr. Cannady. I told them to sit down and I would go and try to find him. I stepped in the back and telephoned the office, and the secretary apologized for not calling me in advance. So when I came out and told them that I was Jim Cannady, the reporters said, "You must be kidding." You see, they expected a person who knew Mr. Frost must be white.

You see, I am always running into this thing. When people hear about me and haven't met me yet, they always assume I am white. They just can't figure out a colored man who knows what I know.

Recently I gave a talk at Syracuse University and when I finished, a white girl came up and threw her arms around me and told me how happy she was to have heard my talk. Evidently, she was greatly thrilled because she wrote her mother and father and told them to go up to Sharon and visit me one Sunday afternoon.

Well, you should have seen the expression on their faces when they saw me! After all the nice things she had said, when they walked in and saw I was black, they were quite perturbed. I tried to make them feel as comfortable as possible by telling them that they had a fine daughter, and how pleased I was to meet people like her who were going to make this country of ours a better place to live.

How did you get to Syracuse?

I was invited by a good friend of mine, Dr. William West, who was then a professor of English at Syracuse University. There were three professors there, and two laymen to discuss the subject of integration. One of the professors and I were the only blacks on the panel. About fifteen hundred students were in this lecture series.

Out of the issue they discussed, I selected three, education, religion and government. I told them that some of the things that had happened to me were premeditated in the thinking of the educators and the religious people, that our government was a product of education and religion. I told them I didn't see much of a solution until we change the technique of education. Only in the higher brackets of education have men and women begun to think seriously about this problem. In grammar schools, high schools and a good many colleges, they haven't even begun to consider it seriously. All of our motivations start back when we are young people, and if you have been motivated badly, it will take much more skill to get it out of you than it would have to avoid it in the beginning.

We have got to tell the truth as it is found, and not put things in education to propagandize, to tear down the concept of other people for your own personal gain. We have got to stop trying to protect something that is superficial and look at the realities of things. American history, for example, is one of the greatest pieces of propaganda you can find. Democracy is the best form of government, but we don't have one. Actually, the hippies are the most democratic people in this country.

A recent example is the treatment given to the wife of Dr. W. E. B. Du Bois. I had met her husband, in fact, heard his last lecture here in the Community Church on Boylston Street, when he was too feeble to leave his wheelchair. He was ninety-two at that time. Well, Dr. Du Bois loved America as much as any man could love it, but after the humiliation and mistreatment that he went through, he had no alternative but to spend his last few years in some place where he had some faith, Ghana.

His wife wanted to come back here, just for a few days to visit. Now, she has never been a very violent woman, always peaceful. Naturally when two people have lived together as long as they, something in common, some of his thinking must have rubbed off on her. I don't see why America has anything to fear, but she was refused a visa to visit the United States. You see, we haven't lived up to the principles which our forefathers laid down for democracy. Abraham Lincoln said, "He who would deny to others that which he has does not himself deserve it."

When I finished, one of the professors told me that he was more than surprised to see me tear down three of the basic principles that they had been trying to outline. So I said, "I would feel guilty if I left this institution without giving you what I consider the ultimate goal if we are to survive: brotherhood." I went on to say that it doesn't matter what color you are, what religion, whether you are a Democrat, a Republican, or a communist, we can all work on brotherhood.

And this includes integration, real integration, especially intermarriage. It is the only way the world will survive. It is much more healthful for a race to intermarry than to stay only with their own kind. A degeneracy sets in when only one group intermarries exclusively within their own kind.

When I finished talking, later in the day, my friend Professor West, invited me to a new high school in Syracuse, about six or eight miles from the city. When we got there, he introduced me to the principal and we had a talk. I told the principal that I would be ashamed of myself to teach in a school as large and as fine as that, and not have one black or one Jew in it. She looked at me and said, "What can I do?" "Well," I said, "you can at least put some black and Jewish teachers in it. How do you manage to get all these Italian and Irish teachers? That looks awfully strange to me." I told her that not only would the education you are giving die, the people who are getting it are dying also.

424

She looked at me and said, "Mr. Cannady, I think you're awfully bitter." I said, "No, I'm giving it to you as I see it." I told her that most people think that the Viet Nam war is the greatest problem we have today, but it isn't. The greatest problem we have today is the race war. Even if we solve the Viet Nam thing, there are gonna be many bloodsheddings, many dark nights before we solve the race problem. And, I told her, you haven't even begun.

Do you know there are groups of Negroes in this country so militant that they know all the techniques of how to destroy? I wonder what a wonderful country we might have had if they could have directed their attention to good deeds and good thoughts. But now they have got two strikes on you. Once, the Negro would have accepted you with open arms. Now, there is a large segment of Negroes that don't want anything to do with you. He's not religious anymore. One of these days he will be very, very ferocious. Any person who has been persecuted, if he ever reaches the top, will do ten times worse than what you would do. He has it on his mind that he will inflict it on somebody and he don't know anybody else to inflict it on but you.

Well, she heard me out and then asked me to talk to her faculty. So I did, and now they have brought some Negroes and Jews into their school.

Tell me about your early life.

Well, I was born in Oxford, North Carolina, about forty miles from Raleigh. I grew up on a farm. My father was a schoolteacher and he farmed on the side. He told me he didn't care whether I was a ditch-digger or what. But if I had an education, he told me I would be able to dig that ditch easier than somebody without it. That was his theory.

He raised eight children and didn't leave us much money, but he did leave us a nice house. We had a hundred and one acres on this lot. Look, here is a picture of the house, mighty nice, isn't it?

My mother was a hard-working woman. Each Monday morning as I was in the field harvesting, I would hear her start the song, "Amazing Grace." She would never start off with the first verse, but always with the third verse — and this puzzled me. The third

425

verse goes, "I once was lost but now I'm found, was blind but now I see." I used to wonder what she could see that I couldn't see. I wrestled with that for many years before I discovered what she saw.

You see she had eight kids, four boys and four girls. And she tried to support these kids, along with her husband, off the income we had. Many a day, as I look back at the problems she faced, it was just not possible to furnish the food because of the economic condition we were in. There were many dark days. This troubled her, and she found comfort in singing, "Nobody knows the trouble I've seen." And she found comfort in the lines, "I once was lost but now am found, was blind and now I see." She saw something in life that most people missed, and that is the image of what God meant to her. She had no troubles that she didn't take to him. The thing that comforted her in those dark hours, that gave her light, was when she thought about her Maker. This is the thing that she could see that I couldn't. I had no knowledge of it.

My grandfather was named Nevison Cannady, a very talented man. He was the first colored postman in North Carolina. Half of my relatives were white, but I didn't know about this when I was growing up. My grandfather was a kind of mixture but my grandmother was very, very fair. You couldn't have distinguished her from a white person.

There is something very interesting here. In Oxford there were two sets of Cannadys. They spelled their name the same way, but one was white and the other was colored. When my grandfather died, they wouldn't let him have his funeral in the colored church. They had it in the First Baptist Church which belonged to the whites. Then when they got ready to lay his soul to rest, they carried him down to the black cemetery.

You see, we have got it in our heads that racism and prejudice is limited to the South. Of course this isn't true. I have made this statement, and some believe it and some don't. I have made the statement that we can have confidence that the South will solve their race problem much earlier than in the North. There are a large segment of white people in the South that are working at it because they realize how much damage has been done. They know

426

more about how black people think about them, and they are disturbed by it.

It even touches little things. Let me tell you an amusing story. When I worked on a certain farm in Oxford, every third week in July they would have what is known as a Revival. After you worked till about ten o'clock, you would go to church and stay there until about four o'clock. On the right side of the road was a white church, and on the left was a colored one. The white one was painted and fixed up, of course. Both of them had their religious service the same week at the same hour. Invariably the Negroes would start singing, "Will there be any stars in my crown?" And the whites would answer, "No, not one!" I remember this very distinctly.

You have been talking with white people now for a number of years. Are you getting discouraged?

Yes. I am. I'm getting discouraged because they don't seem to understand. You see, I haven't inflicted any kind of unnecessary evils on anybody. They are the ones that have inflicted the evils. It is their group that has got to change, not me. They seem to think that I have got to change in order for me to enter their kingdom.

They like to think things will stay as they are. They think I'm pushing them a little too far. I have told them about the book Sinclair Lewis wrote many years ago, *It Can't Happen Here.* I advise them to go back and read this book, and if there are books written about Detroit, California, Watts, about Washington, D.C., read them too. Even with the militia they should read these books. White people have great confidence in their government, and its ability to put down crime and riots. But I never heard of a government solving the problem unless the people did the solving.

It's not like he is incapable of learning. To my way of thinking, he doesn't want to know. He has been taught a certain way, about a certain government, a certain education, a certain religion, and he is going to accept that. But once again, you have an example of not looking at the realities of things.

And what's worse is that white people don't realize what they have done to black people. Almost everything the Negro has done

427

has been based on religion, even his education. And the religion was somewhat mystical, not that they didn't believe it, but the ministers referred to things that, well, you have to call it superficial. It wasn't anything they knew enough about to make it real. This is the pathetic tragedy of the faith of the Negro.

The worst thing the whites have done to the black people is to make them ignorant and keep them ignorant. The fact is that the majority of them today have no way of communicating with anybody except through their own ways of thinking. I am myself an example. I can't even talk to my own people because they say I went to live with Whitey in Sharon. They don't want me. I have very few colored friends. The majority of them don't like my way of thinking. They don't like my approach. Since I moved outside, I don't belong. I sometimes wonder if it will ever be possible for the white man to actually realize what he has done to the black people.

References

1. *New York Times Magazine*, "We Can Claim No Special Gift for Violence," April 28, 1968, p. 25.
2. *Saturday Evening Post*, September 10, 1966.
3. *Commentary*, February 1963, p. 98.
4. *Black Skin, White Masks* (New York: Grove Press, 1967), p. 11.
5. *Home* (New York: Morrow, 1965), p. 89.
6. *New York Times*, July 2, 1970.
7. Memorandum of Chancellor Alexander Heard of Vanderbilt University and President James Cheek of Howard University to the President, July 22, 1970.

8. Kenneth M. Stampp, *The Peculiar Institution; Slavery in the Ante-Bellum South,* Vintage, 1956.
9. *Black Skin, White Masks,* p. 129.
10. *Washington Evening Star,* May 14, 1963.
11. *Chicago Journalism Review,* June 1970, p. 15.
12. *Negro Digest,* February 1960, p. 81.
13. Don Pearce, *Esquire,* March 1970.
14. *Journal of Negro History,* January 1968, p. 7.
15. "Violence in Ghetto Children," *Children,* vol. 14, no. 3, May–June 1967, pp. 101–104.
16. *Manchild in the Promised Land* (New York: Signet, 1966), p. viii.
17. *The Ghetto* (Chicago: University of Chicago Press, 1928).
18. *Kerner Report,* p. vii.
19. *White Over Black* (Harmondsworth, England: Pelican, 1969), p. 28.
20. "The Failure of Black Separatism," *Harper's,* January 1970, p. 28.
21. *Negro Digest,* January 1969, p. 95.
22. *Black Skin, White Masks,* p. 122.
23. *Look,* January 13, 1970.
24. Charles V. Hamilton, *New York Times Magazine,* May 10, 1970.
25. *Who Speaks for the Negro?* (New York: Random House, 1965), Foreword.
26. *Hard Times: An Oral History of the Depression,* Pantheon Books, 1970, Foreword.

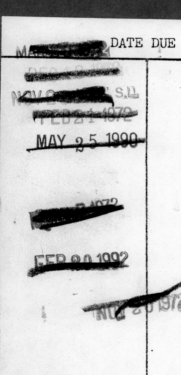